.ibrary & Evidence Research Centre, L(
renew this book please phone 0113 39 20140, or e-m
dsth-tr.stafflibraries@n .n(! You can ls   r   e
k onli   u

Leading Physicians Through Change:
How to Achieve and Sustain Results

Jack Silversin, DMD, DrPH, and Mary Jane Kornacki, MS
Foreword by Donald M. Berwick, MD, MPP

American College of Physician Executives
Suite 200
4890 West Kennedy Boulevard
Tampa, Florida 33609
813/287-2000

Copyright 2000 by Jack Silversin, DMD, DrPH, and Mary Jane Kornacki, MS. All rights reserved. Reproduction or translation of this work beyond that permitted by applicable copyright law without the permission of the College is prohibited. Requests for permission to reprint or for further information should be directed to the Permissions Editor, ACPE, Two Urban Centre, Suite 200, 4890 West Kennedy Boulevard, Tampa, Florida 33609.

ISBN: 0-924674-81-4

Library of Congress Card Number: 00-107870

Printed in the United States of America by Hillsboro Printing Company, Tampa, Florida.

About the Authors

Jack Silversin, DMD, DrPH, and Mary Jane Kornacki, MS, are the founding partners of Amicus, a health care consulting firm based in Cambridge Massachusetts, with clients nationwide. For 20 years, their work has focused on helping executives of physician organizations, hospitals, and health systems across the country to develop shared organizational vision, strengthen leadership and governance, and accelerate the implementation of large-scale change. Their breakthrough work on physician compacts is helping organizations achieve better results from change efforts and improve physician morale and commitment.

A graduate of the Harvard University School of Dental Medicine, Jack holds a doctorate in public health from Harvard and serves as a member of the faculty of medicine at the School of Dental Medicine. He is a nationally recognized speaker on physician culture and change in physician organizations and is a frequent speaker at Institute for Healthcare Improvement, American Medical Group Association, and Medical Group Management Association meetings. He is helping to establish a center dedicated to understanding and promoting change in healthcare settings to be based at Brigham and Womens' Hospital in Boston, Massachusetts.

Mary Jane Kornacki holds a master of science degree in public health from the University of Massachusetts, where she specialized in health education and health behavior. Her special interests include leadership, team dynamics, and the professional satisfaction of women physicians in medical organizations. Her understanding of the principles of adult learning and behavior change is reflected in the models and tools that are fundamental to the pair's consulting work and to this book.

Jack and Mary Jane have collaborated on numerous publications on physician cultures, physician morale, medical group dynamics, governance in physician organizations, and service improvement in health care.

You can visit the authors and learn more about their work through their Web site, www.ConsultAmicus.com. They welcome hearing about your experiences leading physicians through change and how this book affected your approach and results.

Preface

For the foreseeable future, health care organizations face unrelenting change. There are no signs that the forces reshaping health care are going to ease. Patients are saying loud and clear that care is too inconvenient, too rushed, and too impersonal. Businesses outside of health care have proved that costs can be lowered while quality is improved, and their leaders are growing inpatient that medicine does not appear to be committed to this basic premise. Purchasers and government at the state and federal levels are convinced care is too costly and look to managed care and other newer schemes as mechanisms to control costs. A growing chorus of purchasers, consumers, and elected officials is declaring that there are too many errors and too much needless variation in the way in which care is provided and that improvements in quality are too slow in coming.

Whether physicians practice alone, with a few colleagues, or as part of a large group practice, their business success and ability to control their destinies are going to depend increasingly on their ability to respond to the demands of the marketplace. Yet learning how to change has not been easy. Even when under pressure to change and handed a tested method with better results, physicians frequently balk. Organizational change is a challenge in every industry, but physician organizations have shown an extraordinary degree of stability and resistance to change. Asking physicians to agree to make a change as a group is like asking them to all join hands and jump together into uncharted, icy water.

Purpose of the Book

We wrote this book because of our conviction that the process of change in physician organizations can be accelerated. From our experience working with group practices, independent practice associations (IPAs), hospitals, and managed care plans, we know that implementing even changes that benefit doctors and their organizations is no cakewalk. Often we have observed that getting physicians to change looks a lot like the mythical Sisyphus rolling his rock uphill. Boards, executives, and managers expend a tremen-

dous amount of energy trying to move a change forward. They push against gravity and friction and the other natural forces that keep people and organizations at rest. If ever those leading the change ease up, the whole thing comes crashing down. Without constant and strenuous efforts the change goes nowhere.

The premise of this book is that physician organizations have to learn to change or they will either be changed by outside forces or fail outright. We also believe that changing does not have to be painful, protracted, or devastating for physicians. Perhaps Sisyphus could have spared himself his tragic fate if, instead of pushing, he used other strategies to move the boulder over the hill. This book offers the equivalent of taking down the hill and energizing physicians to willingly engage in changes that make practice life and the quality of care better.

Audiences for the Book

We had two audiences in mind when we wrote this book. Both audiences seek to have influence over physicians and have some responsibility for making change happen or for improving the performance of physician organizations:

- The physician leaders responsible for implementing and supporting change in their organizations: medical group or IPA presidents or CEOs, board members, committee chairs, medical directors, department chairs, chiefs, and local site leaders.

- Other leaders who work with physicians on a regular basis and are responsible for supporting their practices: non-physician administrators and managers who work for organizations that partner with or are affiliated with physicians, such as CEOs, COOs, CFOs; medical directors; and board members of hospitals, health plans, insurance companies, and health systems.

Basis of the Change Management Framework

The framework described in this book is built on theories from social science research and nearly 20 years of consulting to physician organizations around issues of leadership, culture, change implementation, and organizational performance.

The issues surrounding how to introduce change successfully to individuals and organizations have been actively researched since the 1960s. Social science researchers have developed many models and constructs to help explain how and why people, organizations and communities change. The framework we are presenting draws on research in learning theory,[1,2] diffusion of innovations,[3] and organization and community development.[4,5] Although this research does not directly address the challenge of introducing change among physicians or other autonomous professionals, it provides a good deal of guidance regarding the fundamentals of change that are a part of the human condition and of organizational life.

The change framework also integrates our personal experience "in the field." We have consulted to leaders of group practices, networks and IPA models owned by physicians, hospitals, insurance companies, and physician practice management companies (PPMs). We have worked with organizations on leadership development, strategy, culture, vision, and change. Our clients reflect markets with different degrees of competition and managed care penetration. We have experience in organizations with wide-ranging compensation plans, including plans based on productivity, on the management of resources under capitated arrangements, and on salary with incentives for a range of behaviors. Our practical experience has allowed us to tailor generic change management constructs to implementing change in diverse physician organizations.

Overview of Contents

The introduction describes a framework for leading change, which is developed in detail in chapters 1-8. Part I, "Change Foundation," which includes chapters 1-3, is devoted to issues that, taken together, build an organization's capacity to develop and implement change. Part II, "Change Levers," consists of chapters 4-8, each of which describes one of the levers in the framework. Part III, chapters 9-11, "Moving to Action," is devoted to taking steps to apply the change model and features a case study of compact change in a physician organization.

Introduction
This section opens with a scenario that illustrates some underlying reasons physician organizations do not readily change and describes the change framework that is the basis for the book.

Change Foundation
Chapter 1 explores the current state of leadership in many physician organizations and the mental models that need to be cultivated to improve leadership's effectiveness.

Chapter 2 deals with the rationale for having a shared vision, the state of vision in many physician organizations, why visions on paper do not necessarily become a useful resource for guiding a physician organization, and how a meaningful and useful shared vision can be developed.

Chapter 3 discusses the impact of current physician compacts (expectations that physicians have of the organization and that the organization has of them) on change implementation and what kind of compact is needed for future success.

Change Levers
Chapter 4 explores in detail the important change roles that facilitate and support change and how to achieve critical alignment among individuals in the roles.

Chapter 5 is devoted to the effective use of participation in the change process. Guidelines are provided for productively involving physicians in changes that will affect their practices.

Chapter 6 focuses on the need to move beyond the status quo and on how leaders can productively create tension to energize physicians to change through "pain" and "pull" approaches.

Chapter 7 describes strategies that leaders can use to address the resistance associated with change.

Chapter 8 examines how leaders can help a change be both implemented and sustained by creating a consistent context for the change that includes financial incentives, non-monetary rewards, resources, training, staffing, measurement, and feedback.

Moving to Action
Chapter 9 applies the change levers to an actual case

example of how a large multispecialty practice changed its compact.

Chapter 10 is devoted to strategies that those who are not physicians or who are not part of the physician organization can apply to influence physicians to change.

Chapter 11, the concluding chapter, describes the mindset leaders need to cultivate to be effective in leading change and actions they can take to start improving their organizations' capacity to change.

Each chapter begins with an assessment that can help the reader get in touch with the current state in the physician organization with regard to the topic covered in the chapter. Every chapter includes sidebars contributed by health care leaders who offer their insights and experience with an issue discussed in the chapter. At the end of every chapter are tools for taking action that can help the reader put the material to practical and immediate use.

The book is organized around the framework for change with the aim of giving you a comprehensive understanding of how to approach significant organizational changes such as those associated with access, quality, and patient service improvements. Reading the chapters in order provides a systematic look at what it takes for change to be successful. However, readers can also jump in anywhere they choose. Those interested in a case study can start with chapter 9 and then go to the chapters on the individual levers most relevant to their situations. Some leaders need to understand better how to build their organization's capability to change. We advise them to not skip chapters 1-3 on the issues that are essential to the foundation for change. If your main responsibility is to implement or support the implementation of a small-scale project and taking on issues such as vision and compact are outside the scope of your responsibilities, focus on chapters 4-8, which describe levers that can be applied to move any change effort forward.

These are daunting times for physicians. They are also exciting times; innovation is afoot everywhere. In health care delivery, trials of group appointments and the Internet are giving doctors new ways of interacting with their patients and new ways for patients to engage in their own health care. New pharmaceuticals are turning once fatal diseases into chronic conditions. One day, the remarkable work on the human genome may vanquish almost all human ills. The signposts on the path to organizational success today read "adapt," "improve," "reduce variation," "teamwork," and "transform." How long will it take physicians to incorporate best practices into their daily work life? Will most be energized by change, or will the vast majority resist and only reluctantly move into the future? Will their organizations develop flexibility and openness to new ways? We believe that, as medicine moves ever forward, knowledge of how to change will be as important to physicians' success and the vitality of their organizations as clinical knowledge and commitment to excellence.

References

1. Lewin, K. *Field Theory in Social Science*. New York, N.Y.: Harper, 1951.

2. Bandura, A. *Social Learning Theory*. Englewood Cliffs, N.J.: Prentice Hall, 1977.

3. Rogers, E. *Diffusion of Innovations*, 4th Edition. New York, N.Y.: Free Press, 1995.

4. Bennis, W. "Theory and Method in Applying Behavioral Science to Planned Organizational Change." *Journal of Applied Behavioral Science* I(4):337-59, July-Aug. 1965.

5. Goodenough, W. *Cooperation in Change*. New York, N.Y.: Russell Sage Foundation, 1976.

Foreword

Some days, you just get a feeling. And, that day, the feeling was bad.

I had been asked to help facilitate the annual "Physician/Management Strategic Retreat" for the senior leaders of a large, prestigious hospital. The stresses were tough and familiar—declining payments, a new competitor entering from the West, troublesome patient satisfaction scores, and a Joint Commission Survey due imminently. No wonder the CEO was worried about declining morale and growing internal conflict. It was still a secret, but he was thinking of moving on.

My task was to help group members think together about their shared future. The work was fragmented; patients reported poor coordination of care; and referring doctors, the chief source of patients for this high-tech hospital, nicknamed the place, "the Black Hole." Yet all the assets were there for superb care and market leadership: prestige; community loyalty; excellent subspecialists; a new physical plant; and a new, young cadre of excited and capable generalist clinicians.

The CEO first reviewed the "current state," as he put it. He skillfully described the environmental threats and opportunities, the hospital's operating statements and balance sheet, the clinical outcomes and satisfaction data he was able to assemble, and basic operational changes that could lead the organization back to firmer ground. "The real key," I recall him saying, "is cooperation. We just can't afford to act as separate players. We are in this together and need to think and act as a whole—like a system." Then he turned to the group and asked for a first round of comments and suggestions.

The chief of medicine—young, charismatic, confident, and brilliant—spoke first. "That's not the key, Bill," he said to the CEO. "The problem here is the bottom-line focus. Nobody in management understands patients. I think the first thing we ought to do is to fire all the pencil-headed dweebs in accounting."

A ripple of uncomfortable laughter rose and fell, like a dirge.

A "service line manager" who reported to the COO countered with a flash of anger. With an icy glare at the chief of medicine, she said, "It's not accounting that's the problem, George, it's the doctors. They're a bunch of prima donnas, and trying to lead them is like herding cats."

A few others chuckled. I didn't. If I had had the option then, at 9 a.m. of a proposed day-long retreat, I would have left and gone home. No progress was in store. And, indeed, none was made. What a waste!

The story is real. But, it doesn't need much disguising to protect the players, because the story is also common. I haven't since heard exactly the phrase "pencil-headed dweebs" repeated in a senior leadership group, but synonyms abound. The "herding cats" metaphor is much more familiar—almost a password in some strategic planning sessions. If I had a nickel for every time I've heard it....

These are poison words. They mark the problem beneath the problem. Good people in troubled settings lapse into rhetoric that they would punish in their 10-year-old children in a setting that calls for decorum. And then they suffer themselves from the wasteful conflict that their words reinforce. The problems create the feelings; the feelings spawn the words; and the words aggravate the problems.

Personally, I agree with the CEO. All routes out of our problems in health care—the big problems, at least—traverse the meadows of cooperation. There are no other options for the long haul. And (this is the key point) a foundation for cooperation—I think a *sine qua non*—is *civility*.

The retreat that day made me shudder; it still does each time I remember it. But I do not shudder because that great hospital was under so much pressure, or even because the level of cooperation was so low. There were plenty of brains in the room to solve those problems. I shudder because these stewards, these leaders, these caring people could not talk with each other in a civil tongue. Termites harm a house no less than incivility harms a system.

In human systems, especially in improvement, everything depends on the ability to have a civil conversation. No conversation, no gains.

Enter Amicus. As this valuable book documents, Jack Silversin and Mary Jane Kornacki have, over nearly two decades, crafted one of the clearest and most effective frameworks the health care industry has yet found to help organizational leaders move methodically toward the changes that will matter. The authors believe—and I agree—that a repeated stumbling-block to clear-headed strategic change in many health care systems has been the failure of capacity of physicians and other leaders to create a meeting of the minds, leading to shared perspectives, shared intentions, and productive innovation.

They explore this gap in vivid detail in this book, and offer in both theory and example a step-wise approach to much more productive interactions between physicians and the organizations with whom they must work to meet patients' needs. Their extensive experience shows through at every step, and the book amounts almost to a manual for change, specific enough to guide actions.

But the actions Amicus counsels are hard to understand or engage in without also acknowledging the underlying view of people embedded in their method. Amicus has a particular view of people. It is a respectful view, full of awareness that human beings, even in conflict, even when they seem patently unwise, are generally not working from meanness and are doing what makes sense to themselves. The model Silversin and Kornacki have created maintains a strong thread of curiosity and genuine inquiry for all involved to understand what, exactly, the world of the "other" is like, from the "other's" point of view. My favorite quotation in the whole book comes not directly from the authors, but indirectly through them from Carl Rogers: "Before presenting your own point of view, it would be necessary for you to achieve the other speaker's frame of reference, to understand his thoughts and feelings so well that you could summarize them for him. Sounds simple, doesn't it? But, if you try, you will discover that it is one of the most difficult things you have ever tried to do."

The respect embedded in that thought perfuses the model and the tone of Jack Silversin and Mary Jane Kornacki. They do not flee the realities, and they are relentless in their insistence that all of the leaders in health care—including physicians—name those realities without compromise or flinching. But in so doing, they also insist on civility as a ground rule. They have faith that that combination—facing reality and civil dialogue—can help even the most jaded and fractious leadership teams to find their way to solutions.

Had they been in the room on the day of that retreat, I think that Jack and Mary Jane would have had the presence of mind that I did not have—to stop the action, face down the language, and ask whether the speakers and their colleagues really, really wished to engage in talk so erosive of their own capacity to hear, and, ultimately, so isolating. They would have confronted the 40 people there with the truth that language does not just classify reality, it creates reality. I tolerated the incivility; I think they might have called the question. The creation of a dysfunctional reality by the choice of bad language is a privilege that responsible leaders simply do not have.

In the well-intended, adolescent quest of health care over the past 20 years to find its way to systematic improvement, it has been common and perhaps more comfortable for both leaders and teachers to focus on learning and adopting the more formal techniques of improvement—measuring, process analysis, process redesign, benchmarking, and so on. These techniques are important, but the softer side of improving systems, equally essential, is to engage the processes of civil conversation that allow us to hear each other and discover the latent system among us, upon which our patients depend and in which we are bound in interdependency.

Compared to drawing a process flow diagram, conversation is extremely difficult. It is made far more difficult if we cannot work from a platform of respect.

That platform is what the authors of this book are now spending their careers understanding and helping to build. When the history of the reinvention of health care is written, albeit 50 years from now, I believe that the contributions of these authors, and their work through Amicus will turn out to have been not just important, but pivotal.

No more "pencil-headed dweebs" talk, please. No more "herding cats." We are in it together, doctors, nurses, technicians, executives, managers—all of us. Amicus knows that we can build the whole thing better, but step one is civility—listening to our friends and neighbors at work, and hearing them, no more or less than we, ourselves, wish to be heard.

Donald M. Berwick, MD, MPP, President and CEO
Institute for Healthcare Improvement
Boston, Massachusetts

Acknowledgments

We spent several months holed up in our office committing to paper observations, experiences, and insights we've garnered over the years working with physician organizations. But writing this book has not been a solitary endeavor. A number of friends and colleagues are owed our deepest gratitude for their contributions.

For adding their own voices and sharing their personal stories, we are grateful to all who contributed sidebars. The contact and interactions we had with each of them made this project more rewarding for us. More important, they provide real world, practical examples of how to lead change that produces results. We want to make particular mention of Dr. Beth Briere's contribution to Chapter 9. By sharing her organization's experience in changing its compact, she has provided a concrete example of a complex task that some might see as amorphous. We thank her for generously giving her time and for her willingness to provide this detailed account.

We were blessed to have had Trish Stoltz on our team from the beginning of the project. To say we couldn't have done it without her is not an exaggeration. She has been our lifeline and keenest supporter. She brought more than her editorial talent to this project; she challenged our thinking and helped us reframe ideas. Her depth of knowledge and the clarity of her thinking have made this a far better book than it otherwise would have been. We will always be grateful for all she has done for us.

Marilyn Libresco is owed a special thanks for her collegiality over the years and for her contributions to our thinking about physicians, leadership, and change.

We are indebted to doctors Peter Lindblad, Shelia Sawyer, Bill Gold, Mark Sheffield, Jeanne Conry, and Craig Green as well as to Ann Gross, Linda Borodkin, and Beth Anctil, who took time out of their busy lives to read drafts of chapters and give thoughtful comments. Dr. Jack Pollard deserves special acknowledgment for providing us with constructive feedback on the entire manuscript.

We also want to express our heartfelt thanks to two individuals—Patti Foley and Charlotte Emery DeBye—not just for their assistance in preparing the manuscript but for nearly two decades of support.

We want to acknowledge Wes Curry at the American College of Physician Executives who believed in this project early on and was supportive throughout the writing and production of this book.

Finally, we are indebted to the many physician leaders who opened their organizations to us and to the front-line physicians who trusted us enough to share their greatest hopes and deep concerns about their profession and organizations. They created opportunities for us to experience and understand the world we describe in this book.

Jack Silversin
Mary Jane Kornacki
Cambridge, Massachusetts
August 2000

Introduction

A Common Scenario

Dr. Bud Jones sits down at the long table in the small and darkly paneled conference room. The practice administrator who is seated and looking grim-faced gets up and closes the door before clearing his throat and carefully choosing his words. "Bud, this isn't going to be easy to hear, but the report I've got here says that the productivity of the group has slipped far behind where we should be. I thought you, as managing partner, should know this before tonight's meeting." He pushes a stack of papers across the table.

"That certainly isn't what I expected to hear from you, Jon. What do you mean by 'way behind,' and what report is this? Where did you get these data? I feel that I'm as busy as I've ever been. There's been no slacking off in this group as far as I can tell."

"I've compared our total patient visits for the past half year with some national and regional data. And, for a group our size, we should be fifteen to twenty percent more productive."

"Jon, I hate to interrupt, but that might be the problem right there. These data you're talking about probably have nothing to do with us. Our practice is different. You can't compare us to physicians in other parts of the country or even to others in town. I would have to see other figures before I conclude we've got a problem. What did our collections run this past year? Besides, none of us joined this group to run patients through like it was some sort of mill. If you're a doctor in the practice across town, you see four patients an hour. You tell me how you can give decent care when you're under the gun like that."

"Bud, you can pick this apart if you want. Overhead has gone up and reimbursement's gone down. Those are facts. I want to put this on tonight's agenda so we can begin to figure out what to do."

"Can't you take something out of overhead? I told you I thought we signed some bad contracts. When they come up again, you'll have to negotiate harder."

"I'd be happy to drive down some overhead costs. The main problem is the doctors so far haven't been willing to standardize anything—not what supplies they order, not how the front desk schedules appointments."

Bud rolls his eyes. "Jon, bring it up this evening if you want, but I would guess the doctors aren't going to be in a mood to have the conversation until they see you take a bite out of overhead."

On his way to his office, Bud asks a receptionist to look up the booking schedules for the four physicians who practice on his unit. All four are booked four or five weeks out for routine care. She reports that this is the way it's always been as far as she could recall. When he walks past an office, Bud sees Ann, one of his partners, eating lunch at her desk and asks for a few minutes of her time.

"Ann, I need your help. Any difference in the past few months in the number of patients you see? Jon and I were talking, and he says we're not being as productive as we should be, given the decline in reimbursements that we've seen."

"Management. It's always the same story. 'You're not good enough. Other doctors in town are going to eat your lunch.' When hasn't he been concerned? About my patients, it feels to me as if I'm working as hard as ever. I'm seeing more seniors maybe, and they take more of my time. But I can't say there's been any appreciable difference in my practice. There's a board meeting tonight, right? I suggest you ask Jon what administration is doing to cut costs. If we're seeing all the patients we can, and there's still a revenue problem, tell him to do his job—get us good contracts and figure out how to make the practice work with less overhead."

That night's board meeting lasts until nearly midnight. Despite Jon's detailed report regarding revenue and expenses, the physicians have difficulty agreeing that they need to change. Jon acknowledges some administrative costs could be trimmed, but he insists that is not where the leverage lies. Without agreement to uniform processes and some standardization, the reductions he can make will have a minor impact on the bottom line. The conversation goes in circles. At one point, the internist on the board becomes exasperated. "I will not go back to my colleagues and tell them they need to work harder. Agreeing to do that would be a betrayal of the trust they've put in me." Jon reminds the group they sat together over a year ago to draft a document of purpose and values to guide the group's future. That triggers a conversation about who did and did not vote in favor of that document and questions about whether all the physicians, in the end, agreed to what was in it. The meeting breaks up without consensus about whether a problem exists and, if it does, what should be done about it. They agree to meet again the following week.

Unfortunately, this frustration-filled scenario is not uncommon. Like most physicians we know, these doctors work hard and pride themselves on giving patients good care. They are committed to what they are doing and do not intend to be obstructionists. When they resist hearing that they need to change, they are acting like normal human beings. Of course they do not want the distraction change involves; they want to focus on what they know best—practicing medicine.

But this group's prognosis may well depend on how quickly it can implement change and turn around performance. Although the administrator is convinced that change is needed, the physicians do not see the situation in the same way. There is not a deep commitment to a shared vision for the practice. Physician leaders are concerned about the backlash from their decisions, are skeptical of data, and believe that it is management's job to identify and fix problems.

Although this scenario might not capture the dynamics around change you experience in physician organizations, we have seen elements of this scenario in most of the physician organizations with which we have worked. Some of what impedes change responsiveness and success appears to occur regardless of organizational size, structure, ownership, or governance. To be effective, any management approach must take into account these dynamics when they are present. The framework presented in this book is based on the commonly occurring determinants of success or failure.

The Amicus change management framework shown in figure I-1, page xvii, consists of:

- Three issues (referred to as the change foundation) that build the capacity for implementation of all organizational changes.

- Five levers that leaders can apply to enhance implementation of any specific change.

What follows is a high-level orientation to the components of the framework. Each foundational issue and lever is explored in subsequent chapters.

Foundational Issues

Leadership, shared vision, and culture and compact are the foundation of the framework. In our experience, these foundational elements represent the most common reasons large- and small-scale changes are not successfully implemented in a timely way in physician organizations. Leadership is ineffective, doctors are not in agreement around a vision for the organization, and physicians' expectations of their practice life are incompatible with what change requires of them. When a physician organization invests in building a foundation for change by addressing these issues, it benefits enormously. There are many ways that leadership, shared vision, and a realistic compact strengthen an organization; the chief benefit is increased ability to move quickly to implement change as market forces shift.

Leadership

Given the traditions in medicine and the history of most physician organizations, leadership is often weak. Physicians do not typically see themselves as followers; therefore, they do not readily acknowledge leaders to have any more authority than that required to call meetings or to represent physicians' interests. Effective leadership among physicians calls for more than a skill

FIGURE I-I. Amicus Change Management Framework

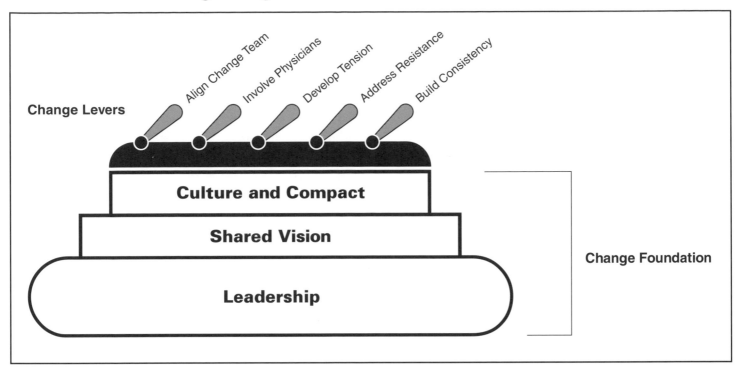

set; it takes a mindset on leaders' part that they are responsible for the whole enterprise, and it takes recognition on physicians' part of leaders' authority. Effective leadership almost always calls for a new dynamic between leaders and others in the organization.

Shared Vision

Consultants and academics have used the term vision to mean different things; in our change management framework, vision describes where the organization is headed. A useful vision paints a clear picture of where the organization will be at a future point and speaks to those elements that distinguish it from competitors. To serve as a foundation for successful change, a vision has to be inspirational yet reality-based.

The power of vision to support organizational change is ultimately not a function of the particular words chosen to describe it. Its potency depends on the extent to which it is meaningful to and widely shared by all members of the organization. It is useful as the context for implementing change only if there is shared agreement that it represents a future state that is desirable for both individuals and the enterprise.

Culture and Compact

The other foundational issue that significantly affects a physician organization's ability to implement change is its culture. The culture defines normative behavior

and typically is a barrier to physicians' embracing changes that call for new behaviors. Physician organizations tend not to consciously create their culture so that it can support their vision and business plan. Instead it is allowed to evolve from the compact that exists between the organization and its physicians.

The physician compact is the *quid pro quo* or "deal" between the physicians and their medical group, IPA, hospital, or strategic partner. It defines what physicians expect to give and what they expect to get in the relationship. Typically these expectations are not written down and formalized, but they do shape physician behavior and in turn the organization's culture.

Culture and compact potentially affect the implementation of every change involving physicians. Many of the demands for new physician behaviors—for example, to add hours to their schedules, share staff, or follow practice guidelines—are not consistent with the practice life they believe they were promised. This makes changes that require different expectations on physicians' part particularly challenging to implement.

The Five Change Levers

Once leaders have established the change foundation, those responsible for supporting and implementing change can most effectively employ the change levers

The Framework Applied to a Change

BY PAUL HACKMEYER, MD

Paul Hackmeyer is Chief of Staff at Cedars-Sinai Medical Center in Los Angeles, California. Cedars-Sinai is an 877-bed acute care facility with almost 2,000 medical staff members.

As Vice Chief of Staff, I was in charge of Cedars-Sinai's Quality Improvement Committee (QIC). The monthly reports to the QIC from 14 subcommittees varied widely in their quality focus and format. The reports were supposed to summarize ongoing quality improvement activities. However, the quality of the reports was an impediment to QIC's fulfilling its mission and being able to monitor improvement within the institution. I undertook an effort to get all subcommittees to establish indicators that could be tracked, recorded, and presented in dashboard format. I had learned the Amicus change model in a workshop, and I used it to guide my efforts at changing the reporting process. The project was to change the reporting structure in the QIC first and then export the model if successful. By the end of one year, we achieved almost 100 percent compliance, with 12 out of the 14 committees presenting in the desired format.

One benefit of the model was being able to understand what the change process would require of me even before I began. If I had gone about this change as I had others, I would have tried to effect change on my own and not figure out who I needed to involve up front in the process. I would not have anticipated resistance and adequately prepared for it. Last, I would not have kept the goal for the project in front of everyone, constantly and consistently.

I began by getting clear on what I wanted the reports to accomplish and by sharing this goal with others. Making the picture of what would be different after the change a shared goal was an important step.

Identifying key players in the change process is critical. I knew I couldn't do this alone, so I identified key support people from quality improvement and key physician leaders to share what the change would look like and what it would accomplish. I wanted these people to all communicate about the change in the same way. Many projects fail because those trying to promote it are inconsistent and send mixed messages to the physicians.

to move any specific change forward. Each addresses a vital aspect of the change management process. Even though change is impeded when foundation issues are not addressed, the levers can still help in the design and execution of a change process that gets results.

Align a Change Team

This lever addresses the kind of leadership any specific change requires and describes three distinct change roles that need to be played: sponsor, agent, and champion. It focuses not just on development of a leadership team but also on the process that leads to alignment among team members. Alignment is a key issue, because it results in consistency that minimizes back-door politicking and mixed messages.

Involve Physicians to Enhance Change Design and Implementation

In the experience of many physician leaders, involving physicians does not always produce better results. Ineffective involvement does not just complicate change efforts; it also frustrates those who were asked to offer input as well as those who say they want it. Yet, the participation of those who will ultimately have to change is essential. This lever uses physician participation to design and implement change. When used properly, this lever enhances physician commitment to a proposed change and makes it more workable, without bogging down the overall change process.

Develop Tension for Change

To leave the comfort of the status quo, most individuals need to believe that change is truly imperative and that there is a more attractive alternative. This is the lever leaders use to energize change. It involves addressing complacency, where it exists, and communicating urgency for and the benefits of change. Leaders get physicians ready to change by helping them understand the price of not changing (what we call "pain" strategies) and by creating a picture of a future state that attracts and energizes them toward it and away from the status quo ("pull" strategies).

Address Resistance

In our experience, leaders who seek to help change happen in physician organizations often give short shrift to the affective component of the process. In addressing resistance, leaders help those involved in a change let go of what is familiar and predictable, express their concerns or ambivalence, and commit to new behaviors and perspectives. Being able to apply this lever requires leaders themselves to make an emotional transition and commit to the new way. It also means leaders have to be proficient in surfacing others' emotions and then in responding appropriately.

Build Consistency

Willingness to stick with a change fades quickly if the environment sends inconsistent messages or provides inconsistent support. This lever identifies how leaders can build a consistent context for change by providing physicians and team members with the capacity to follow through with implementation. Capacity includes resources, time, staffing, and appropriate work design. Consistency is also built through financial and nonfinancial rewards and through the way in which feedback is designed and delivered. Building the consistency to support change is often critical for success; a change effort can flounder in an inconsistent environment, even when leaders and implementers are deeply committed to its success.

In our experience, no magic bullet exists for accelerating organizational change. For example, only modifying the physician compensation formula to provide an incentive for a change rarely results in sustained change. Sharing data in the absence of perceived urgency also will not motivate anyone to adopt a change. Inviting physician participation in designing the change does not lead to sustained implementation if physicians do not have adequate resources and other supports that contribute to a consistent environment. Those who seek to influence physicians need to acknowledge the complexity and challenge involved in successfully integrating change in a physician organization. The challenge is best met by applying a system-

In this case, I wasn't looking to other physicians to come up with the new way—I had a protocol I wanted them to buy in to. However, as the project took on a life of its own, contributions from the participants emerged. I also understood that consensus might not be possible and that moving forward is the responsibility of leadership, despite lack of unanimity.

I used our upcoming JCAHO survey to create tension to get people to make the change. I also positioned as an "attractor" the ease of reporting the information required. This stage did involve a lot of hands-on communicating on a personal level with the doctors involved. Without this effort, the change would have failed.

The model reinforces that resistance is natural. Understanding that resistance will occur helped me prepare to hear it and respond. I found I was able to validate the resistance some doctors had to changing the reporting system without allowing the project to be abandoned because of some opposition.

I was pleased with how this change unfolded and the results achieved. Within a year, all but two reports were coming to QIC with exactly the information that the committee needed. It made the committee more functional, and, by using the reporting protocol, the quality of the subcommittees' work has been improved.

Any new behavior needs to be reinforced to keep it from reverting back to what it used to be. Constant feedback from the Medical Executive Committee and other committees and task forces to QIC and its subcommittees has communicated that what they do makes a difference.

I have shared the Amicus model with other physician leaders in my organization, and they have responded well. It helps identify who will be most important to the change and helps organize an approach to "get things done." Those who use it find the model makes the process of change much more manageable.

FIGURE I-2. Types of Individuals Seeking to Influence Physicians

		PHYSICIAN	
		YES	NO
RELATIONSHIP TO THE ORGANIZATION	INSIDE	Medical director, department heads, site leaders	COO, administrator, department manager
	OUTSIDE	System or insurance company medical director	System CEO or CFO, insurance company executive

The Framework in Daily Life
LOIE LENARZ, MD

Loie Lenarz is Senior Medical Director for Fairview Clinics and is responsible for 22 primary care clinics in the Twin Cities of Minneapolis and St Paul. Fairview Clinics is part of Fairview Health Services, a large health care system of clinics, hospitals, pharmacies, home health, long-term care, and other related services.

With such complex changes in health care, many issues need to be addressed. By being deliberate about a change foundation, and by thinking through the levers in a systematic and thoughtful way, the change happens much more readily and effectively. If leaders say, "Such and such has to change," without detailing how to make it happen, the change is much less likely to be successful. With the time pressures we are all under, it makes more sense to take an organized and thoughtful approach to change so you can get it right the first time.

The Amicus change framework is most useful when it's in the hands of the whole team responsible for leading the change. Having it in front of you and talking through each lever leads you to a plan. It helps bring clarity about who needs to be involved and how. This conversation also starts to build the team, and helps people get clear on the work involved and how, collectively, the team is going to get it done.

When approaching change, a very important consideration is culture and compact. Change that involves a shift in culture is by far the most difficult to achieve, and when culture is the root cause of not being able to make change, it is essential to apply a remedy that addresses this issue. Superficial solutions won't suffice, although it's tempting to try this first.

I have become convinced of the need for effective individuals to fill all of the change leadership roles—sponsor, agent, and champion. One of my responsibilities is interfacing with other leaders in our large system. When progress in making a change is slow, it's often because we, as leaders, don't have clarity about who the sponsors are, who the agents are, and who the formal and informal champions are. Perhaps we haven't tapped into these potentially important catalysts, or, worse yet, we may have agents or champions who are actually preventing the change.

Another way I've used the change role descriptions is to fill open medical director positions. Ideally, the new leader would be someone who could listen to doctors,

atic and comprehensive approach to leading change. In the sidebar on pages xviii-xix, a medical center chief of staff explains how he used this model for a specific change, and in the sidebar left and on page xxi, a medical director in a physician organization shares how she draws on various parts of the model in daily life.

Physicians, Insiders, and Outsiders

The framework can be used to guide change efforts with any group of staff in health care organizations. However, the intent of the book is to apply the framework to supporting change among physicians. This is not meant to imply that physicians are the only ones who matter or that they single-handedly achieve results. In our experience, physicians have the most influence on the implementation of most operational changes that aim to improve organizational performance. Whether it is improving clinical quality, access, service, or coding and collections, physicians are critical. Physicians also have a powerful influence on staff's receptivity to change. Physician and administrative leaders deeply believe that, if they can only get the doctors "on board," everyone else will follow. When Willie Sutton, notorious for robbing banks, was asked to explain his actions, he allegedly responded, "Because that's where the money is." We believe focusing on physicians when it comes to implementing change is critical, because that is where the greatest opportunity lies.

We have found it helpful to categorize those trying to influence physicians to change from two perspectives:

- Is the individual a physician?

- What is the individual's relationship to the organization?

Figure I-2, page xix, gives examples of roles that illustrate the various possibilities. In the upper left quadrant are the leaders who themselves are physicians and members of the organization. Of all four categories, these individuals, in our experience, have the greatest leverage with physicians involved in change efforts. However, even these individuals are seen as "not-exactly-like-us" by other physicians, a label that has implications discussed in more detail in Chapter 1.

Individuals in the other three quadrants are typically seen by physicians as "not-at-all-like-us" from one or both perspectives. Like many professions, medicine can be described as a guild or lodge. The connotation is that, beyond a specialized body of knowledge, insiders share traditions and a special degree of loyalty to one another. The profession was set up to protect the economic interests of members, and the alliance among members is typically strong. Health care administrators, managers, and executives, regardless of their skill set and the bonds they establish with the physicians with whom they work, are not treated the way fellow physicians are. Those who work for other organizations—health plans, insurance companies, PPMs—tend to be viewed by physicians as outsiders, with motives not necessarily in physicians' best interests.

We use the term "outsiders" to refer to all those who are not inside both the profession and the organization. We are not making any judgments in this terminology. In our experience, it aptly describes physicians' views. The better those outside the profession or organization understand how they are seen, the more effective they can be. Being mindful of physicians' perceptions can help them interpret behavior appropriately. It also points out that some paths are more fruitful than others.

We wrote this book for all who are responsible for supporting and leading physicians through change to improve the value of the care they provide—for physician leaders such as Bud Jones and for administrators who, like Jon, are accountable for overall organizational performance. It is our goal to provide readers, regardless of where in the matrix they fall, with information that is useful and actionable. We believe the framework and guidance we offer can help accelerate positive improvements that make care better for patients and work life better for physicians and the staff who work with and support them.

work with them so they can be professionally satisfied and productive, and get the group to function together as a team. In these situations, I evaluate each doctor who is or could be a candidate in terms of his or her ability to be a sponsor for change. The doctor needs to be able to "straddle" the worlds of clinical medicine and administrative medicine and to have a commitment to each. Using the change role descriptions also helps me sort out the doctors who function best as informal leaders or champions and those who could be effective as formal leaders.

Involving physicians in a change has so many pluses you can't skip over this step. Physicians are independent thinkers, and effective group participation can be hard to come by without facilitation. Most of what we do in clinical practice reinforces our sense that when we're with the patient, we're on our own. On our own we need to gather data, assess what's important and what's not, and make a decision. When physicians collaborate or solve problems together, an entirely different skill set is called for. When working together, physicians can bring their own agendas to the table and won't even be aware they're doing it. Our inclination toward independent thinking can pervade group work. I find there are times I need to consciously remind myself what skills I need in such situations. Having someone facilitate these groups can help physicians shift into this other skill set.

I believe that many of the operational changes that could strengthen our business or make life better are resisted because of the deep unhappiness in our profession. Most doctors I know didn't go into medicine to practice the way we do today. The biggest disappointment is the changed relationships we have with patients. We simply cannot spend the time with each patient we think would be best and still get out of the office at a reasonable hour. The insurance forms, regulations, and productivity demands all mean doctors have to be very creative about how they parse out their time. For some physicians, being asked to change is the straw that breaks the camel's back. So, as the framework points out, leaders have to be sensitive to doctors' emotions and be prepared to deal with resistance that change so often provokes.

Contents

PART I

Build a Foundation

Leadership

Assessing the Current State

In your experience, what do physicians want their physician leaders to do? What criteria would they use to assess their leaders' effectiveness?

How do these expectations influence leaders? In what ways do they limit or support effective leadership?

How clear are the physician leaders you work with about their roles and their responsibilities?

Not very clear  Extremely clear

| I | 2 | 3 | 4 | 5 |

What do you observe that led you to select this number?

Physician Leadership as a Steady State

How physicians see their leaders' role is the primary driver for how physician leaders themselves see and fulfill their responsibilities. What matters most is not what leaders have learned in executive management programs or in other leadership development activities; what matters is the beliefs and assumptions that the organization's physicians hold about leadership and the expectations they have because of these beliefs and assumptions. Physicians' mental models[1] of leadership behavior determine leaders' mental models. And leaders' mental models of leadership determine their behavior as leaders. When leaders act in ways that fulfill physician expectations, they positively reinforce those expectations. In doing so, they also strengthen the influence that physicians have over the role that they as leaders play. This leadership steady state, illustrated in figure 1-1, page 4, can be observed across many different physician organizations. Moreover, it contributes in a fundamental way to the difficulties these organizations encounter when they try to implement the changes needed in the health care industry today. Consider the following scenario.

FIGURE I-I. Leadership Steady State

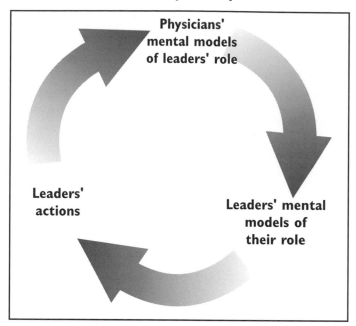

The Typical Leadership System in Physician Organizations

Dr. Maddy Lesnik is much-admired as the chief of her department. The doctors in the department consider her the best chief they've had in years. She is a good politician and can be outspoken when it's called for. She has fought for and won budget increases for three years in a row. She brought a couple of clinical stars to the department—one of whom is young, with an ego the size of a yacht. He rubs staff and other physicians the wrong way, but Maddy defends him to the hilt, claiming that his clinical acumen outweighs any interpersonal problems he leaves in his wake. Her attitude is, "This organization should be big enough to include good doctors like him." She juggles all of her many responsibilities skillfully and was recently named the organization's clinician of the year.

Maddy believes that her success is, in large part, due to her ability to get resources for her doctors and to relieve them, as much as possible, of "administrative nonsense." She also knows that it is important for her to spend time in clinical practice and not be seen as an ally of administration. The last thing she would ever want to be called is "a suit."

Other chiefs have difficulty with Maddy's style. In meetings, she monopolizes conversation and is not above bullying colleagues to gain an advantage for her doctors. She doesn't hesitate to point out that morale in her department is high. "Who else," she asks, "can say that?" One chief just rolls his eyes because he knows that these physicians have never adequately covered for one another and that Maddy chooses to ignore the squabbles over coverage and other internal issues. When the medical director asked every department to develop and implement one clinical guideline during this fiscal year, she got her doctors exempted. She argued that time away from seeing patients would only stress her doctors and wreak havoc with her access targets.

Given the strength of her personality, other leaders don't want to tangle with her. As a result, her department is seen as marching to its own drum, a situation that is beginning to concern the board. She is only now reluctantly working with purchasing to standardize ordering of common supplies, a year after other departments were brought into a centralized purchasing system. And she is intent on having the information technology (IT) department supply monthly reports even though they mean extra work for IT staff and the parameters tracked aren't of the highest priority to the organization. The topic at the next board meeting is the increasing red ink in the financial report. The board chair is concerned enough about the situation in Maddy's department to add it to the agenda even though he knows that more than one board member has a certain level of admiration for Maddy's successes.

Let's examine the leadership steady state as it is revealed in Maddy Lesnik's actions.

Physician Mental Models of Leaders' Roles
Across a range of organizational settings, physicians' mental models of leadership are consistent. Physicians tend to view leaders as their advocates who are responsible to secure resources, protect their interests, and keep "them" (nonphysician administrators) from interfering in doctors' lives. For example,

FIGURE 1-2. "Old" Leadership Steady State

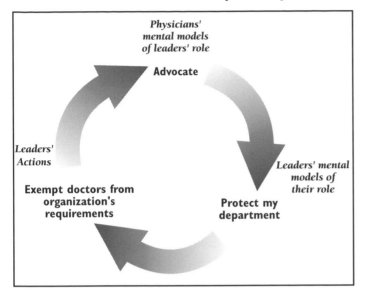

the doctors in Maddy Lesnik's department look to her to represent their interests to higher-ups. The general expectation is that a chief will act as a scout and carry messages into the larger organization and back to the department. Most important, the physician leader "takes care of his or her own" and brings resources back to constituents. When the leader's efforts are successful, department colleagues appreciate the leader. In Maddy's case, her doctors' esteem for her reinforces her approach. She is led to view her effectiveness in terms of protecting the departments' interests regardless of the impact on the organization down the line. A steady state is established that we like to think of as the "old" steady state, or the steady state of traditional physician leadership, shown in figure 1-2, above. Reflect on the figure and on the frequently quoted reminder of Donald Berwick, the leading thinker on improvement in health care, "Every process is perfectly designed to produce the results it gets."

In any leader-follower dynamic, followers influence leaders, and leaders respond to and stay in touch with their followers. For example, few political leaders would consider running for office without tapping public opinion through focus groups and polls. Followers shape the candidate's stand on issues. Once elected, officials who want to remain in office continue to take the pulse of the electorate. Through favorable legislation and other means, they repay their supporters. Likewise, in business enterprises,

leaders stay in touch with other organization members lest they get too far ahead and lose touch with what matters to them. In our experience, however, this dynamic is skewed in physician organizations where leaders are reactive to an inordinate degree. When physicians expect their leaders to represent and protect their interests, and in some cases elect them to do just that, these criteria define success in the role and make it difficult to wear the mantle of any other kind of leadership.

Mismatch of the "Old" Steady State and the Organization's Needs

The "old" steady state, as advantageous as it may be to a department, can compromise the effectiveness of the whole organization. Consider the negative impact on overall organization performance of these situations, all too common under department-centered leadership:

- A physician's rudeness adversely affects staff morale, but is tolerated.

- Physician coverage is not adequate to provide good patient access and service, but is tolerated.

- A physician who resists making changes is allowed to opt out, and is tolerated, weakening the capacity of the clinical team.

The "old" steady state reflects traditional physician values, attitudes, and beliefs and the leadership that naturally evolved to meet physicians' expectations. Independence, for example, is a dominant feature of physician cultures. As a result of their training and professional socialization, physicians look to themselves, not leaders, for answers, and they defend their autonomy as the foundation of good medical practice. Within an organization, they follow the direction of others reluctantly, especially if they have not been involved in setting the course.

Another aspect of the old steady state that is also deeply ingrained in physician cultures is the reluctance to confront colleagues even when it may be the only way a situation can be resolved. There are two reasons. The first is that leaders often see their role as protecting physician autonomy. That makes it difficult for leaders to even envision confronting physicians about their behavior. The second relates to the emphasis physician leaders place on building collegial relationships with those they lead. Maddie's reluctance to confront inappropriate behavior among her physicians is not atypical. Even the board and other chiefs are not direct with her when her behavior undermines the enterprise.

Until external pressures for lower cost and improved quality began to force change, autonomy and an individualistic orientation worked well for physicians, even in group settings, hospitals, and faculty practices. Acting collectively was not required for success. Being a loosely knit "team" of individuals, all pursuing the same goal of providing good medicine, was the norm and was sufficient for most organizational purposes. In this context, the purpose of leaders was to represent local interests in organizationwide venues, secure resources, and occasionally rally physicians against an enemy—hospital administration, insurance companies, nonphysician management, or even other physicians in their own organization.

A fundamental shift in the market has profoundly changed the need for leadership in physician organizations. Physician organizations can no longer afford to primarily serve the needs of physicians; they must focus on meeting the needs of patients and other customers. Putting patients in the center of all the organization's work calls for a new perspective among leaders and among all physicians in the organization.

The traditional steady state of leadership doesn't support organizational success today because each physician doing his or her personal best isn't enough to improve quality and service or to reduce costs. Meeting the needs of purchasers and patients will require physicians' working collaboratively. The traditional steady state protects the core belief that physicians practice best when they are given the resources they ask for and then are left alone.

Ways to Change Physician Leadership by Changing Leaders' Mental Models

Many physician leaders find themselves caught between physicians' expectations of them and pressure to meet customer needs, which requires dramatic changes in how physicians work together. They appreciate that improvement requires a kind of leadership

FIGURE I-3. "New" Leadership Steady State

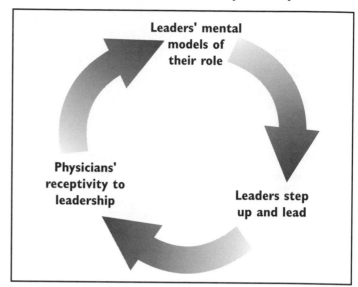

that is not possible under the old steady state and that it is unlikely that physicians will spontaneously choose it. Kotter says that, when the outside environment undergoes dramatic shifts, the organization has to respond, which increases the need for effective leadership. "More change always demands more leadership."[2]

If the "old" leadership steady state is inadequate for the challenges facing physician organizations today, what should take its place? In some organizations, a "new" leadership steady state can already be observed that offers the promise of promoting collective action among physicians to meet the challenges they and today's health care leaders face (figure 1-3, above).

Moving to the "new" leadership steady state requires leaders to take the bold step to redefine their mental models of leadership and thereby redefine leadership for the organization. Leaders proactively shape their role instead of reactively filling the role created for them by the expectations of their physicians. The possibilities for leadership expand. Exercising leadership in this way may represent a stretch for some. Actions include holding other physicians accountable for performance, working as a leadership team, and working to support even decisions they may have voted against. By physician leaders' acting in ways that support organizational performance and make life better for physicians, others come to a different view of what leaders do; over time their expectations of leadership shift, and their new expectations reinforce the new mental models that leaders have adopted. Getting to the "new" leadership steady state requires disrupting the old one. In any such cyclical dynamic, all parties share responsibility for keeping the cycle going; physicians and their leaders both contribute. "Everyone is responsible for problems generated by a system," Senge writes, but "that doesn't mean that everyone can exert equal leverage in changing the system."[3]

The most effective method we have seen for moving to the "new" steady state is for leaders to use their leverage to disrupt the old one. The call for a different kind of leadership is unlikely to swell up from physicians' ranks. Leaders must create disequilibrium in the "old" steady state, but this can be very challenging. Physician leaders are physicians first and leaders second. Many benefit from the traditional leadership system themselves. Furthermore, if they try to lead in ways consistent with the new steady state, they come up against the culture that sustains old beliefs about leadership. The culture can dilute the impact of their actions and pull them back into their comfort zone. (The power of culture to undermine new models of leadership is explored in chapter 3.)

Some breakthroughs in leadership systems come about through retreats designed to get leaders to explore barriers to their effectiveness and come to agreements about new mental models and behaviors. This usually happens when the most senior physician leaders understand the limitations of the old steady state and commit to taking action to recreate the organization's leadership. But that's only one way to move toward the new steady state. The more natural course of change begins with one or two leaders who perceive a need and enroll other leaders in the cause until enough are convinced that carrying on with traditional models of leadership in the face of increasing complexity and change is unsustainable.

Level One: Individual Examination of Leadership

In our experience, many physician leaders have to navigate some very tricky waters. On one hand, they are limited by others' perceptions and can lead only to the extent "permitted" by colleagues. A chief was described to us by one physician in his department as "not one millimeter above the rest of us." On the other hand, they are expected to implement strategy and improvements. The "pinch" felt can be the impetus for a personal exploration of the kind of leadership that is needed.

If you feel caught between the expectations of those you lead and what the organization needs to do to succeed, consider how you personally can challenge the prevailing views of leadership. This starts with personal reflection and action and involves:

- Getting clear on your own assumptions and determining if they need to change.

- Considering new mental models of your leadership role.

- Beginning to experiment with acting in ways consistent with new mental models.

Get Clear on Your Own Assumptions and Whether They Need to Change

Reflecting on two issues as parallel tracks can generate new insights and deepened conviction about the need for a different approach to leadership. One track is clarifying your own personal views of what leadership is in general and what model of leadership guides your behaviors and interactions in your leadership role. After giving thought to how you see your role, consider the second track—the demand for leadership being generated by external change. What kind of leadership is called for to develop change readiness and adaptability among the physicians you lead? Exploring both your leadership model and the organization's need for leadership helps you assess whether your model can support success as you go forward. Tool 1-1, pages 18-19, is provided to guide you in this exploration. As you do this work, keep in mind that the assumptions guiding physician leadership in the past were appropriate to their time and setting. It's not a matter of criticizing the "old" leadership steady state or the behaviors (your own or anyone else's) driven by it. The only issue for consideration is whether current mental models will support success of the enterprise as it goes forward.

If Maddy Lesnik had thoughtfully tried to reconcile the demands for leadership brought on by outside pressures and her own beliefs about her role (e.g., not wanting to be seen as a "suit," protecting an "outlier" doctor, focusing on her own department's needs with little regard to the whole), it would be clear that doing what "works," if it's defined exclusively by her mental models, is destructive.

Consider New Mental Models

What new mental models are most useful to leaders who need to develop a true patient orientation and a receptivity to change among physicians? There is no one right model, but, in our view, a few are fundamental to getting to the "new" steady state. Also, it's not necessary to leave behind all the assumptions that support the "old" steady state. Some will always be important (e.g., as a leader, I am responsible to support physicians to be the best clinicians they can be). Mental models of leadership that support organizational success include:

- Put advocacy in perspective.

- Make patients and other customers the focus of daily work life.

- Facilitate physicians to work collectively.

- Confront inappropriate physician behavior directly.

- Be responsible to other leaders and be a team player.

- Go first—move on and model changes before expecting others to.

- Remove barriers and facilitate others to take responsibility.

- Provide spiritual leadership—meet physicians' need to feel connected and acknowledged.

- Build trust, avoid actions that can be construed as purely political.

- Communicate to and from other levels in the organization—even "bad news," such as information about competition, customers' perceptions, and budget and performance shortfalls.

When thinking about what basic view of a leader's role is most appropriate for you, think in terms of the competitive pressures and the extent to which your organization currently is focused on meeting its customers' needs. The most important criteria for leadership going forward relate to what it will take for the whole enterprise to take on a customer-orientation

and make other changes in response to the market in order to thrive.

Begin to Experiment

For a whole leadership system to shift, just about every leader in the organization needs to take on different behaviors. However, a single leader who translates awareness about mental models into action can have an impact. Individual leaders have many opportunities to "try on" new mental models and to experiment with new ways to lead.

Base your experiments on which mental models you believe are most suitable, given the challenges to your department and organization. Here are some ways to put into action mental models associated with the "new" leadership steady state.

- *Put advocacy in perspective.* When physicians ask you to advocate on their behalf for more resources, educate them about how their request will affect others or why it is important to live within the budget. Ask them to help you find resources in the current budget that could be re-deployed to fund requests.

- *Make patients and other customers the focus of daily work life.* Physician leaders need to help everyone in the workforce put patients and other customers at the center of daily work. Physicians are the irreplaceable human resource in the care delivery system, but they cannot be at the center of what drives the organization. Keep patients' perceptions and satisfaction in the forefront; continually ask how physicians can make the process of getting care easier and better for patients. Bring attention to "the voice of the customer" by sharing verbatim patient comments, both positive and negative, about the department or the organization.

- *Confront inappropriate physician behavior directly.* Hold physicians accountable. Many physician leaders we know avoid this responsibility because they interpret holding someone accountable as "getting heavy" on him or her or being confrontational. This perception unfortunately cuts off a good deal of leverage a leader could have. Confronting inappropriate behavior could be simply expressing your disappointment in someone's behavior—e.g., "I'm disappointed you didn't keep your word and follow up on that matter." This can be a powerful communication and all that is needed to get a physician's attention and change a behavior.

- *Be responsible to other leaders and be a team player.* Support decisions by the leadership team of which you are a part—the board, the council of chiefs, a group of site managers—even when you do not agree with the decision but understand the logic for it. Avoid relying on "rules management" and conveying to other physicians that the board or the medical director is "making us" accept a new policy or change.

- *Remove barriers and facilitate others to take responsibility.* Strike a balance between removing barriers that block physicians from meeting patients' needs and supporting physicians in their taking responsibility to fix problems or to work though interpersonal conflicts themselves. The barriers that are within your purview to remove, take down. But when physicians ask you to work out a situation that they should address themselves, do not allow them to shift the burden to you.

- *Provide spiritual leadership.* Part of leading is connecting with others on a human level and providing a sense of optimism. In physician organizations, this has never been more needed, yet it is still largely overlooked and undervalued. You can fill this void by listening with empathy, inspiring confidence, and acknowledging physicians' effort.

- *Build trust and avoid actions that can be construed as being purely political.* Leaders may not be conscious of how their actions undermine others' trust. Even when leaders think they are trustworthy, others can misconstrue their actions. Engaging at any time in behavior others think untrustworthy creates a filter through which others later evaluate and sometimes misinterpret behavior. Actions that destroy trust include not sharing information, not getting back to requests in a timely way, acting in one's self-interest, not discussing the "elephants" in the room that cause problems, and not dealing with sacred cows. To build trust: keep your word, follow through on commitments, acknowledge mistakes, take actions

that make physicians' daily practice life better, refuse to cut special deals, steer clear of backdoor politics, and involve physicians in meaningful dialogue and input.

When experimenting with new behaviors, be prepared to persevere. When you try something new, many physicians are likely not to notice or, if they notice, may think it's a passing fad. A useful approach is to choose one behavior that you repeat and work into your daily interactions with physicians. Keep up the new way, and others will notice in time. Keeping a daily log and reviewing it regularly can be a good way to support your commitment. (Tool 1-2, pages 20-21, can help you develop a plan to incorporate one new leadership behavior into your physician interactions and track its effect.)

The steps down this path need not be lonely. Especially if thinking in new ways about leadership and taking new actions are contrary to the norm in your organization, it may be helpful to build in some support. Professional associations, educational conferences and workshops, and electronic and organizational networks are some of the ways in which physician leaders find like-minded colleagues. Look to colleagues in your own organization as well for support and to share your reflections on leadership and the demands for change faced by your organization.

Level Two: Collective Action

Leaders need to move from personal insight and experience to engaging other leaders to consider and ultimately agree to shift the way they view their role. The process could begin as informally as sharing ideas with other leaders willing to reflect on their roles and on the challenges facing the organization. Share with them your personal views of leadership and your experiments in being a different kind of leader. Engage in conversations about how the dynamic among leaders reinforces current mental models. Resist trying to convince anyone of the need for change; instead, use questions to lead to discovery of what works and what does not work in the current leadership system and of what the organization needs as it goes forward.

The goal is to ripple through one or more levels of leadership. Those you engage, in turn, will have opportunities to talk to other leaders. This process might take some time, but it is one way to build the critical mass of support needed to address these issues more formally, at a retreat or in a structured series of meetings. A productive discussion about leadership is unlikely if leaders have not already recognized the liability represented by the "old" leadership steady state. Limiting discussion of the issues to a single meeting or retreat is likely to generate only superficial agreement, or perhaps even cynicism.

Opportunities exist in the course of daily interaction with physicians to open up dialogue regarding mental models of leadership. Whenever you are involved in planning a leadership skills training program, ask others to consider if there is something more fundamental than skills that needs to be taken into account. How would those trained be able to use the skills they learn if this fundamental level is not also discussed? You might also ask other leaders to consider what they think contributes to the shortfalls between targets for organizational performance and results achieved. Ask them to think about how leaders' roles and their view of leaders may contribute. Tool 1-3, pages 22-23, can help you identify ways to get others to consider how mental models held by physicians in the organization influence leaders' actions.

When a critical mass of leaders demonstrates a willingness to have a group discussion about these issues, it is time to create an opportunity for an in-depth dialogue among senior leadership groups. Who is included in these discussions depends on the traditions in your organization. For example, if the board, senior management, the medical director, and chiefs have a history of meeting together, that might be the best group. Alternatively, if the board and senior management always meet separately, not together, for strategic discussions, start with these groups separately.

When designing the agenda for these discussions, keep in mind that the main objective is to have a full discussion of the differences between the "old" and "new" leadership steady states and of the implications of moving to more empowered and effective leadership for your organization. It is helpful for leaders to understand that transitioning to the kind of leadership that is necessary to be successful in today's

environment requires more than change in any one individual. It requires a change in the dynamic that has been reinforced among leaders and between leaders and the rest of the organization. The discussion should make explicit that other foundational work to improve organizational change capability—for example, work on developing a shared vision and a new compact—depends on leaders moving to a "new" steady state and that it is up to the current leaders to generate that shift. Without this recognition, these powerful tools and efforts to use them are likely to be viewed as one more "flavor of the month."

While these discussions need to be customized to each organization, an example of goals, an agenda, and pre-work for this kind of retreat is provided in figure 1-4, page 11. It is important to create an environment that encourages participants to be open to new ideas as well as to take risks to fully share their perspectives. Setting and enforcing ground rules and providing effective facilitation can be helpful. It is also useful to keep the discussion as concrete as possible. Work to link the discussion of mental models to real examples of how they affect day-to-day behavior and organizational performance. If physicians find the term mental models too abstract or see it as jargon, do not insist on it. Substitute expressions such as "how I see my role as a leader," "what I hold myself accountable to do as a leader," or "my beliefs about leadership."

Be realistic about what you can achieve. Although the commitment of some individuals, including the board chair, the CEO, and the medical director, is essential, it is unlikely that every leader will agree to the concepts and commit to work toward a new steady state. To expect 100 percent agreement is a set-up for disappointment. Each leader can only move at his or her pace. Pushing for a new steady state only increases resistance and slows the process. It may not be necessary to get total buy-in to shift the steady state. Most important is agreement among the key leaders, and as many more as possible, to make a conscious effort to lead in a new way.

Step Up and Lead

When leaders collectively develop new and different views of their leadership roles, they set the stage for the "new" leadership steady state. When they step up and lead in ways consistent with their new views,

FIGURE 1-4. Retreat to Consider Views of Leadership: Objectives and Agenda

SUGGESTED PRE-WORK:

- All participants should complete Tool 1-1 prior to the retreat. This gives everyone an opportunity to start thinking about current mental models of leadership.

- For background on leadership mental models in physician organizations, participants should read "New Dynamic for Medical Group Governance: Enhancing 'Followership' and Organizational Performance." Silversin, J. and Kornacki, M., *Group Practice Journal* 49(2):27-34, Feb. 2000.

RETREAT OBJECTIVES:

- To explore current mental models of leadership.

- To identify how these mental models influence leadership's effectiveness and the organization's ability to change.

- To choose new mental models of leadership roles and explore what these new mental models would mean for how leaders lead.

AGENDA:

- Review objectives and agenda.

- Set ground rules.

- Present background on mental models. For resources, see Peter Senge, *Fifth Discipline*.

- Describe current mental models of leadership by sharing responses to the Track 1 questions in Tool 1-1.

- Discuss the impact, positive and negative, of prevailing mental models and the extent to which physicians' expectations of leaders shape leadership behavior in the organization.

- Present a high-level overview of the challenges facing the organization and review responses to the Track 2 questions in Tool 1-1.

- Review mental models that can potentially drive different leadership behaviors. These include:

  - Put advocacy in perspective.
  - Make patients and other customers the focus of daily work life.
  - Facilitate physicians to work collectively.
  - Confront inappropriate physician behavior directly.
  - Be responsible to other leaders and be a team player.
  - Go first—move on and model change before expecting others to.
  - Remove barriers and facilitate others to take responsibility.
  - Provide spiritual leadership.
  - Build trust, avoid actions that can be construed as purely political.
  - Communicate to and from other levels in the organization—even "bad news," such as information about competition, customers' perceptions, and budget and performance shortfalls.

- Decide if new mental models are needed and, if so, which you would collectively adopt to drive different leadership.

- Brainstorm what it could look like if all leaders were to lead from the preferred mental models.

- Identify what stands in the way of acting in congruence with the preferred mental models and what supports exist.

- Commit to a few new behaviors.

- Decide on a way to measure progress and next steps in the process to develop different leadership. (Consider skill development needs, changes in meeting agendas, revised job descriptions.)

- Summarize commitments.

- Evaluate the meeting.

they help to change physicians' mental models and, over time, their receptivity to this kind of leadership.

By "step up and lead," we do not mean to imply that physician leaders do not lead now—they do. In our experience, however, many are leading in ways too narrowly prescribed. They feel torn when others expect them to carry the banner for a change that they anticipate physicians will resist. To step up and lead means to lead from a different set of mental models of the leader's role. To make their new mental models visible to the organization, leaders may take the following actions:

- Start doing things differently in everyday work life.

- Add value by helping make physicians' daily lives easier or better.

- Use development and implementation of a shared vision, compact change, or another large-scale change effort to educate all physicians about why and how leaders need to lead for the whole and what the implications are of doing so.

- Clarify the roles of the board and physician management and enable each group to fulfill its unique role.

Start Doing Things Differently in Everyday Work Life

When all leaders begin to make their new mental models visible in action, organizational norms will shift. Think about an organization you know well—perhaps your own—and what would happen if every leader adopted the new mental models and started to practice the new behaviors described earlier in this chapter. For example, what if every leader understood the roles and responsibilities of leaders for building trust and began to avoid actions for political reasons alone? If Maddy Lesnik, the other chiefs, and the board members in her organization were to step up and lead from a new and different set of mental models of leaders' role, they would be well on their way to dissolving the "old" leadership steady state that prevails in that organization. Instead, they would work collaboratively to lead for the whole organization. Doing what is best for the organization would replace their current silo mentality.

Add Value for Physicians

Physicians will not have any greater respect for leadership if all leaders do is pressure them to change and

to work more. Leaders can add value for physicians by making physicians' daily work life easier or more rewarding. Leaders need to focus some of their attention on listening to physicians' concerns and responding. If processes are broken, get involved and fix them. This does not mean to get engaged in work physicians should be doing. Consider the case of two physicians who cannot get along. One approach is to separate them, even though doing so makes life less convenient for the support staff and doesn't deal with the underlying friction that is eventually bound to threaten quality of care. A better approach is to facilitate a conversation in which the doctors figure out how they will work out their differences in a constructive way. Similarly, if physicians complain about inadequate support staff, do not shrug off the concern by pointing to the budget or press for an increase in staff without objective evidence of the need. Adding value means helping physicians explore all the options and working with them to find a solution that meets their needs within the organization's real constraints.

Use Other Change Processes to Educate Physicians

Change processes offer an opportunity to educate all physicians about why and how leaders need to lead for the whole and what the implications are of doing so. Shoring up your organization's foundation for change may involve developing or deepening a shared vision or creating a new physician compact. Either would involve a number of physicians and set the context for a discussion of the kind of leadership the organization needs. (Vision development is addressed in chapter 2; compact change, in chapter 3.)

Communicating the need for different leadership by linking it to major change efforts and specific actions works better with physicians than talking about leadership in the abstract. For example, a chief medical officer might say, "As part of the plan to improve patient access to care, it is necessary to implement new scheduling, and chiefs and pod leaders will be responsible for working with physicians on the following changes...." Chapter 9 describes the process one medical group undertook to create new expectations of group membership among physicians and staff. This effort touched every physician and happened over the better part of a year. It involved many discussions among physician leaders regarding their roles in this change. The change effort provided an ideal way for leaders to become clear on what kind of leadership the organization needed and also gave them a very public communication role. Leadership behavior by the end of the process was very different from before it.

Clarify the Roles of the Board and of Physician Management

The board's job and management's job are, for the most part, distinct. The board is responsible, in partnership with senior management, to set vision, strategies, and policies, including compensation; to approve the budget; and to oversee the performance of management, in particular the effectiveness of management in achieving the organization's desired financial and quality results. Ultimately, the board is responsible for the organization's financial and quality performance. The board delegates to management the responsibility to turn policies and strategies into tactics and work plans. Leadership effectiveness is improved when those involved in governance and physician management understand and fulfill their respective roles and responsibilities.

In many physician organizations, these different roles and responsibilities are not clearly defined. Not uncommonly, boards focus time and attention on what should be management's purview, for example, overseeing the supply budget or physician scheduling instead of developing strategy. This role confusion undermines management's authority and encourages backdoor politics, such as physicians' circumventing management and taking issues directly to the board. Precious board meeting time is wasted on issues best handled by others. The board leader and the chief executive are responsible for ensuring that board members have the knowledge and the skills they need to perform effectively as a board. (The sidebar, right and page 14, provides an example of what one physician organization has done to improve its board.) Board development work typically includes educating board members about the health care industry and the organization's market, as well as about the responsibilities of health care boards and members' roles. Board members often benefit from learning how to conduct productive

Creating Effective Governance
BALTEJ S. MAINI, MD

Baltej Maini is President and Chief Executive Officer of Fallon Clinic, a 240-physician multispecialty group practice located in Worcester, Massachusetts. Fallon Clinic is part of the Fallon Healthcare System, which includes a not-for-profit HMO and a research and education foundation.

The board of directors of any organization plays a vital role in providing leadership to the company and its senior management team. For years, the Fallon Clinic Board of Directors functioned well in that capacity. However, amid significant losses in 1996, the board found itself operating ineffectively.

What had happened? First and foremost, the board had lost some of its focus. As a result, board members often found themselves involved in day-to-day operations instead of looking at the big picture and providing strategic direction. In addition, communication among physicians, administrative leaders, and board members had disintegrated. Staff physicians felt disconnected from the very board that represented them.

Our task was to revitalize the board and, in the process, reenergize administrative leadership and the organization. Our first step was to understand who we were as an organization and where we wanted to go. We reexamined our mission, vision, and core values, revised them where necessary, and rededicated ourselves to their principles.

From that process, we got a clearer picture of how the board could be reorganized to better achieve its purpose. We took several steps, including reducing the number of board members from 12 to nine, with the majority of seats assigned to primary care physicians to ensure fair representation. We also revised the bylaws to clarify ambiguities, scheduled meetings quarterly rather than monthly (adding informal meetings when necessary), and designed meeting agendas to be more efficient.

To extricate board members from day-to-day operations, we developed a new leadership team that included a chief financial officer, a director of human resources, and a medical director. With the medical director in charge of physicians and other managers, the board could step away from acting as the go-between whenever physicians had concerns.

We also provided board members with more relevant, timely, and detailed information and committed ourselves to complete candor and honesty. This helped board members to understand more easily where operations were broken and where staff physicians encountered significant difficulties. Board members thoroughly review the information prior to meetings and prepare to engage in meaningful conversation about the topics at hand.

We have further strengthened governance by developing a formal process to evaluate the president's performance and that of his direct reports. A process whereby individual board members evaluate each other is also being developed.

There have been other improvements as well:

- We established ground rules to promote open and honest communication geared to the benefit of the whole organization.

- To ensure a consistent message, we provided written talking points on major board decisions to each member.

- Major votes are decided by unanimous decisions, a process that encourages honest and open conversation, as well as the sharing of opinions.

- To improve operations and governance, we encourage relationships between board members and senior managers that are founded on trust.

- We have restructured the medical staff to ensure accountability for resolving conflicts without interference from board members.

All these steps have helped to form a board of directors whose sole purpose is to lead the organization into the future. The process of building governance that is distinguished by strong leadership demands careful planning and great care. However, the benefits are enormous.

How do you achieve this type of board? First, it is important to clearly define and separate the roles of management and the board. If necessary, use a facilitator or a consultant to encourage open dialogue and to keep the process on track. Make it a habit to meet with opinion leaders both on and off the board, because their influence can be far reaching. Most important, get input from staff physicians. If physicians don't buy into the need for governance, they have the potential to defeat the purpose of the board and to derail its mission.

At Fallon Clinic, the changes we have made in governance have had a positive impact. Profitability has improved and capital has increased. Staff at all levels of our organization have a clearer vision and sense of

purpose that translates into consistently high quality of care for our patients. And Fallon Clinic's mission in the community is more widely understood. We feel our efforts to improve our governance and physician leadership are paying off.

meetings. This work can be done through a variety of board development activities, including educational retreats,[4] policy discussions, and special communications from the board chair, such as newsletters and recommended readings.[5,6] To ensure the board's effectiveness, the leadership also has the responsibility to provide appropriate committee structures and staff support and to ensure that sound processes are in place to recruit and select new members.

Develop Capacity to Lead

New Skills

Historian Garry Wills elegantly defines the leader as "one who mobilizes others toward a goal shared by leader and followers."[7] Leaders, in essence, have the skill and the tact to take those in their organization to a different place, one they might not have chosen on their own. Providing spiritual leadership and promoting discipline are two essential skills that are new for many physician leaders. Developing skill in providing spiritual leadership is essential in order to mobilize others toward a goal.

Providing spiritual leadership means meeting human needs and fostering the sense of optimism that, by working together, physicians can create a positive future. To be followers, physicians would need to trust leaders and perceive that they care about their best interests. To go along, physicians also need to have confidence that there is a plan shaped by sound judgment and analysis and that a leader can execute the plan. The skills associated with demonstrating and promoting discipline come into play.

Promoting discipline involves the knowledge and the skills leaders use to become and stay focused on the key determinants of organizational success. Promoting discipline requires that physician leaders:

- Develop strategy based on a sound understanding of the industry and the market.

- Develop focus, distinguishing between what is "nice to do" and what is essential.

- Acquire and use budgeting and financial skills.

- Set and communicate clear targets.

- Use data and measurement in setting targets, analyzing performance, and providing feedback.

Our observations of physician organizations suggest that many physician leaders need to work on both dimensions of leadership. Even when physicians agree that a new kind of leadership is called for, many are not prepared to act in ways consistent with the new mental models. Without education and support to help them follow through on their intentions, many leaders slip back to familiar patterns. The sidebar, right and page 16, relates the approaches that one leader has taken to develop physician leaders.

A Process of Education over Time

The goals of new leadership are twofold: to re-focus physicians on the roles leaders and followers should be playing and to lead the organization to success. Because of the steady state dynamic between leaders and followers, if physicians' mental models do not change, the job of leaders is much more difficult. Changing leaders' view of their role and thereby reshaping how physicians see their leaders and what they expect of them requires a considerable investment of effort and time. The process can be accelerated by explicit education and by continually linking the new roles for leaders being played out in the organization to other change activities. For example, board elections provide an opportunity to educate constituents about the role of board members as stewards for the whole organization and to discuss the differences between responsibilities of the board and responsibilities of management.

Receptivity to Leadership

When leaders are effective and demonstrate to physicians how the organization as a whole and physicians in particular benefit from effective leadership, physicians become more receptive to the new brand of leadership. In the process, physicians develop a new view of their own role as followers—a role that physicians traditionally have not been comfortable in or seen a need for. A breakthrough occurs when

Developing Physician Leadership
THOMAS C. ROYER, MD

Tom Royer is Chief Executive Officer of the CHRISTUS Health System, an integrated delivery system consisting of 40 hospitals, 108 physician clinics, multiple long-term care facilities, and numerous outpatient programs and ministries in more than 60 communities in Texas, Louisiana, Arkansas, Utah, and Oklahoma.

I want physicians working for me who inspire confidence in their patients simply by walking through the door. But leading physicians with strong clinical egos presents several challenges. These physicians need to understand how to be team players outside of clinical areas. Doctors understand the concept of teamwork in the operating room very well. But in other arenas, doctors often want to be in control. Another challenge is getting them to move away from individual thinking and toward global, program, or system thinking. A third challenge is getting them to understand and respect the role of administrative colleagues. Our solutions in health care today have to balance effectiveness, efficiency, and fiscal soundness. Physicians are in the best position to make judgments on effectiveness of care. But we need to listen to administrators and financial people on other issues, and physicians don't always appreciate their contribution.

It's been a real joy to me to help other physicians develop as leaders. I've used a number of strategies that other leaders might employ, including:

- Provide doctors a book list and create a physician leadership library.

- Offer workshops on specific leadership topics identified through a needs assessment.

- Hold semi-annual leadership retreats.

- Involve physicians in the strategic planning process as a way to increase their business literacy.

- Conduct one-to-one meetings with direct reports, with a frequency determined by how much attention each person requires.

- Share best practices through an intranet. As a resource for leaders, CHRISTUS posts best practices in our four core areas: clinical and technical change, service, community value, business literacy. The database includes the sponsor of each best practice so one leader can talk with or visit a colleague who has been successful.

- Offer affinity group meetings as a venue for professionals to meet with their colleagues across a large system—for example, CMOs with other CMOs—to dialogue about standards of performance.

One of the greatest mistakes physician leaders make is working too long with the wrong people. When a physician is not performing up to expectations, you only compound the problems by not dealing with it in a forthright manner. If you've done all you can to help someone be successful, but they don't have what it takes, you must change horses. Holding other physicians accountable, for most physician leaders, is the hardest of all their responsibilities.

When I teach other leaders about holding physicians accountable, I discuss the need to occasionally "weed the garden." The weeding process only occurs after a thoughtful performance appraisal process that guides you to identify goals, objectives, tactics, and measures. This is an excellent way to get physicians involved and taking responsibility for results. Coaching and mentoring physicians to be successful is the next step. However, after you've put the effort into developing a good performance review and you've taken time to coach for improved performance, if success is not measurable, a transition plan should be developed for the individual. This task is understandably hard, and one should never get so callous that you do it without empathy.

As a corollary to holding physicians accountable, leaders have to set high standards and inspire others to reach for them. Sometimes a bold statement is needed to get doctors' attention, and I'm not beyond staging a little drama to do just that. At one time, when I was the leader of the Henry Ford Medical Group, it was below the median for patient satisfaction scores according to a survey conducted in medical groups across the country. Our physicians thought the data were wrong. I knew something beyond the written report was called for to focus them on the reality. At an all-staff meeting, I placed myself on a gurney, dressed in a patient gown, and gave a five-minute presentation to let the doctors hear the "voice of our patients." This was most effective in getting their attention. Our physician leaders learned to read patient satisfaction data, develop action plans, and seek out best practices for using feedback and aligned incentives. In 18 months, our patient satisfaction scores were at 84 percent, only eight percentage points from being best in class. Motivated physician leadership made that success possible.

physician-followers recognize the legitimate role of their board or governing body in making decisions and delegating authority to carry out policy and decisions to others. Such recognition can be a signal that the "new" leadership steady state has been established. Ideally, physician-followers are far from passive. Physician-followers take responsibility to understand business and market realities, internalize the link between the organization's economic health and their own, accept responsibility to attend and participate in meetings, understand the necessity of collective action, and acknowledge that the organization's vision prevails over individual interests. They proactively engage with board members to stay informed and to express their views and give feedback to leaders on the congruency between what leaders say and how they act.

Fully understanding and acting out the leader and the follower roles do not happen quickly or easily in physician organizations. It takes patience and commitment. In our experience, however, unless physicians can be helped to understand and accept these roles, their organizations remain stuck in the "old" leadership steady state and remain disabled from responding effectively to the challenges they face.

Take Responsibility—Avoid a Victim Mentality

Taking responsibility and getting drawn into a victim mentality are opposite states of mind. One of the earliest observations we made about life inside physician organizations is that a victim mentality is fairly typical. "It's not worth trying that. We gave it a go five years ago and it didn't work." "The managers are hopeless, totally tuned out of reality." "We've always done it this way." "Why are you telling me? I can't do anything about it." Some would argue that the issues with which physician leaders deal are out of their control, that they are the victims of efforts to contain costs and other larger forces, and they would resent any implication to the contrary. The market may be demanding that you take costs out of your system, but how you meet the challenge is in your control.

To take responsibility means to accept your contribution to current reality. When leaders take responsibility, they own their part in the current dynamic. Leaders who adopt a victim mentality minimize their

FIGURE 1-5. The Victim Box

CAUGHT IN THE VICTIM BOX
The Space of Impossibility

possibilities and choices and externalize the cause of problems. Figure 1–5 illustrates the condition we call "being in the victim box."

The victim box is having a mindset of "no," "we can't do that," or "we tried that once before." As long as they are inside the box, leaders are constrained in their ability to think creatively and proactively. The victim mentality is a serious impediment to breaking out of the "old" leadership steady state. If leaders believe they can do little to change physicians' current expectations of them, that the current situation is as good as it gets, or that the dynamic is "bigger" than they are, they will not make the necessary investment or take the risk to change the situation. It is easy to fall prey to such a mindset. All it takes is two or three physician leaders who feel their hands are tied to discourage others from taking action.

Taking responsibility for actions and choices is like finding the pot of gold at the rainbow's end. The insight, "if we contributed to this state, then we can change it," is empowering. Leaders who are not in the box realize that, by working collaboratively and supporting each other, they can move to a more effective mode of leadership.

Success Requires Leadership that Facilitates Collaboration

Golf is a wonderful sport. No one excels at it without innate skill, the ability to concentrate, and openness to coaching and feedback. But winning at golf does not take a group effort. Golf is a solo sport. Health care used to be much more of a solo endeavor. Great clinicians were rewarded with success largely because of personal achievements.

Today, succeeding at health care is more like winning at basketball. Bill Bradley has written that "the society we live in glorifies individualism, what Ross Perot used to champion with the expression, 'eagles don't flock.' Basketball teaches a different lesson: that untrammeled individualism destroys the chance for achieving victory. Players must have sufficient self-knowledge to take the long view—to see that what any one player can do alone will never equal what a team can do together."[8]

If delivering the best health care and thriving as an organization both take collective effort, are physician leaders working from the most appropriate, most helpful mental models? It is up to each leader to explore this question and find creative ways to engage others in this issue. New mental models are the essential first step to establish the "new" leadership steady state, which represents the foundation for all other changes the organization must make in order to meet and exceed the requirements of patients, families, and other customers.

Tools for Taking Action

TOOL 1-1: Clarify the Meaning of Leadership: Personal Views and Organizational Requirements

PURPOSE: A personal exercise to help leaders clarify how they view leadership and what is required, given the organization's challenges.

INSTRUCTIONS:

• Answer the questions under Track 1 and Track 2. Take enough time to be thoughtful about each answer. Put your thoughts in writing to help clarify your thinking.

• Next reflect on your answers and consider what changes, if any, are called for in your personal view of leadership.

TRACK 1. Personal views of leadership

Think about the truly great leaders you admire outside of health care. What do they do that you call leadership?

In what ways are you a leader?

What kind of leader do physicians want you to be? What are the manifestations of their mental models of leadership?

How does what others expect of you influence the way you lead, in particular, when you need doctors to work together to implement a change?

TRACK 2. The organization's ability to change and succeed

Think about your organization's record with regard to change implementation. How successful has the organization been in adapting to changes in the external environment?

What was successful?

What has not gone well?

Overall track record regarding change implementation?

Usually unsuccessful ←————————————————→ Usually successful

| 1 | 2 | 3 | 4 | 5 |

How challenged is your organization likely to be over the next three to five years?

Consider the potential impact of the following forces:
- Changing patient expectations
- Competition
- Trends in reimbursement
- Recruiting and retaining high-quality physicians and support staff
- Acquiring and integrating new technology into clinical practice, such as an electronic medical record and on-line doctor-patient interactions

Not very ←————————————————→ Highly

| 1 | 2 | 3 | 4 | 5 |

Aligning personal leadership and organizational needs

In what ways, if any, do you need to expand or change your view of your leadership role to better support implementation of change?

TOOL 1-2: Practice New Leadership Behaviors

PURPOSE: To support you in integrating a new leadership behavior into your daily work life.

INSTRUCTIONS:

- Choose a leadership behavior with which you want to experiment. It should be one that is new to you, ideally one that is consistent with the expanded definition of leadership that came from using Tool 1-1. Some examples of the kinds of behaviors you might consider:

  - Put advocacy in perspective.
  - Make patients and other customers the focus of daily work life.
  - Facilitate physicians to work collectively.
  - Confront inappropriate physician behavior directly.
  - Be responsible to other leaders and be a team player.
  - Go first—move on and model change before expecting others to.
  - Remove barriers and facilitate others to take responsibility.
  - Provide spiritual leadership.
  - Build trust; avoid actions that can be construed as purely political.
  - Communicate to and from other levels in the organization—even "bad news," such as information about competition, customers' perceptions, budget and performance shortfalls.

- Identify the opportunities you have to manifest this behavior.

- Create a simple data collection form to record your actions and others' reactions. (See sample next page.) Keep it with you; a three-by-five index card works well. Make a few notes each time you try out your new behavior. At first, others may not notice. By recording your experience, you can create support for yourself even if it takes a while for them to recognize the change in you.

- Review your record daily to assess your feelings and progress.

- Feel free to add new behaviors as you develop competence in the skills you are experimenting with.

- If you are experimenting with integrating new leadership behaviors at the same time as one of your colleagues, it can be helpful to discuss your experiences with each other.

BEHAVIOR I'M TRYING ON:

Where I was (occasion/place/people)	What I did	How others reacted

TOOL 1-3: Discuss Mental Models

PURPOSE: To identify ways to get others to consider the mental models of physician leadership that prevail in the organization and to move toward different mental models if a shift would support the leadership required for organizational success.

INSTRUCTIONS:

Using the worksheet on the facing page:

- Identify up to three people who you think would be receptive to a conversation about prevailing assumptions about leadership and their influence on achieving the organization's vision. Think about individuals who are generally open to new ideas, who have been hampered in their roles by others' views, or who have the authority to organize a meeting or more formal approach to exploring this issue.

- For each individual, identify what action or approach you will take to engage him or her. Some ways include:

  - Have direct conversation.
  - Share something you read and found of interest, and follow up to get reactions.
  - Share the Track 1 and Track 2 questions in Tool 1-1. Propose that you both think about and share your responses.
  - Share your own experience if you have experimented with new leadership behaviors, as suggested in Tool 1-2.
  - Share your thoughts about how physicians' expectations reinforce leadership behaviors and how this dynamic could influence the organization's ability to make the necessary changes to meet customer needs and performance targets.

- For each person, identify how you can introduce the subject so that it will be of interest or have relevance.

Who	What action or approach	How to position the issue to be of interest

CHAPTER 2   Shared Vision

Assessing the Current State

Does a written vision statement exist for your organization?

_____Yes   _____No

If yes, to what extent does it guide leadership in setting priorities and making decisions?

Not at all ← ──────────────────────── → Always

1   2   3   4   5

If you were to poll four or five physicians in the organization, how likely is it they would:

Share a similar understanding of where the organization is headed?

Not likely ← ──────────────────────── → Very likely

1   2   3   4   5

Be committed to playing a role in making the vision a reality even if that means more work or personal sacrifice?

Not likely ← ──────────────────────── → Very likely

1   2   3   4   5

Shared Vision Supports Change

Lee Chen, Vice President for Marketing and Business Development, is meeting with the faculty practice planning committee to develop business plans for the coming year. Given all the potential projects on the table, Lee decides that it might be useful to review the organization's vision statement to order priorities and focus plans. His department put a lot of effort into developing the vision statement to provide the organization with a tool to help develop business strategies and align work efforts. He asks if anyone has a copy of the vision statement handy. None of the five doctors thinks it will be particularly useful to their discussion. Trying to be supportive, one of them tells Lee that, if he really wants to go to the effort, he can go to the Medical Director's office, where the vision statement is hanging on the wall.

If this sounds familiar, your organization is not unique. In many physician organizations, vision has not been a useful concept. Physicians tend to dismiss it as idealistic and impractical. Too often, once developed, the vision is not used in any meaningful way to support the organization. In our experience, however, creating a shared vision and applying it in organizational work are fundamental to leading and implementing major change.

Mission and Vision Defined

The terms "mission" and "vision" are used commonly, and often interchangeably, in management literature today. However, the terms represent two distinct but related concepts. An organization's mission is its core purpose—the most basic reason it exists; it relates to the need in society or in the community that the organization fulfills. Collins and Porras[1] describe the core purpose as that which remains fixed while strategies and business practices change to adapt to new market conditions, trends, and consumer needs. For example, the mission of an IPA, let's call it the Elmwood IPA, is "to be a vehicle for physicians to negotiate with insurance companies and work collaboratively to reduce the cost and improve the quality of care." Those who founded the IPA thought long and hard about their reason for starting the enterprise. In their mission they tried to capture why the business exists and what, as they looked out into the future, would be the purpose for some time to come.

Vision as a Competitive Strength

BARTON WALD, MD

Bart Wald is President and CEO, Physician Associates of Greater San Gabriel Valley in Southern California. This IPA of 800 physicians was first started in the early 1980s by two physicians who grew the network and then sold it to a corporate for-profit physician management company. In 1999, many of the physicians in the network formed a new professional corporation to purchase the IPA and its management company.

I consider the entire effort that led to our physicians' successfully acquiring the company as being vision-driven. In the beginning, my personal vision was of a crusade to take back the organization and restore it to physician ownership for the ultimate good of the physicians and their patients. This occurred while the industry was going through tremendous convulsions and uncertainty—as it still is—so that our vision was perhaps more emotional than practical, but it struck the right chord with many of the physicians.

The challenges of developing support for and commitment to the board's vision are great, but I don't consider them insurmountable. Communication is a challenge, as our doctors are dispersed over several hundred square miles and for the most part are in one- and two-doctor practices. More fundamentally, physicians, I suspect, are in general more skeptical and less inclined to look to a vision statement for inspiration. Given their practical nature, they look inward or to their professional code of conduct for that type of emotional connection. Also, like most physicians in southern California, our doctors have been battered by health plans, political interventions, regulatory agencies, and intense competition; a degree of helplessness, if not hopelessness, permeates the physician community.

But, even with those obstacles, the board and I believed that developing our vision early in the life of the new organization was a critical step. (The vision for this IPA is shown in figure 2-2 on page 28.) We see it as one of our competitive strengths that will distinguish us from other IPAs. Our vision speaks to being a virtual group of physicians who work together to share their knowledge and best practices. By including this statement, we are acknowledging the need to achieve a higher degree of integration and

FIGURE 2-1. Characteristics of Mission and Vision

MISSION	VISION
• The purpose or reason to exist • Endures over time • Resonates with professional values and identity	• Translates the mission into a picture of the future • Points the way forward • Changes as environment changes • Inspires and is relevant to all organization members

Many physician organizations have similar themes in their missions—delivering care and improving quality of life for individuals and communities. An organization's mission may reflect a religious affiliation or a public health orientation; it may reference a particular population group, such as women or the indigent, or a geographic area, such as the inner city or a multistate region. Most organization members understand the concept of mission and can relate to it intellectually. We find, however, that many organizations run into problems translating mission into a vision that is compelling and that actually serves to support organizational success.

An organization's vision is a vivid word picture of what it is striving to look like and be known for. The time frame in a vision statement is the future. It describes the organization relative to its market and identifies what distinguishes it from others. The Elmwood IPA's vision serves as an illustration here. "Our IPA will be a high-performing, 'must-have' group and as such will be able to get premium reimbursement for its services and will attract and retain excellent physicians. Our reputation is a function of our ability to deliver high-quality care that meets or exceeds measures important to insurers and that meets consumers' expectations for access and service." The sidebar, left and page 27, describes how one IPA in Southern California is using its vision to develop a competitive organization.

The mission and vision taken together lead people to understand what business the organization is in and what is important to success. Figure 2-1, page 26, provides an overview of the characteristics of each of them. Mission describes the organization's fundamental business, today and far into the future. Vision describes a future state that is a stretch from present reality. In this respect, it acts to fuel organizational change. A vision cannot be achieved without change; moreover, any vision will likely change itself as new trends and technologies emerge. The Elmwood IPA vision speaks to working toward outstanding quality and service—both important to insurers and payers today and likely to be important to them for the foreseeable future. But, if another feature of care delivery becomes critically important for an organization's success—demonstrating particular technological competencies, for example—it should be reflected in the vision. The vision supports the dynamic and changing part of organizational identity, whereas the mission or purpose reflects that which is fixed and endures over time.

A vision is useful only when it gets beyond platitudes and "feel good" statements. The cynicism that many physicians have toward the concept of vision is based on their experiences of vision statements that ring of "motherhood and apple pie." A useful vision is strategic, in that it is based on the mission and grounded in current and future business realities, describes the organization relative to its market, and identifies what distinguishes it from its competition.

A shared vision should connect not just with people's intellect but also with their hearts. It should include language that, at some level, stirs the soul and defines the goals everyone is working toward. Finally, the vision has to transcend position and status and be appealing to everyone who is a part of the enterprise. It must be seen as relevant and meaningful by support staff, managers, physicians, and executives.

Figures 2-2 and 2-3, pages 28 and 29, provide examples of vision statements developed by physician organizations to address their unique challenges and opportunities. Figure 2-2 is the statement developed by the board of an IPA in Southern California (also see sidebar on pages 26-27). Figure 2-3 is the vision statement for the Q and R Clinic, the medical group component of the Medcenter One Health Systems in Bismarck, North Dakota.

collaboration than IPAs have traditionally done. It also indicates that one of our priorities will be to invest in technology that will enable us to overcome the fragmented IPA model. We included language about being advocates for patients to acknowledge that professional responsibility. Yet we balance that responsibility with the need to practice efficiently and reduce the waste of medical resources that is inherent in health care but that is deadly in today's competitive medical and financial environment. Finally, our vision announces that we intend to be an essential physician organization for our customers: patients, health plan, and purchasers. This position will be required to achieve the market leverage necessary to compete for scarce resources, that is, the funding for health care services. Our physicians are tired of being "rule-takers," and we offer them the hope of once again being leaders as the health care system continues to evolve. The bottom line of what we've developed for our vision is that it communicates to all the doctors that this IPA is different. It's not simply another vehicle through which they get managed care enrollees. It's going to be a more critical component of their professional lives; they will have to do more, and they can expect more back in return.

We have begun to share this vision at meetings throughout our network. Physician responses are variable but generally positive. However, results will say more to the doctors than any speech will. The board is responsible for keeping us on track for meeting the vision. For example, becoming a virtual group will require a mandate that all offices be electronically linked. If a doctor's office doesn't have that capacity, how can they be a part of our enterprise, which must use electronic communication in order to meet its financial and professional goals?

We're going to keep talking about our vision and use it to guide us in strategic as well as tactical decisions. It's going to be a critical tool as our market and organization evolve.

The Importance of Shared Vision

Shared Vision Provides a Context for Change

Regardless of what drives change—market pressures, the desire to be leading edge, or both—a shared vision supports wide-scale change implementation. A vision that doctors buy into and own creates an environment conducive to change. Without it, what individuals are striving for economically, personally, and professionally will prevail. These personal visions of individual organization members often clash with what the organization needs to do to succeed. The lack of shared vision becomes a significant barrier to change.

Consider what happens when an organization tries to implement fundamental change, such as improving access to boost patient satisfaction. Without the context of a shared vision, the various individual changes required, such as scheduling adjustments, productivity incentives, and changes in vacation policy and coverage, can appear to be disconnected from each other or from any larger purpose. When physicians ask, "Why are we doing this?" leaders need to be able to respond, "Because it supports where we all agree we are headed." Otherwise, they are likely to find themselves debating the merits of each separate idea.

Shared Vision Sets Priorities

A shared vision helps individuals recognize their priorities and take appropriate actions to make the vision real. When the mission and vision resonate with physicians and staff, fewer policies are needed. The famous one-page commitment to salesperson empowerment at Nordstrom department stores—"Use your own best judgment"—works only because all employees understand why they are there: to serve customers.[2] When the guiding light is that clear, giving people latitude to use their own judgment produces great results. In health care, front-line empowerment training was a costly management fad that produced disappointing results for many organizations. Missing was one essential element—a clear shared vision. It is hard for people to feel empowered without it. A clear and shared vision makes it safe to take actions that move the organization closer to where everyone has said they want to go.

For leaders, the vision helps identify and maintain focus on a few changes that have the highest leverage to take the organization into the future. Some leaders believe that they can drive several complex changes at the same time. That approach tends to produce change fatigue in the organization; in

FIGURE 2-2. Vision Statement for an IPA

Physician Associates of Greater San Gabriel Valley (California) Vision Statement

Physician Associates of San Gabriel Valley is a virtual physician group that shares a common vision of the health care system. As physicians, we are advocates for our patients' well-being. Each physician sees him- or herself as responsible and accountable for providing the best possible care without being wasteful. Our organization supports each physician in a manner that promotes excellence in quality, access, and service to all of our patients. Our superior reputation results in our being an essential physician group for health plans, employers, and members. Acting together and focusing on results enables us to be successful and to be a leader in the ongoing evolution of our health care system.

return, results suffer. Here is one not uncommon scenario:

The yearly strategic planning retreat ends by listing the "must-do's" for the next year. When the "must-do's" get posted on the walls, participants gulp, seeing the amount of work that needs to get done. However, everyone agrees that all of it is important. Several months later, the board is frustrated that many imperatives are not much closer to successful implementation than when the retreat ended.

Numerous seemingly disconnected changes stand little chance of being adopted and sustained. Leaders who, instead of making hard choices, insist that many changes must be undertaken simultaneously contribute to stress, frustration, and cynicism among physicians and staff. Physicians end up viewing every change as another fad and respond, not unreasonably, "If we keep our heads down, this too shall pass." The work of leaders is to separate real imperatives from those that are desirable but not necessary. A vision that is meaningful and shared helps. Tough choices between competing strategies and investments demand good decision support, of course, but a vision anchored in the core purpose provides valuable guidance. The importance of

FIGURE 2-3. Vision Statement for a Medical Group in a Health System

Q & R Clinic Vision Statement

OUR RELATIONSHIP WITH MEDCENTER ONE

Our relationship with Medcenter One is a partnership built on collaboration, mutual respect, cooperation, sharing power and information, and valuing each other's contribution and expertise. As physicians we take responsibility for participating in governance of the system and for contributing ideas and solutions to problems that will advance system success. Administration works with physicians to facilitate the group's stability and success and, in turn, the system's success. We work as equal partners with administration regarding the day-to-day operations of our practices.

Administration and physicians acknowledge our interdependence. We share our expertise and educate each other. The quality of our dialogue and interaction build trust. We fully air and resolve our disagreements in private and present a unified position publicly. Both physicians and administration accept full accountability for keeping commitments and for achieving agreed-to targets and results.

THE GROUP CREATES VALUE FOR THE SYSTEM

The physicians of the Q & R Clinic contribute to the economic success and growth of Medcenter One by:

- Consistently delivering high-quality, efficient, humanistic patient care.
- Building a cohesive, stable physician group that builds long-term relationships with patients and the community.
- Developing a cadre of skilled physician leaders that provides leadership to physicians and the medical perspective and expertise to administration.
- Participating in developing contracts and positive relationships with employers.
- Fostering strategic collaborative relationships with our competitors.
- Enhancing physician recruitment and our community image through educating students and residents.
- Educating our peers.

HOW PATIENTS EXPERIENCE OUR GROUP

Our patients are treated in a timely manner with respect. Our communication with patients is honest and sensitive. They experience seamless care as they move through our integrated system. By supporting one another's patient treatment plans, patients experience consistent care and have increased peace of mind regarding their care.

We are patient advocates in terms of providing the best, appropriate care and by demonstrating responsibility for their financial resources.

HOW WE ARE VIEWED IN OUR MEDICAL COMMUNITY

Our group is respected as a team of organized, skilled physicians who are proud of their role in the group and in the community.

POSITIVE OUTCOMES TO OUR GROUP

The following benefits accrue to the physicians in our group:

- Stable or increasing income.
- Being a member of a stable group of physicians.
- Enhanced job and professional satisfaction.
- Pride in our system, group, and work.
- Growing patient volumes, which decreases nonproductive internal competition.
- A more positive professional environment

Vision As Driver Of Change

ROBERT PEARL, MD

Robert Pearl is the Executive Director and CEO of The Permanente Medical Group, Inc., with more than 3,700 physicians, the largest physician group in the country. The Permanente Medical Group is the exclusive provider of care to the members of the Kaiser Foundation Health Plan in Northern California.

Leadership in health care requires vision and the ability to communicate this vision to both physicians and staff. A shared vision allows the organization to take a long-term rather than a short-run perspective and to discipline those who work for personal gain instead of the common good. A clear vision requires that one's strategy be explicit and comprehensible. If a strategy and vision are unclear, or if they portray the goal as becoming the best at everything for everyone at all times, the organization will flounder.

Upon assuming the position of Executive Director and CEO of The Permanente Medical Group, I recognized that we were an organization in chaos because of the lack of a clear vision. Historically, our program—Kaiser Permanente—had been the low-cost leader in a market in which the competition was solely fee for service. The entry of for-profit managed care organizations eliminated this competitive advantage, and we became undifferentiated from the rest of health care. Our strategy became to maximize our "value" by creating a balance between quality, service, and cost. This value proposition failed to communicate to the organization in general, and physicians specifically, exactly what we needed to do on a daily basis. Lack of vision led to loss of focus. Our failure to differentiate ourselves in the minds of members resulted in membership loss, the need to slash prices, successive years of $100-200 million losses, a progressive three-year decline in service as reported by our members and patients, and a demoralized medical group.

With new leadership, a new vision to become the health care leader through a strategy of price parity with service, access, and quality differentiation was developed and communicated. Although this vision required increased efficiency in order to generate the capital needed to rebuild our facilities, add new technologies, and expand our program, the new vision resonated with physicians.

The vision of price parity and service and quality differentiation was translated into five imperatives—primary

vision in providing organizational focus is discussed in the sidebar at left and page 31.

Past Experience Colors Perceptions of the Vision and Its Value

For at least a decade, organizational development consultants and others have advised leaders to develop a shared vision for their organizations. Almost all physician organizations have put some effort into this activity. However, many are deriving minimal benefits from their vision statements or from the processes that led to them. Instead of being a vital part of decision making and daily life, the vision statement languishes unused. In some situations, mergers and affiliations compound the challenge. Merger activities often distract physicians, staff, and their leaders from the work of getting clear about where they need to go as a physician organization. Moreover, these activities may render an existing vision statement obsolete.

If your organization has, without much success, created and used a vision statement, or attempted to, we invite you to give this issue a second look. For many organizations confronted with immediate pressure to improve their performance or to reduce costs, a visioning process may not seem to be the best use of time. In our experience, however, investing in a shared vision, and giving the time and attention to do it right, is not just worthwhile; it may be crucial. Even the best changes are likely to languish or to be short-lived if organization members do not have a common view of what the organization must become. As Peter Senge has written, "The easy way out usually leads back in."[3] Without shared vision, the gap between good ideas and implementation so typical in physician organizations is likely to continue to be the norm.

Barriers to Shared Vision in Physician Organizations

In our experience, physician organizations tend to have a difficult time developing meaningful shared visions. They struggle to define and use a shared vision for a number of reasons:

- **Physicians fail to see the practical value of a vision.** Physicians typically prefer to deal in the real, the concrete, the practical, and the "now." However, vision statements tend to be idealistic, imaginative, inspirational. As a result, physicians often see little value in developing or using a vision, especially if they fail to understand its relationship to producing results today.

- **Physicians fail to recognize their interdependence to achieve results.** Physicians are trained to be independent and self-reliant. They view their success as a function of their own efforts, not as the result of their interdependence. Until recently, physicians were able to enjoy the benefits of organizational membership—contracting, sharing overhead, developing referral relationships—and still retain considerable autonomy. This experience makes it difficult for them to embrace the need to work interdependently toward a shared vision.

- **Physicians share a pragmatic focus on income and lifestyle.** The vision most physicians would recognize they share relates to their income and lifestyle goals. The relative importance of income and lifestyle varies by organization and by the age of the physician cohort. Physicians, for the most part, readily acknowledge that providing excellent clinical care is their focus; some would add service. However, doing what it takes to achieve the organization's vision often becomes secondary when it interferes with satisfying their personal income or lifestyle objectives.

The Evolution of Shared Vision

In physician organizations today, having a vision that resonates with physicians and staff and that serves as a source of focus and alignment is the exception, not the rule. We observe that physician organizations tend to fall into one of three stages of evolution when it comes to having and using a shared vision:

- **STAGE 1. Individual visions supersede broader organizational vision.** In the first stage, the business is driven by a collection of personal visions that are roughly aimed at the same end—maximizing individual physician income or maintaining quality of professional life. Sharing common personal visions is a form of shared vision, but not an effective one. Many physician organizations remain in this early stage of shared vision until there is concerted effort to shape something different. When physician autonomy is the core value deeply held by many or most physicians, it is difficult to move beyond this stage.

care appointment supply to match expected demand, closer linkage of members with their personal physicians, timely access to subspecialty care, convenient telephone access, and an improved care experience for our members when they visited our medical offices. These imperatives translated the vision into the hard work of meeting member expectations, but the vision also provided the incentive and motivation for success.

The sharing of a vision is a constant effort and requires communication in all forms and at every opportunity. It has been said that it takes 17 exposures to learn a foreign language word, and it takes at least this many exposures to understand a vision and become committed to taking the necessary steps to put it into practice.

Ultimately, the success of any vision is measured by whether it leads to the outcome on which it is predicated. Visions and strategies that lead to better outcomes for patients and greater satisfaction for physicians will be reinforced through their success, while those that have misjudged the market or have failed to be implemented will wither away over time. At this point, one year later, we have reversed the financial setbacks of the past and have now generated $150 million toward capital reinvestment. Similarly, rather than having experienced another year of deterioration, for the first time in four years, there has been a significant improvement in patient satisfaction scores. Of equal importance, surveys of our physicians indicate an improving level of professional satisfaction.

To create a leadership vision requires knowledge of the marketplace and an understanding of the people of the organization. The vision must be appropriate to meet the challenges of the external world, and it must be communicated to people internally and successfully implemented. The ability to create and implement a shared vision defines success versus failure in medical groups, health care organizations, and in business overall.

There are several drawbacks to Stage 1 vision. When individual visions prevail, the organization is unable to respond quickly to shifts in the market to implement change. Tension and divisiveness increase in the face of declining reimbursement rates and mounting pressure to improve. There is typically little recognition that success lies in physicians' collective effort.

- STAGE 2. Shared vision on paper only. In the next stage, a written vision statement exists, perhaps even one developed with appropriate data and input from physicians. However, physicians and others regard it with only shallow commitment or indifference. At this stage, leaders use the vision inconsistently to guide decision making and are unable to get others to take responsibility to make it real. Communication about the vision is usually in a public relations context. For example, it is likely to appear on official documents and marketing tools but is rarely brought forth in committee meetings.

There are drawbacks in getting stuck at this stage. A visioning process and a vision statement cannot by themselves build understanding and commitment. Nevertheless, having gone through the effort to develop a vision statement, many leaders think their work around vision is complete. They fail to realize that, for the majority of physicians, it is "business as usual." Moreover, if they asked doctors and staff to participate in a visioning process at one time, it is often difficult to go back and try to get deeper commitment.

- STAGE 3. Shared vision embedded in organization. In this stage, individuals throughout the organization understand the vision and feel committed to achieving it. Leaders rely on it to make decisions and to formulate policy; the vision drives leaders' actions. Physicians, by and large, understand and support the vision and have a sense that it relates to their daily work life. The vision is used to identify important change efforts and to set targets that often serve as the basis for performance feedback.

This is the ideal state for which high-performing organizations strive. One danger sometimes associated with this stage is that individuals may be so wedded to a particular vision that it becomes static. This happens when vision is treated as mission should be—as a stable part of identity. If the vision does not change to reflect trends and innovations, it undermines rather than furthers the mission. To be useful, the vision needs to be reexamined and challenged periodically to be certain that the direction and priorities for going forward still make sense given the mission of the organization, its current structure, and the realities of the marketplace.

A Process to Develop Shared Vision

If your organization is at Stage 1 in the evolution of a shared vision, initiate a process to move toward a shared vision. If you have a vision that is not used or that has little real meaning (Stage 2), explore why your earlier efforts were not effective and what steps related to vision development make sense now. (The section "If It's Not Your First Time" later in this chapter is designed to guide this inquiry.) If your vision was useful once (Stage 3), but no longer seems relevant or attractive, consider revising it. Going through at least a part of the process described below can help renew your organization's vision.

A process to develop a meaningful and relevant shared vision includes the following steps:

- Organize data and other inputs.

- Create a draft.

- Involve others in improving the draft.

- Make the draft final and engage in dialogue about its application.

- Apply the vision.

Organize Data and Other Inputs

A useful vision is based on the business reality the organization faces today and in the likely future. To start the process, assemble information from several sources:

- *Your organization's mission.* The foundation for any vision is the organization's mission. To develop an effective vision for the future—to know where you are going—you must first understand what business you are in and why. If there is confusion about the mission, take the time to get clear. The board of trustees and senior executives are the ones to take this on. (Tool 2-1, pages 38-39, is designed to help leaders identify or refine their organization's mission.)

- *Reliable data that reflect market reality.* A vision should represent a stretch, but not create so much tension that it is demotivating. A useful vision incorporates a wide range of data—demographic data, customer requirements, competitor and organization performance, market conditions, and forecasts.

- *Trend data that suggest what will be important for success tomorrow.* Because the vision paints a picture of the future, it is essential to consider data related to what current and future customers are likely to expect from your organization in the years ahead; these may be wants and needs that have not yet been thought of. Enrich your vision conversations with information about demographic, societal, economic, technological, and industry trends. The local Chamber of Commerce and health benefits managers are often good sources for this information. Local colleges and universities may have faculty who can offer advice.

In addition to market demands to reduce costs, many other forces appear certain to have a strong hand in shaping the future of health care. The Internet, alternative medicine, and self-care are a few of them. The demand for access and service is expected to skyrocket as baby boomers age.[4] How will decoding the human genome transform medicine and affect your organization? Think expansively, and be creative. Resist the temptation to settle for a future in which your organization does what it does today, just somewhat more and somewhat better. Instead, ask yourself what trends are likely to transform everything about the way the organization pursues its mission, and what will that transformation look like? Collins and Porras[1] suggest that a compelling vision has only a 50-50 chance of success; it requires more than a little luck.

- *Your organization's capabilities and strengths.* Your capabilities and strengths, as well as what makes your organization unique, are all useful inputs. Crafting a vision statement is an opportunity to promote traditions or assets that set the organization apart. For example, if a track record of forming caring relationships with patients is part of the organization's identity, include it in the vision. Likewise, if the organization has earned recognition for its capability in data collection and management or for its clinical centers of excellence, clarify the importance of such expertise for the organization's future success and include these ideas in the vision.

- *The vision of the larger enterprise.* If the organization is part of a larger system—a medical group within an integrated delivery network, for example—the organization vision should link to the system vision. Consistency between the vision of each component and the system as a whole reflects the interdependence of parts within a system that share a common aim and promotes alignment of strategic priorities, resource allocation, and work efforts.

Create a Draft

Although others will have a hand in the process, drafting a vision is typically the responsibility of top leaders, such as the board of trustees and senior executives. They create a first draft to share with others in the organization. We have found it most useful when leaders share their work and encourage others not just to react to it, but to rework it. The leaders who drafted the vision need to have some passion for their work but should remain open to others' input and revisions.

This work is best done over the course of a few meetings. Tool 2-2, pages 40-41, can help leaders develop their thoughts and begin to draft a statement. At a first meeting, strive to be clear about the organization's mission. For example, if the mission includes education and research, the organization's vision of the future will be quite different from that of an organization whose mission is solely the delivery of patient care. At the same meeting, take the time to understand all the environmental influences affecting the organization and its ability to pursue its mission. Review and discuss the data you have available that describe the context in which you will be doing business in the future. Then begin the discussion that will provide substance for the initial draft.

To get started, establish how far into the future you want to look. For many organizations, a three- to five-year time frame for the vision feels right. Some suggest pushing the time out to 10 years or more. There is danger in setting the future state too close to today if it results in tactical or strategic thinking, rather than the expansive visionary thinking that should be the aim. In working with physicians, it can be useful to ask them to think 10 years out to stimulate creativity and then to ask them to pull back and think in concrete terms about the next 3-5 years.

Here is one way to proceed. Given the mission, who are the organization's key customers? Identify both external customers, such as patients and payers, and internal customers, such as physicians and other members of the organization. Ask everyone in the group to think forward and to imagine what it would be like to overhear each of those customers describing an experience with the organization in glowing terms. What do they say? Use their words, and speak as they would.

- When the organization has succeeded in making the vision a reality, what will patients and families say about us?

- What will other physicians in the community say about us? What will payers and insurance companies say about us?

- What will our suppliers and other partners in the community say about us?

- What will our colleagues in other parts of the system say about us?

- What will we say about ourselves?

Recording these comments should yield a rich set of vivid words and phrases that can be used to construct the first high-level draft of a vision. At a second meeting, review these words and phrases and organize them into a draft; assess how well it fits the criteria for a meaningful and potentially powerful vision. Is the draft a vivid word picture? Does it help you to see the future? Would it energize others in the organization? Would individuals at all levels relate to it? Does it seem to address what you understand the organization needs to do differently to succeed?

At another meeting, but early in the process, challenge the draft vision in order to test leaders' commitment. This is where the work gets hard. This step takes the vision from theory to practice. Many visioning exercises fall short because they fail to deal with the practical implications of having a vision and the difficult situations leaders will encounter in trying to apply it, to make it real. "What if" questions can help leaders get clear on their commitment to the draft vision. For example:

- What if one department refuses to consider any vision other than the implicit one it already follows? What would leaders do?

- What if there is an unexpected budget crisis. How would this affect the priorities in the vision?

Involve Others in Improving the Draft

Sharing the draft is the next step in the process. The process of getting input will depend on the size and complexity of your organization. A balance needs to be struck between having leaders define the vision and getting ideas from other levels in the organization. (Chapter 5 deals in detail with the subject of involving members of the organization effectively in making change.) In general, the goal of this step is to enrich the draft with others' ideas, build commitment, and educate others about why you are engaging in this process.

- *Involve physician in a meaningful process.* Involving physicians in a meaningful way in the vision development process greatly enhances their support for the process and their commitment to the vision. The size and complexity of the organization determine the best method for soliciting their input. If possible, involve all physicians in the discussions. All 100 physicians at the Q and R Clinic shaped and reacted to the vision shown in figure 2-3. Some of the work was done at all-physician retreats, with numerous between-retreat discussions extending over a three-month period.

  If all players cannot be included, design a cascading process that involves multiple levels of representatives. In a large organization, one way to get input is to organize small-group discussions led by one or two members of the senior leadership team. This approach allows a cross-section of physicians to participate and provide their feedback and input. Other methods that can be used to support wider participation and feedback are electronic bulletin boards, open meetings, and voice or e-mail.

- *Requirements to make involvement meaningful.* Set the context to facilitate productive discussions. Physicians need to understand why the organization is going through this process. Also share assumptions and data on which the draft was based. Giving participants information about market conditions, customer expectations and trends, competition, and the organization's strengths and capabilities prepares them to constructively react to and modify the draft.

Let physicians know how their ideas will be used and who has responsibility for final decisions regarding the vision so that they will have realistic expectations of how their input will be reflected in the final document.

To ensure that all physicians feel their ideas are valued, use a process that fosters honest conversation with senior leaders, even disagreements if there are divergent points of view. If physicians believe that they cannot say what they really think or that their input will not be taken seriously, the process is sure to break down. It will turn out to be little more than a rubber stamp for whatever leaders decide the vision should be, and physician ownership will be minimal.

Make the Vision Final and Engage in Dialogue about Its Application

Those responsible for the final vision sort through all the input to develop a statement that is as powerful as possible. As in any participatory process, it is important to close the loop and get back to those involved. One method is to have the leaders involved initially take the vision statement to other levels of the organization, in small groups if possible. Their role is to review the vision, asking what it means personally to individuals and how it might shape what they do in their daily work. Chiefs and department managers can also lead such discussions in their departments.

It is also useful for leaders to talk about how they intend to use the vision and the ways in which it can be made part of organizational life. In these discussions, it is helpful to point out that the vision is dynamic and will be revisited to ensure its fit with industry trends and marketplace changes.

Apply the Vision

A vision is kept alive only if it is integrated into the daily life of the organization. The following approaches can be useful:

- Take every opportunity to communicate the vision and how it can be used. Tie it to decisions and use it to explain the rationale behind strategies, policies, and changes.

- Apply it when setting goals and making decisions, including the difficult choices involved in allocating resources and choosing which strategies to pursue and which to drop.

- Provide regular feedback to organization members regarding the state of the vision and the organization's performance relative to it.

- Build a human resource strategy that supports managers, physicians, and staff to help achieve the vision. This could include providing opportunities to develop essential knowledge and skills or to get coaching and mentoring.

- Incorporate key elements of the vision in performance feedback and in conversations about career development and opportunities for advancement.

- Use it in recruiting and hiring physicians and staff to attract individuals who can contribute to the vision.

Tool 2-3, pages 42-43, is provided to help leaders review ways in which they could apply the vision to their organization's daily life.

The process described here is one we have found effective in physician organizations. It is not the only way to arrive at a shared vision. Helpful resources abound. Burt Nanus describes a process in detail in his book, *Visionary Leadership.*[5] *The Fifth Disciple Fieldbook*[6] offers strategies for building shared vision. *Built to Last* by Collins and Porras[7] deals extensively with developing both mission and vision. Any of these resources can help you educate others about the power of shared vision and create an effective process in your organization to develop one.

If It's Not Your First Time

For organizations stuck in Stage 2—the vision exists but only on paper—it can be difficult to focus energy on visioning and ask others to do the same. Based on previous efforts, many physicians may conclude that investing again in developing a vision will not be any more worthwhile than before. If physicians in your organization hold this perception, consider taking the following steps:

- Determine why past efforts did not produce results. Was the vision a "motherhood and apple pie" statement without a connection to the true business reality? Was the effort viewed cynically because it felt like another "flavor of the month?" Was the vision, once created, not used to guide decision making or changes?

If these reasons contribute to a lack of enthusiasm for vision, leaders need to take some responsibility. It is important to distinguish between failure of the vision in how it works to support change and overall performance and failure in the design or implementation of the visioning process. Learn from past experience and re-commit to an approach more likely to produce results. Instead of complaining about the unwillingness of physicians to engage in a dialogue about vision, put energy toward creating a meaningful new vision and using it.

- Design your efforts to be different this time. Create a plan that takes into account lessons learned from experience.

- Assess the commitment of other leaders. To succeed, the board and senior executives must be willing and able to invest their time and energy. Without that agreement up front, effort is certain to be superficial and will not drive real change in the organization. Start only after you have their commitment to see the process through and to use the vision, once developed, in their decision making.

Determine What You Can Do, Given Your Position

If You Are in a Position to Initiate a Process

Those at the top of the organization need to be the prime movers in developing and implementing a vision. Involving others is essential, but responsibility for the vision ultimately rests with the board of trustees and senior physician and administrative management. As a group, they must own and visibly support the effort. No single leader can do it alone.

- *Assess the state of shared vision.* If the vision is not being used or is not meaningful to all levels of physicians and staff, make this a priority issue. Often, when leaders sense the need to develop commitment to a shared vision, they look for a sign of support from other physicians. Some fear getting too far out in front of physicians; they hesitate to pick up the ball and run with it. It is important to remember that the demand for a clear vision is not likely to bubble

up from lower levels in the organization. Developing the vision is leaders' responsibility.

- *Get others to see the value in developing shared vision;* no one leader can carry this ball alone. Use your influence to educate others about the need for shared vision and about how it can benefit the organization. Identify reasons to take this on that others can personally connect with. Some benefits to vision that might get others' attention are that it:

  - Provides focus and helps decide which strategies and activities to pursue.

  - Supports change implementation.

  - Provides a benchmark against which to measure performance.

  - Meets a human need to be connected to something beyond self-interest.

  - Helps potential recruits determine if they would fit in.

- *Seek expertise to support the process.* For example, get good data support and expertise to analyze your current situation and to make projections going forward. In addition, consider involving someone to help facilitate conversations around vision and to help plan a process. This person could be an internal consultant or an external one who has worked with other physician organizations and appreciates physician cultures.

- *Develop a thoughtful process that is leader-led and includes participation.*

If You Are Not at the Top But Are in a Position to Influence Others

You may personally experience the effects of not having a shared vision, such as inconsistent and changing priorities, but you may not have the authority to initiate a process to address the situation. There are several approaches to influencing the top to take ownership for a vision-setting process:

- *Proceed with a positive mindset.* Avoid letting baggage from the past cloud your interpersonal effectiveness. Let go of any frustration aimed at leadership for not playing as strong a leadership role as you would want them to.

- *Invest in working with individuals who could move a process forward.* Focus on supporting or educating leaders who have the enthusiasm and skills to make a persuasive case to other leaders.

- *Tailor your message about the value of developing a shared vision so that it is relevant to specific individuals.* Some benefits may be more salient than others to the individuals you want to approach. Consider what is important to each person you want to influence.

- *Offer to help those who need to take the lead.* Recognize that the effort leaders put toward vision will likely come at the expense of other organizational priorities; be sensitive to what leaders can take on and how you and others can help them leverage their time. Your help might be needed to staff a process, to help in the assessment or planning stages, or to react to draft documents

- If your influence extends only to your local work unit, *reflect on how you and your colleagues can benefit from having a shared vision for the work for which you are responsible.* Adapt the ideas in this chapter to your own area. The process can be as straightforward as talking with physicians and staff about what they understand their common aim to be—what they are trying to accomplish together—and how they want to be known in the future by their patients and by others in the organization.

Tools for Taking Action

TOOL 2-1. Clarify the Organization's Mission

PURPOSE: In working with other leaders, to clarify the organization's mission—its core purpose or reason to exist. This work sets the stage for developing a shared vision.

INSTRUCTIONS: (adapted from Collins and Porras,[1] see worksheet on page 39)

- Begin by writing down your " top of mind" response to "What is our mission? Why do we exist?" This is your level 1 response.

- Move down to the next row. Reflect on your Level 1 response. Push deeper. Ask why this is important. What need is being served? For example, a Level 1 response might be that the organization's mission is to provide comprehensive health services. A Level 2 response might be, "This is important because comprehensive services mean fewer gaps or hand-offs and more continuity." A Level 3 response might be, "This is important because continuity should mean that needed care comes sooner, and that should cost less and produce better outcomes."

Move through the levels until you think you have captured the fundamental reasons for the organization to be in business. This activity should help you surface, and connect the organization to, the enduring needs of society in general and those you serve. It should allow you to see what they would lose if your organization went out of business.

Level 1.

What is our mission? Why do we exist?

Level 2.

Reflect on your Level 1 response. Why is this important? What is the deeper need we are filling?

Level 3.

Reflect on your Level 2 response. Why is this important? What is the deeper need we are filling?

Level 4.

Reflect on your Level 3 response. Why is this important? What is the deeper need we are filling?

TOOL 2-2. Draft a Vision

PURPOSE: To support a leadership group in drafting a vision to use as a basis for discussions with other levels in the organization, a first step in the development of a shared vision.

INSTRUCTIONS:

Working on vision is a multi-step process. The first step is gathering and sharing information that will help shape the vision. Individuals might answer the questions below on their own first and then share answers at a meeting. Thorough and open discussions of all points of view will make for a rich conversation. The notes taken of the conversation and summarized can be gotten back to participants as a starting place for crafting a draft of a vision.

Ideally, the draft vision captures what will make the organization distinct. The vision should take into account:

• Your organization's mission.

• Reliable data that reflect market reality.

• Trend data that suggest what will be important for success tomorrow.

• The organization's capabilities and strengths.

• The vision of the larger enterprise if the organization belongs to a system.

Think in terms of a three- to five-year time frame, and consider what will it look like when your organization is achieving its mission and thriving as an organization.

When the organization has succeeded in making the vision a reality, what will patients and families say about us?

What will other physicians in the community say about us?

What will payers and insurance companies say about us?

What will our suppliers and other partners in the community say about us?

What will our colleagues in other parts of the system say about us?

What will we say about ourselves?

TOOL 2-3. Apply the Vision

PURPOSE: To stimulate thinking among leaders, or your own thoughts, about what actions to take to embed the vision into the daily life of the organization. This tool is useful for planning how to communicate a new vision or to revive one that is still relevant but not as "alive" as you would like.

INSTRUCTIONS:

- Review the list of opportunities in the worksheet on page 43, and add others that you identify.

- Select up to three opportunities that you think offer the most leverage for making the vision real in the organization.

- For each opportunity, decide what specific actions leadership will take to get the most out of it.

- Decide who should take action. It may be you alone, the leadership team, different groups of leaders, or all of these players.

Opportunities to Apply the Vision	What Actions Will Be Taken?	Who Should Take Action?
Apply the vision when setting goals and making decisions (e.g., how resources are allocated, choosing which strategies to pursue and which to drop).		
Communicate the vision broadly and frequently (orally and in writing).		
Tie the vision to the rationale for decisions, strategies, policies, and changes.		
Provide regular feedback to organization members regarding the state of the vision and performance relative to it.		
Provide opportunities to develop knowledge and skills necessary to achieve the vision.		
Incorporate key elements of the vision into performance feedback.		
Incorporate key elements of the vision into career development.		
Use the vision to recruit individuals who can contribute to it.		
Use the vision to select physicians and support staff.		
Other		
Other		

CHAPTER 3   **Culture and Compact**

Assessing the Current State

1. Consider the culture of your organization and its impact on change.

   How has the culture supported implementation of a change? Think of a specific example.

   How has the culture acted as a barrier to implementing a change? Again, think of a specific example.

2. Consider what most physicians regard as "the deal" they were promised when they joined their organizations. To what extent can the organization today fulfill that perceived promise and still succeed as a business?

   Not at all ◄————————————————————► Completely

   | 1 | 2 | 3 | 4 | 5 |

Culture in Physician Organizations

Organization culture is like the air we breathe. It surrounds us, and we take it in. Air quality affects our health and how we function. Yet, it is transparent, and most of the time we do not see it or think about its effect on us.

Culture is made up of individual and collective values, attitudes, and beliefs that translate into unwritten rules of behavior. These rules, or norms, clue us in to what others in the organization expect of us, and they allow us to predict their behavior. Thus, culture has a significant impact on how people in an organization relate to one another and communicate. For this reason, understanding organization culture is key to designing and implementing change effectively.

Many factors determine an organization's culture: its history and the values of the founders; where it is located; its products and services; the nature of the industry it belongs to and the business imperatives it faces; the kind of employees it attracts; and, in particular, the values, attitudes, beliefs, and actions of its leadership. One well-known thinker in the field of organizational culture has defined it as a pattern of shared assumptions that a group learns and uses to solve both internal and external problems and that has worked well enough to be considered useful and is therefore taught to new members.[1] Internet start-up companies live or die by the speed with which they get innovative products to market. The culture tends to be entrepreneurial: employees are linked in dynamic networks and teams; the organization is flat, with a few layers at most between management and the front-line; and individuals have substantial authority to make decisions and take action. Long hours are the norm; in return, employees have the opportunity for intense involvement in highly creative work and the promise of significant financial rewards within a few years if the company does well. The entrepreneurial culture of such high-tech start-ups supports what it takes for them to succeed.

In contrast, the culture in many physician organizations does not support what the organization must do to meet customer needs today and be ready for more change in the future.

> "Nobody gets into my schedule until they talk to me. I don't care about any PR campaign to the public about access. I call the shots when it comes to adding patients into my day."

> "We're not having any luck getting the two cardiologists to sit down and talk about what's bothering them. They complain to their nurses about each other, but that's as far as it goes. I guess the only thing left is to separate them. Let's move Dr. Conrad's office so that they'll be on different floors."

> "It is true that Dr. Brady shouldn't have yelled and thrown the chart. You know what he's like. He may be a bear some days, but he's a great clinician. He's the doctor I'd want taking care of me."

> "We all seem to have different ideas about how to treat lower back pain. Who's to say one way is better than another. My suggestion is that we each do what works for us. I don't think any of us joined this organization to do cookie cutter medicine."

These snippets of conversation speak volumes about the culture in which these and many physicians practice. The power of culture to block change is considerable. Regardless of how beneficial a change is likely to be—new clinical guideline, new scheduling approach, different staff mix—if the change requires actions inconsistent with the organization's current norms, it will be difficult to introduce and, once implemented, a challenge to maintain. Moreover, when changes fail because of the power of culture, members of the organization become more cynical about, and more wary of, future changes. Failures reinforce the existing culture and build a reservoir of resistance to future change.

The culture of physician organizations tends to reflect values, attitudes, beliefs, and norms that physicians develop during their training and professional socialization. In many cases, these elements fit with the traditional style of practice for most physicians half a century ago, when medicine was essentially a cottage industry and they practiced on their own. Independent practice, even in group settings, is one example that remains strong today. In the past, physician-driven cultures supported, or at least did not impede, a medical organization's success. By offering its physicians considerable independence, for example, a medical group could attract and retain top talent. Today, however, leaders in many physician organizations have come to recognize that the organization's culture is a barrier to doing what it takes to reduce costs and improve quality and service.

Even when physicians and leaders recognize that the culture makes it difficult to improve and innovate, it has not been easy to re-wire physician cultures. Attempting to re-create the culture by discussing values, attitudes, beliefs, and norms is unlikely to be successful. Physicians will view it as a cerebral and impractical exercise. One approach we have used that has produced breakthroughs is to do what we call "peeling the onion." This means to peel back the layers represented by decisions and actions, the layers represented by values, attitudes and beliefs, and to look within at what we call the physician compact, which is at the core of culture in physician organizations.

Physician Compact: The Core of Culture

Compact refers to the "give" and the "get" that physicians expect as members of their organizations. It is a concept Harvard Business School's Chris Argyris first described in the late 1950s as the psychological contract between an organization and its members.[1] Another well-known management expert, Edgar Schein, wrote about intangible contracts in *Matching Individual and Organizational Needs*.[2] The downsizing of companies in the 1980s had a major impact on the old assumptions about lifetime employment in exchange for being loyal to a company.[3] In 1996, Paul Strebel, in a *Harvard Business Review* article, called the reciprocal obligations that define a relationship between an organization and employees a personal compact.[4] Typically, the compact is not written down or formally acknowledged, although some elements may be embedded in various organizational policies and agreements

We saw the application of the compact concept to our work with physician organizations. It was clear to us that, in many cases, the unstated expectations that made up the "deal" physicians were promised when they joined their organization had become a barrier to adopting improvements. The compact shapes what physicians consider normative or appropriate behavior. New demands on physicians that fall outside of what they understand as "the deal," such as working extended hours, following practice guidelines, or implementing new models of care delivery, often provoke the response, "I didn't come here for that."

What physicians see themselves responsible to "give" can vary from one organization to another. In our experience with many different physician organizations, however, regardless of the location, size, and type of practice, physicians consistently expect to "get" autonomy, protection, and entitlement.[5,6] These expectations are so universal that we have come to regard them as the three pillars of the physician compact. Together, they represent a formidable roadblock to change.

Autonomy

Physicians expect to be able to care for patients without interference and to retain control over daily operations related to their practice. In an organization, the promise of such autonomy gives physicians the best of both worlds: support from their clinical and administrative colleagues and the right to do things their own way. Autonomy shows up in the lack of standardization common in many physician organizations. In essence, each physician is saying, "If you don't tell me how to practice, I won't tell you."

Protection

Physicians expect the organization to buffer them from market forces and change. In return for surrendering a measure of independence to join a group or an IPA, they expect protection from the vagaries of the market.

Entitlement

Within a group or an IPA, one of the most common entitlements is freedom from the business side of the practice. In this case, the "give" and "get" proposition goes like this: "I do my part by seeing patients. It's somebody else's job to get the best contract and make the enterprise work." Other common entitlements from the physician perspective are yearly increases in compensation, a steady stream of referrals from organization colleagues regardless of how one behaves toward them, and the right to be away from the practice for CME or for vacation when they want to be.

For most physicians, these elements describe much of what they expect as organizational members. The degree to which physicians hold these expectations is associated with their experience and years in practice. Physicians who "came of age" in the era of managed care typically expect less autonomy, protection, and entitlement than do their older colleagues.

How the Traditional Compact Blocks Change

The traditional compact makes it difficult to forcefully lead for change, and, when change is suggested, physicians generally see it as an option they can take or leave.

> Dr. Singer, the service line chief, is not looking forward to meeting with Dr. O'Grady. She anticipates he will not be pleased to learn that he cannot take the vacation time he had arranged. For many years, the physicians in his department worked out among themselves when each would take vacation. At times, three physicians took the same week off, and chaos ruled. The staff would reschedule as many patients as possible, and the remaining physicians would take on the extra burden. Everyone found this stressful, and patients invariably complained about access. To make the group more patient-focused, the board revised the vacation policy to allow vacation only when adequate coverage can be ensured. Dr. O'Grady is the first to be told that a planned vacation must be rescheduled and that the old practice of "working it out" among the doctors has to change. Dr. Singer meets with him and goes over the new vacation policy, widely circulated and discussed in recent weeks. She points out other weeks when his being away would not negatively affect access. Rising out of his chair to signal the end of their meeting, Dr. O'Grady responds, "I

work hard for this group. I have sacrificed, given my free time, covered more than my share of the holidays. I have always expected to be treated fairly, and I am sadly disappointed by your edict. I am not just angry; I am humiliated. Just tell me where I need to go to get this straightened out."

This scenario illustrates three major ways in which the traditional compact retards implementation of important changes in physician organizations.

The Traditional Compact Subverts Collaboration and Improvement

The traditional compact strongly reinforces a "practicing alone together" mentality. This position conflicts with the interdependence and the cooperation required to implement many changes, particularly those that improve the organization's performance, such as maintaining and improving patient access or meeting organizational productivity goals.

The Traditional Compact Undermines Leadership Authority

The typical physician compact weakens the authority of elected boards, physician managers, and administrators, thereby reinforcing a cycle that thwarts change implementation and further undermines the credibility of leadership (figure 3-1, right). When the compact promises autonomy, protection, and entitlement, physicians are unwilling to surrender authority to their leaders. Although they expect leaders to be their advocates, they do not accept them as coaches to help them change or as "bosses" with responsibility and authority to hold them accountable for results. Therefore, leaders have little leverage to sanction changes the physicians do not support in the first place. The inability to sanction change compromises the leverage leaders have to make change happen, which, in turn, results in ineffective implementation. Failure to establish a strong track record with regard to making changes to improve performance undermines physician confidence in leadership and further reinforces their belief that delegating authority to leaders is a bad idea.

The Traditional Compact Erodes Physician Morale

Physicians today get the message from many different directions that they are not as valued as they once

FIGURE 3-1. The Impact of Compact on Change

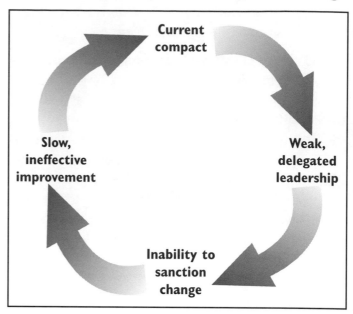

were. They expected to trade years of training and personal debt for a high degree of control over their professional lives. In reality, many find that, instead of calling the shots, they are responding to the relentless demands of one group after another. Business and government demand that physician organizations, and their physicians, do more and better for less. Patients make new demands for access and convenience. They come and go as their benefit plans change. And more and more of them challenge their physicians, coming to appointments armed with information from newspapers, the Internet, and pharmaceutical company advertisements. Hospital owners demand better access and higher productivity. Accrediting bodies, HMOs, and other payers demand measurable evidence of high-quality care. From the physician's perspective, practicing medicine today means marching to many different drummers. It is anything but autonomous.

The mismatch of the traditional compact and today's health care industry environment is the source of much physician frustration and disappointment. Changing "the deal" is one way to address physician morale. In our experience, conversations that confront and address the dissonance between current reality and the old compact enable physicians to let go of their old expectations, to move away from victim box thinking, and to develop expectations that support the organization in its efforts to succeed and thrive. Being proactive in addressing the need for new, different expectations—a new compact—opens up positive energy.

How the Organization Reinforces the Traditional Compact

People, policies, and practices in physician organizations frequently serve to reinforce rather than challenge the traditional compact. Three of the most common ways include how new physicians are recruited and hired, how leaders see their role relative to the organization's physicians, and how the organization addresses inappropriate or unhelpful physician behavior. In each case, leaders who wish to begin compact change work should consider the possible benefit of removing these inadvertent reinforcers.

Recruitment and Hiring Reinforce the Compact

Recruitment brochures and other materials aim to make the organization attractive, and so they may reflect a culture and a work ethic that appeal to physicians even when what is promised cannot be delivered. Physicians themselves tend to communicate their own current expectations of practice life to doctors being recruited. When they talk informally with recruits, they often express what they think new doctors would want to hear and downplay the ways in which life inside and outside the organization is changing. The compact gets re-created with each new hire as the expectations of practicing physicians are passed on to the new recruits.

Leaders' Mental Models of Leadership Reinforce the Compact

A chief who sees his or her job as getting resources and representing the department fits the expectations of many doctors. Typical expectations physicians have of their leaders include, "go to all the meetings you want, just don't tell me what to do." By falling into the expectations, a physician leader unintentionally encourages his or her physicians to practice as they see fit. This leader's actions reinforce all three pillars of the traditional compact: autonomy, protection, and entitlement.

The Organization's Tolerance for Physician Behavior Reinforces the Compact

If the organization tolerates inappropriate behavior, the compact is reinforced. For example, it is not uncommon to find physicians who behave in ways that are not in the interests of their organizations. Such behaviors include yelling at staff, being late with charge slips, and refusing to follow clinical guidelines. In many cases, the response of leaders is to look the other way or to rationalize the behavior in some way, essentially to "make the tent bigger" and let the offender in. Often, the offending individual is not asked to change or leave the organization until leaders have exhausted all other responses, including those that impose on or inconvenience others or put the organization at risk. By failing to hold such physicians accountable for their behavior, leaders expand the definition of what is acceptable and at the same time reinforce the old compact.

A New Physician Compact

Many physicians and leaders in physician organizations are coming to appreciate the scope of the mismatch between the deal they bought into and today's business realities. A growing number of them recognize that doctors are not intentionally digging in, nor are they fundamentally uninterested in improvement. Rather, physicians' expectations of practice life have remained essentially the same, while many aspects of health care have changed radically. Seeing this reality without judging physicians is the first and a critical step in the process to realign physician expectations with what the organization, and they, need for success.

If the physician compact in your organization is similar to the traditional compact that has been described, you are probably familiar with its impact on improvement efforts and other changes. Tool 3-1, pages 56-57, can help you clarify the physician compact and determine how it has added value and how well it fits with the organization's needs today. The questions provide a framework for sharing your observations about the compact with others and for encouraging them to consider thoughtfully the issues raised in that exercise. If enough leaders agree that the compact represents a liability, you are ready to consider a process to develop a new one. No compact is inherently better than another. The value of any compact is how well it incorporates expectations that support achieving the organization's vision.

The effort to develop a new compact will pay off if the process includes:

- Discussion at a philosophical level about what the organization needs, and will expect, from its members in order to be successful.

- Development of new expectations to guide physician behavior—expectations related to both what physicians "give" and to what physicians "get."

Real Compact Change Requires a Philosophical Shift

Once leaders conclude that the current compact is a liability, many are ready to move forward quickly to develop a list of new expectations and behaviors for immediate action. For example, they may want to get doctors to participate in department meetings, return colleagues' phone calls and e-mails, and demonstrate respect for support staff. However, it is unwise to move straight to generating expectations without thoughtful discussion of how the current compact operates, how it adds value, and how it undermines the greater good of the organization. Attempting to develop a new compact simply by listing expected physician behaviors is not likely to be constructive for at least three reasons:

- Simply listing new expectations circumvents the most important and powerful part of the compact change process—developing a deep understanding of the fundamental shift that physicians have to make in how they see themselves relative to the organization. Physicians will not embrace new expectations—and accept what most will see as the loss of important rights and privileges—unless they fully appreciate why a new deal is called for.

- Without understanding the fundamental shift, physicians are unlikely to move beyond the "talking stage" and be willing to undertake meaningful change. Without insight into the nature of the new compact and what it requires at a fundamental philosophical level, physicians are apt to pick apart any list of new expectations and squabble over what should be included and what level of specificity is appropriate. The focus on the most important aspect of the compact change process—education about how external changes are driving changed expectations of organization members—gets lost.

- Physicians are likely to feel demeaned if the compact discussion results in nothing more than a list

of acceptable and proscribed behaviors. They would view such an approach as inappropriate for dealing with professionals and could easily end up feeling further constrained and alienated.

A process that first grapples with the fundamental shift that compact change requires stands a better chance of producing a meaningful compact. In the novel *Even Cowgirls Get The Blues,* Tom Robbins offers an irreverent take on how avoiding fundamental issues that are philosophical in nature plays out in life. "I believe in political solutions to political problems but man's primary problems aren't political——they're philosophical. Until humans can solve their philosophical problems, they're condemned to solve their political ones over and over and over again. It's a cruel, repetitious bore."[7]

Substituting "physicians who practice in organizations" for "man's" and "humans" explains why so many changes turn into political footballs or consume valuable meeting time in endless debate. Physicians' apparent inflexibility often stems from the organization's failure to engage them at a deep and respectful level in discussing what the organization needs and what they can reasonably expect to get from the organization in return. For example, if both the organization and its physicians do not agree that the most basic driver of organization success is meeting patient and

FIGURE 3-2. Comparison of Old and New Physician Compacts

OLD COMPACT	NEW COMPACT
GIVE:	**GIVE:**
See patients	Be patient-focused
Deliver quality as you define it	Foster interdependence
	Delegate authority
	Be accountable
GET:	**GET:**
Autonomy	Market-sensitive organization positioned to compete
Protection	Opportunity to influence governance (elections and participation)
Entitlement	Input into local decisions
	Compensation linked to organization and individual performance

FIGURE 3-3. Fallon Clinic Physician Compact

RESPONSIBILITIES OF FALLON CLINIC TO PHYSICIANS

1. **Build an adaptive physician-directed group.**
   - Provide the opportunity to work with and contribute to a leading medical group practice.
   - Allow physicians to define strategic direction and policies while management assumes responsibility for operational functions.

2. **Support local control.**
   - Allow physicians as much input as feasible, within the efficient operation of a large, multispecialty group, to impact practice management at the local level.
   - Foster innovative health care delivery that will optimize value to our patients and other customers.

3. **Employ sound compensation practices.**
   - Link compensation of physicians and managers to individual and group performance.
   - Ensure that compensation methodologies balance the goals of clarity and fairness and are consistent with the best practices in the marketplace.

4. **Recognize physician contributions.**
   - Appreciate and acknowledge contributions to patient care and to the organization.
   - Respect the well-being of physicians as individuals.

5. **Maintain open channels of communication.**
   - Foster candid communication among governance, management, and physicians.

6. **Meet specific expectations of physician owners.**
   - Provide financial reward for the building of equity in a successful medical group.
   - Communicate, whenever prudent, significant issues affecting the enterprise.
   - Ensure accountability of board and management to shareholders.
   - Maintain ongoing evaluation of the compact to ensure the success of Fallon Clinic.

RESPONSIBILITIES OF PHYSICIANS TO FALLON CLINIC

1. **Focus on our patients.**
   - Understand and meet patients' needs as patients define them.
   - Be collectively accessible to patients when they need and want to be seen.
   - Take responsibility to develop long-term doctor-patient relationships.

2. **Strengthen interdependence.**
   - Build relationships and teamwork within the group that enhance the total patient care experience and add to the value of our business.
   - Treat one another with mutual respect.
   - Acknowledge and appreciate each physician's and staff member's contributions to patient care.

3. **Delegate authority.**
   - Provide appropriate input into decisions and then delegate authority to elected and appointed leaders.
   - Work as a physician/partner with administrators; demonstrate respect and support for administrative actions and decisions.
   - Accept the dual role of owner/employee and provide input into the practice. As an owner, elect the governing body and new shareholders. As an employee, support and carry out the policies and decisions of the governing body.

4. **Acknowledge ownership.**
   - Take responsibility for the success of the whole enterprise.
   - View departmental and individual decisions in light of group goals and vision.
   - Make decisions that affect quality of service and costs in ways that build the group.
   - Acknowledge that individual prerogatives have limits when they conflict with the best interests of the group.

5. **Insist on quality.**
   - Behave in ways that facilitate achieving Fallon Clinic's quality mission as defined in the mission statement and the Quality Improvement Program.

6. **Engage in innovation.**
   - Develop, accept, and adopt new ways to add value to the consumer and to improve the performance of the group.

FIGURE 3-4. The Luther-Midelfort Compact

WHAT CAN YOU (PHYSICIANS, STAFF, ETC.) EXPECT FROM OUR ORGANIZATION?	WHAT CAN OUR ORGANIZATION EXPECT FROM YOU?
A physician-led organization that manages with integrity, honesty, and open communication. A commitment to recruit and retain superior physicians and staff. Provision of support to physicians and departments as they strive to accomplish organizational goals. A commitment to make the changes needed to ensure future success.	A focus on decision making that serves the needs of our patients and their families. A commitment to treat all members of Luther-Midelfort with respect and to embrace a team approach to achieving optimal patient care. A commitment to professional development, including: • Current knowledge within an individual's area of expertise. • Use of objective measures of clinical outcomes to improve the care given to our patients. A recognition that personal change will be needed to accomplish organizational goals.

payer needs, physicians will almost certainly resist new scheduling or access models that require them to be flexible about when their day will end.

Figure 3-2, page 50, illustrates a striking difference in the give and the get in the old and new physician compacts. Whereas the traditional compact is to a large extent physician-centered, the new compact is customer- and market-focused.

The Value of New Expectations to Guide Physician Behavior

Effective compact change requires that physicians recognize the need for a basic shift in what they expect of organizational life. Physician leaders and others can then develop specific expectations to bring the high level framework to life. This means translating general concepts, such as patient focus and accountability, into behavioral descriptions that make explicit what each element of the compact means. The goal of this work is to create a few vivid and specific illustrations in order to be able to communicate, "This is what our organization means by this part of the compact." The goal is not an exhaustive list of every possibility. With broad agreement about the underlying purpose of the compact, the exact expectations serve more as a guide than as a prescription. Tool 3-2, page 58, can help you identify the philosophical basis of a new compact that would be relevant to your situation. Chapter 9 is a case study of the process one physician organization used to define and implement a new compact.

Compact discussions should clarify not only what physicians must "give" but also what physicians should expect from the organization—what physicians will "get." This discussion clarifies the kind of working environment the organization will commit to provide for physicians. To identify this part of the compact, consider:

• What is meaningful to physicians. The "get" part of the deal must matter to physicians and make the organization an attractive place in which to practice from their perspective.

• What physicians need in order to accomplish what the organization is asking them to do. For example, physicians must get timely, high-quality data if they are to succeed in managing their practices to meet organizational productivity standards.

Figures 3-3 and 3-4, page 51 and above, provide examples of compacts from two medical group practices. The Fallon Clinic compact includes examples of behavioral expectations for the various compact elements. The example from Luther-Midelfort is more succinct and philosophical. In their own organizational contexts, each is useful.

Ways to Change Physician Compacts

Two approaches are used to change physician compacts:

- Chipping away at the old compact.

- Engaging in an explicit process to define a new compact.

"Chip Away" Approach to Compact Change

The less direct approach is to take bites out of the old compact by asking physicians to make periodic, and generally incremental, behavior changes. Examples include extending clinic hours, adjusting vacation schedules, and adhering to drug formularies and other practice guidelines. Typically, these changes are introduced without reference to the underlying "give" and "get" expectations of the physician compact or whether they also have to change.

Almost all physician organizations have had experience with this approach to changing physician behavior. A new policy or operational change requires adjusting a long-held expectation, yet no conversation takes place about that expectation or its relationship to the change. This approach inevitably slows implementation of the change and makes it more difficult. The board, physician leaders, and administrators set themselves up to fail with this approach. As long as physicians believe the old deal is in place (or is expected to return), when the very leaders who were supposed to "protect" them from change begin to sponsor change, the physicians lose trust and respect. The job of physician leader becomes all the harder.

Explicit Process to Create a New Compact

Far more effective than chipping away at the old compact is to design and implement an explicit process to create a new compact. The sidebar on pages 53-54 describes the value to one physician organization of developing a new compact. A successful process has three characteristics:

- It is leader-led.

- It includes all physicians.

- It follows up on implementation.

As in vision work, the board and senior leaders need to own and be visible sponsors of any process to change the compact. These leaders are responsible for identifying

Creating A New Physician Compact
RANDALL L. LINTON, MD

Randy Linton is the Chief of Staff at Luther-Midelfort, Mayo Health System, an integrated health care system based in Eau Claire, Wisconsin. Working in partnership with Mayo Clinic, Luther Midelfort's more than 180 physicians offer primary, specialty, and subspecialty health services for patients at 11 clinic locations and three community hospitals.

We began the process of compact clarification because we sensed that multiple compacts existed within our group. In order to meet significant future challenges, we felt a need to be clear about our mutual expectations. In many ways, we were evolving into a group different from the one we had been in the past. Although our newly recruited physicians were attracted to the emerging organization, some of our veteran physicians were frustrated and longed to return to the group they joined many years ago. The compact gave us a vehicle to clarify for all physicians who we were and where we were going.

Changing an organization's physician compact is not a "memo exercise." Compact discussions reach into the delicate core of a physician's relationship with his or her group.

Our process began by developing a clear consensus among senior leadership. The leaders of our group felt that it was part of our obligation to the group as a whole to clarify our compact. Senior leaders drafted an early version of a compact that was tested with physician leadership groups and individual physicians. To set the stage for further compact discussions, we led a discussion with the entire physician group titled "Before and Now at Luther-Midelfort" that was designed to ground compact discussions in real-life examples.

We spoke about what it was like to be a member of our group "before" (that is, some time ago) and what it's like to be a member of our group today. For example, "Physicians don't need to worry about the business issues" (that was before) and "Physicians are expected to know and manage our costs" (that's today). After this introduction, we presented a refined draft of our compact and held small group discussions to give all physicians the opportunity to explore and confirm their commitment to the new compact.

We also learned the power of individual words. In our compact we initially used the words "Luther-Midelfort" when referring to our organization. But, from input received, we found that for discussion purposes "our group" was a better choice of words. We have a long history as a multispecialty group practice, and our physicians more readily related to their commitments and expectations as part of a group of physicians.

It is crucial that leaders commit to real and honest dialogue. In our group, one-on-one conversations with "concerned physicians" have been very productive. One should not start this process unless leaders are prepared to devote the time to listen to and address these very personal issues.

The process of clarifying the physician compact will draw the attention of others. In our case, the aspects of our compact that deal with the expectations of teamwork and respect have drawn the interest of the nursing staff. They are now watching to see if this is real or just talk.

A key lesson of our year-long effort of compact change is that the process is as important as the product. Our process of compact development has been one of dialogue and self-examination. It is through this experience that we, as physicians, can achieve clarity of the commitments that are required to meet the needs of the patients we serve.

what the current compact is and how it "shows up" as behaviors and expectations. The leadership group may need more than one conversation to come to terms with how the compact compromises the organization's performance and how their own actions reinforce the old expectations. Owning the need for compact change requires leaders to engage in considerable personal reflection and honest conversation about what they and others need to let go of and what will take its place.

This group can develop a draft compact built on an understanding of what will drive success. This kind of leadership discussion can benefit from the dedicated time and working environment that retreats can provide. How explicit leaders want to get before bringing the compact before all physicians will vary. Having something in writing to share with physicians can help stimulate discussion. As with vision, for participation to be meaningful, those asking for input need to be open to learning from others and willing to modify their work accordingly.

Physician participation is essential to the process. Any discussion around a compact requires setting the context and making the case for change. Physicians need to appreciate the downside of the old compact and

how a new one benefits them as well as the organization. Making the case for compact change and involving physicians in some process to develop a new one, or to react to drafts prepared by others, takes time. In larger organizations, this phase could take months. As part of the process, group or department meetings provide a forum for physicians to come to terms with letting parts of the old "promise" go, as they consider the new expectations necessary for future success. Compact work involves deep and personal physician values—values that for many physicians help define their professional identity. As a result, giving up old expectations and embracing new ones calls for a significant psychological transition. (A process to address psychological transition is discussed in chapter 7.)

The easier part of any compact change is getting physicians to understand and accept the need for a new compact and then getting these new expectations down on paper. The real challenge, according to Gary Weisenberger, who led compact change in his medical group, begins after "the ink dries. To be useful and meaningful, expectations must become part of the fabric of organizational life. The aim is for the new expectations to translate into new norms for behavior." See the sidebar on page 55 for a description of how his organization is making a new compact part of organizational life.

Again, this is largely work that leaders need to do. Effective strategies for leaders to embed the new compact into daily life in the organization include:

- Acting as role models of the desired new behaviors.

- Providing feedback, in particular recognition of physicians demonstrating new behaviors.

- Aligning physician compensation and other incentives with the new expectations.

- Ensuring that the organization fulfills its commitment to physicians under the new compact.

- Taking steps to ensure that new recruits clearly understand the new compact before joining the organization.

The Power of New Compacts
The traditional compact is a significant roadblock to the kind of improvements physician organizations must make to thrive. Defining a new compact has the potential to transform disappointment, resistance, and struggle

into hope, willingness, and alignment toward common goals that match the requirements of key customers. Comparing today's realities with yesterday's promise is a source of disappointment and frustration for many physicians. A new compact can help shift the focus of physicians, and everyone in the organization, from looking backward to looking ahead. The aim is to redirect everyone's attention to the difference between today's realities and the vision and promise of tomorrow. Developing a new compact can be liberating and energizing. It allows the organization and physicians to work in partnership to apply physicians' considerable intellect, creativity, and energy to improving health care in ways that add value for their patients, themselves, and the organization.

Making a New Compact Real
GARY WEISENBERGER, MD

Gary Weisenberger served as Board Chairman during development and implementation of a new physician compact at Cincinnati Group Health Associates, an independent 120-physician multispecialty group formed in 1974. It is led by a seven-member physician Board of Directors.

"This is pretty ridiculous." That was my initial reaction to hearing about the physician compact concept. It seemed so basic and oversimplified that I didn't see how it could be useful. Initially, it would have been very easy to just drop the whole thing right there. But an administrative leader and our quality manager clearly saw how our group had to deal with issues raised in the compact to move ahead as a business. Fortunately, they didn't drop it. These two champions encouraged me and facilitated my education regarding this concept. Now I firmly believe that the compact shift we've been going through is absolutely necessary to sustain us as a successful group.

Learning the theory and hearing practical examples was my first step in becoming enlightened about the compact. The power of the concept started to sink in when I heard what others had gone through. When I mentally applied the compact to our own group, it was easier to see its effect. I could see why change had been so hard for us to make. I also knew that any effort to change the compact needed to come from me as chairman of the board. The two individuals who first got the message could not have led compact change in our group—it had to come from the highest level in the organization.

As the sponsor, I worked with our Board of Directors. After helping them to understand the message of the compact, we took it to our core physician leaders and then, through a retreat, to all physician-owners. For us, the work around the compact was all based on a significant change in our thought processes. In the past, physicians mainly concerned themselves with the group's responsibility toward them. The compact work was designed to get them to understand their reciprocal responsibilities to the group. Getting this message out and focusing conversation on this philosophical shift was the initial step of compact development. A year and a half later, the next step is still ongoing. We are keying policies, performance reviews, governance, and management off the compact.

All our directions are based on the principles outlined in the new compact. The compact has given physician managers a context for holding physicians accountable, with processes such as a formal physician behavior policy. Our revamped compensation policy reflects expectations beyond putting in 30 hours a week. An ownership factor that amounts to up to 10 percent of compensation is directly based on a physician's alignment with compact expectations and is determined by front-line physician leaders. Yearly reviews reflect compact expectations. We've had to clearly delineate the responsibilities of the board, the medical director, and vice presidents in implementing the compact. That has helped us get clear in general on how we should be working together.

The point over which our physicians struggle the most speaks to shareholders' having two roles: employee and owner. For an employee, one compact expectation is that you accept that the organization at times will make decisions in its, not your, best interests. The compact also identifies owner responsibilities, such as setting an example for staff. Wearing both hats continues to be a struggle. This clearly is not easy, and it's not superficial. I would say this is the most complex and powerful part of our new compact.

We still have a distance to go to get the compact ingrained in everyday life. We're trying to completely turn around physicians' thinking from "What is the group doing for me" to "What do I need to do for the group." That does not happen overnight. What will get us there is the leadership groups', myself included, making it a priority and keeping it in front of people continually. That means talking it up, keeping it visually in front of people, coaching physician managers in how to make the compact real, and continually reinforcing physicians' responsibility to each other and to the group. My initial thoughts of the compact being like motherhood and apple pie have changed dramatically; I understand now it is the basic shift needed to remain a successful group.

Tools for Taking Action

PURPOSE: To guide personal reflection or to stimulate conversation among members of a leadership team. The aim is to explore the impact of the current compact on organizational performance.

INSTRUCTIONS:

• Answer each question below. Share your answers if you are working on this as part of a group.

• Consider how well the current compact serves the organization, given the challenges the organization faces and the need for physicians to engage in change.

Historically, what has been the physician compact?

• To what extent do physicians have the following expectations of what they **get**?

	Low				High
Autonomy	1	2	3	4	5
Protection	1	2	3	4	5
Entitlement	1	2	3	4	5

• What other expectations do they have of what they get?

• To what extent do physicians have the following expectations of what they **give**?

	Low				High
See patients	1	2	3	4	5
Deliver quality care as they define it	1	2	3	4	5

• What other expectations do they have of what they give?

How has this compact added value to the organization?

How has this compact been reinforced by physician and executive leadership?

How well does this compact serve the organization today? Specifically, how does it influence physicians' readiness and willingness to engage in needed change?

TOOL 3-2: Facilitating the Philosophical Shift to the New Compact

PURPOSE: To help leaders identify the basic philosophical elements of a new compact to support the organization's vision.

INSTRUCTIONS:

• Begin by completing the box labeled Old Compact Basics. Your work from Tool 3-1 provides the input for this step.

• Based on what you think the physician compact needs to be to achieve the organization's vision, consider each element of the old compact one at a time. Use the vision as a filter. Determine how each old expectation needs to change to "pass through" into the new compact.

■ If an element of the old compact is compatible with the vision and leaders want to bring it into the future, write it in the box labeled New Compact Basics.

■ If the overall element is important for the future but some aspect is no longer valid, write a new formulation to bring forward. For example, perhaps a high level of autonomy is no longer appropriate in general but is required in certain circumstances. In that case, you might want to include "autonomy when it adds value to service or quality of care" as a "get" in the box titled "New Compact Basics."

■ Review what you have listed as the New Compact Basics. Do the "give" and the "get" define an adequate compact for supporting the vision going forward? If not, modify or add elements until you feel that you have a draft that accurately reflects the philosophy of a new compact. Reviewing the compact examples in this chapter may give you ideas and direction.

OLD COMPACT BASICS   **NEW COMPACT BASICS**

GIVE:	GIVE:
GET:	GET:

PART II   **Systematically Employ Change Levers**

Align a Change Team

Assessing the Current State

How would you characterize the level of alignment among leaders that typically occurs during efforts to implement change in the organization?

Not at all aligned ⟵——————————⟶ Completely aligned

| I | 2 | 3 | 4 | 5 |

What has been the impact of this level of alignment on past efforts to implement change?

How effectively has the organization used:

Change sponsors to sanction a change, provide visible support and remove barriers, and hold others accountable?

Not at all effectively ⟵——————————⟶ Extremely effectively

| I | 2 | 3 | 4 | 5 |

Change agents to teach new methods and tools, facilitate group work, and provide essential technical expertise and staff support?

Not at all effectively ⟵——————————⟶ Extremely effectively

| I | 2 | 3 | 4 | 5 |

Change champions to participate in the change and invite the curiosity and win the support of colleagues?

Not at all effectively ⟵——————————⟶ Extremely effectively

| I | 2 | 3 | 4 | 5 |

A Change Starts with a Cast

The starting point of a change process is creating and aligning a team to launch the effort and oversee it through completion. This team consists of individuals who play three distinct roles: sponsor, agent and champion. As a team, they have the responsibility to manage and support a process that results in implementation. They plan for participation and seek input; help create a felt need for the change; manage the emotional component of the change process; and work to align resources, rewards, and feedback to deliver a consistent message to help the change be sustained. The change team also plans and sequences the operational details of change implementation.

A systematic effort to put a change team together begins with identifying who has the knowledge, skills, status, and expertise to implement a change. Identifying the cast and clarifying how individuals will support the change ensures that the three roles are played. The team is most helpful when all team members are aligned around the critical issues of what the change is and why it is being made. The size of the organization, the complexity of the change, and the need for a highly coordinated approach to the change process all help determine whether the change team is a formal group that meets regularly or a looser network of invested individuals who know their parts but have little formal interaction as a group.

Three Change Roles

Three distinct roles support a change to happen:

- *Sponsors:* Prime movers who have authority to sanction a change and hold others accountable— for example, the CEO/president, board members, department heads, and site chiefs. Their status gives the change legitimacy. Their visibility and expressions of support communicate the priority of a change. They are responsible for using their positions to remove barriers.

- *Agents:* Individuals who support sponsors and provide guidance, education, and technical help to those working on a change. Typically, change agents are internal consultants, such as human resources staff, information services staff, and reengineering and quality improvement professionals.

- *Champions:* Opinion leaders whose voices and actions help others become interested in the new way or develop commitment to it. They can be individuals who command the respect of colleagues within a department or across the organization. Particularly effective as champions are physicians who have shown themselves in the past to be early adopters of change.

Change flounders and often fails in physician organizations either because leaders in the organization do not understand and provide for these roles or because those invited to play them are not clear about their roles and about how to fulfill their responsibilities. Consider the following scenarios:

- *The medical director assigns the chief of internal medicine the responsibility to develop and implement new access standards for the department. The chief takes the charge very seriously and holds department meetings to get input. A month into the process, one member of the department speaks up at a meeting to voice opposition to the need for standards. The chief is taken aback to hear this physician report that he has met with the medical director to find out if standards really are warranted. According to this doctor, the medical director indicated he would not support standards that members of the department found too radical.*

- *As part of the strategic plan approved by the board, primary care departments will develop clinical guidelines for several high-volume conditions, such as diabetes and asthma, before the end of the year. The physician who fills the part-time role of quality director gathers a group of physicians to develop the diabetes guideline. He throws himself into this effort, fully expecting that the physicians who are collaborating on guideline development will also pilot the guideline in their own practices. The doctors involved like and respect the quality director and even enjoy being part of the project. However, they feel no accountability to him and vary in their willingness to pilot the guideline. Annoyed and frustrated, the quality director recognizes that the payoff for the time invested will be minimal if he cannot get the guideline tested and implemented. When he asks the chiefs to support him, they reply, "The doctors will get on board when they see the benefits. We can't tell them what to do."*

In both cases, well-meaning and hard-working physicians end up feeling undercut or unsupported in their efforts to do what leaders indicated had to get done. Clarifying roles and aligning efforts can minimize the frustration illustrated in these examples. The sponsor role is a particular challenge if the "old" steady state is the prevailing leadership model in the organization. Both these scenarios illustrate leaders who appear reluctant to step up and lead (i.e., the medical director in the first scenario and the chiefs in the second). Their current mental models of their roles don't support effective sponsorship.

The Role of the Change Sponsor

Sponsors are sometimes referred to as those who "own" or have the responsibility to implement a change. Owning has to do with providing support, visibility, status, and personal commitment to a change. The authority to sanction change is the hallmark of this role. Sponsors are the most critical members of the change team, because, ultimately, they are accountable for making a change happen.

Take the case of Dr. Ellen Lightfoot, who is learning about sponsorship. As the chief of family medicine, she uses much of her three hours a week of administrative time to stay in touch with or move along several significant changes in her department. During a typical day, she engages in several responsibilities related to change sponsorship:

- She has breakfast with the pod of physicians and their support staff that is piloting group appointments. She asks questions to ascertain problems being uncovered and what, as chief, she can do to make the next phase of the pilot go smoothly.

- Before going off for her morning schedule, she has a brief meeting with Tom, the quality improvement facilitator, who is the primary change agent for the group appointment innovation. They will be making a joint presentation later to other chiefs at the chief medical officer's meeting. They review their respective parts of the presentation, and she asks Tom to put the team's data into a run chart in time for the meeting.

- At the chief medical officer's meeting over lunch, she and Tom review the status of the group appointment pilot and answer questions. Then Ellen outlines how the chiefs in other departments can support the pilot and solicits their help. Enthusiastic about the early results, she earnestly shares her conviction that this project can be implemented with positive results for the whole organization. She and Tom had given the chief medical officer an update earlier and asked him to communicate support for their work. He ended the meeting endorsing Ellen's project and asking her how she thought he could best help at this stage.

- Late in the afternoon, she drops in to visit with one of the pilot physicians who expressed tremendous ambivalence when the project began but who offered very constructive comments at the breakfast meeting. Ellen has noticed that this doctor and the two nurses who work with him at his group appointments are becoming more positive and constructive. She wants to let him know how grateful she is that, despite his initial skepticism, he has stayed with and supported the project.

- Before leaving for the day, Ellen seeks out the one doctor who did not attend the morning meeting, one of two physicians in the department dragging

his feet. Her objective is to give an unequivocal message about the need for him to get on board. This week he left his group appointment early because he claims the receptionist made a scheduling error. He sees the group appointment pilot as the first step down the slippery slope toward inferior care. Now sitting across from him, Ellen expresses her disappointment in his recent behavior and goes over her expectations.

Sometimes, when a middle-level or front-line physician leader such as Dr. Lightfoot is initiating a change, it is useful to have a leader with greater authority sanction it and give it prominence. The imprimatur of a higher level leader helps ensure that the change is taken seriously. In this case, for example, Ellen benefited from asking the chief medical officer to demonstrate sponsorship regarding the change she wants to make happen. In the case of foundational changes, such as vision development and compact change, sponsorship from the very top of the organization is essential.

Senior leaders who are sponsors can be particularly helpful by visibly demonstrating their support. For example, a chief executive officer who considers a particular change important could express his or her commitment by addressing the need in written communications and presentations; by attending department meetings or convening special meetings, such as town hall meetings and lunches; or by spending time one-on-one with individuals whose support is essential for success. In addition, senior leaders use their authority to remove barriers and to ensure that financial and other resources are available to those making the change. They also ensure that management at all levels is working to demonstrate support, remove barriers, and provide resources and guidance. (Chapter 8 is devoted to how leaders create a consistent environment that sends an unequivocal message that a change is important.)

The Importance of Ongoing Sponsorship

The responsibilities of the sponsor do not end once a change is under way. Given the number of responsibilities those in sponsor roles have to juggle, using them to launch a change might appear to make best use of their time. However, the support of sponsors is often needed most when those who are involved in the change, and will have to work in a different way, are deciding if they are willing to do so, based on the preliminary results. Sponsors help physicians to accept and commit to a change—to "cross the bridge," as we have come to call it. After a change has been tried but before it has become routine, physicians often stop to consider whether they should cross back over the bridge to where they started. At this time, sponsors can have considerable influence on physicians' willingness to stick with a change. Actions that sponsors can take to reinforce a change include:

- Make rounds and spend time with the individuals making the change to find out how it's going. This communicates that the change is important, and it allows for an in-person assessment of progress. It also provides opportunities to acknowledge everyone personally for their efforts to date.

- Continue to link the change to personal, departmental, and organizational benefits.

- When applicable, share personal experiences of the change. If a sponsor has firsthand experience with a new practice, he or she can use that experience to build confidence in others by sharing a personal story about what difficulties occurred, if any, and how the change ultimately affected his or her practice.

- Seek out physicians who are resisting. Some physicians may be reluctant participants. Sponsors have an important role to play in talking through physicians' concerns with them.

- Link the change to the organization's vision and compact. Talking about how any one change relates to the broader organizational vision and goals reinforces the understanding that the change is not an isolated activity but is directly connected through the vision to a set of activities critical to the organization's success. If the organization has defined the physician compact to include openness to change, bringing the compact into conversations about a specific change is one way to help reinforce that expectation.

Guidelines for Generating and Spreading Sponsorship

Sponsorship can come from a leader at any level of the organization who believes that improvement is needed. Sponsorship can originate at the board or the front line. Foundational changes—for example, vision development and compact change—require sponsorship across many levels of the organization and include both physician and administrative leaders. Other major changes also require similar broad sponsorship. For example, when the leaders of an IPA wanted all physician members to become linked electronically, sponsorship for the change had to come from the board, the chief executive officer, and the medical director. In a multispecialty group practice, an operational change as substantial as converting to an electronic medical record or switching to a call center system to schedule patients might require sponsorship from the department chiefs and site or module leaders as well as from the board and the senior executives. The more challenging the change project is, the more sponsorship you will want to have.

Sponsors also take steps to help others embrace the role. Senior executives have some advantage in spreading sponsorship through their formal authority. In reality, however, they frequently rely on their informal influence to recruit other leaders to be sponsors. Some guidelines for generating and spreading sponsorship are:

- Determine as clearly as possible what you want or need other sponsors to do. Others are much more likely to help—and to work effectively—if you make a specific request. The statement, "I'd like you to come to the meeting tonight to learn why this change is important to the business strategy," is certain to work better than the general plea, "I want your support."

- Ask others to demonstrate support in ways that take advantage of their strengths—for example, meet with recalcitrant individuals or lead a small-group meeting. Consider sponsors' strengths and your own needs carefully so you can avoid asking them to take on responsibilities they are likely to be uncomfortable with or unable to fulfill.

- If you have been disappointed in the willingness or ability of an individual to serve as a sponsor, be certain that person understood what you needed and what you hoped he or she would do. It is often very helpful to let go of any baggage, clarify, and ask again for what you need.

- Communicate why this change is important. Potential sponsors are more likely to step up to the role if they see implementation of this change as a high priority. Consider how to communicate the importance of this change in terms that are meaningful to the potential sponsor, such as the reputation of the department or organization, quality of patient care, or your acknowledgment or approval.

Even a senior leader might be ambivalent about being a sponsor for a specific change. He or she may be overwhelmed with other responsibilities, uncomfortable with holding physicians accountable, or unconvinced about the change. In trying to get a particular leader to agree to the sponsor role, it helps to be sensitive to these realities.

Ways to Enhance the Effectiveness of Sponsors and Sponsorship

The sponsor role can be a difficult one for physician leaders, because it requires sanctioning change and holding others accountable. Indeed, weak or inconsistent sponsorship is a principal reason change fails in physician organizations. Weak or inconsistent sponsorship results when physician leaders back peddle or withdraw their support in the face of opposition. It is important to listen to and empathize with physicians' concerns, but, when leaders display ambivalence about the importance of getting on with a change, they become ineffective change sponsors and change implementation is more difficult.

Physician organizations that have begun to address the change foundation issues of leadership, vision, and compact are typically better able to develop effective physician sponsorship. When leaders already understand their role as developing followership, when the organization's vision paints a picture of the future that is attractive to physicians, and when the physician compact puts individual prerogatives in balance with doing what is best for the organization, the environment for sponsorship is set. When the issues of leadership, vision, and compact have not been addressed, developing sponsorship remains challenging.

The Role of the Change Agent

Change agents play important support roles in change implementation. They serve as guides, educators, facilitators, and cheerleaders. Typically, change agents are internal consultants—organizational development consultants, quality improvement professionals, and members of departments with technical expertise, such as information services and decision support. They play a supportive role; typically they are not in a position to hold accountable those they help to design and implement a change. Change agents frequently are assigned to a project. Other times, they may volunteer. More than one agent can be involved in any one change. For example, a clinical quality improvement team might work with a quality improvement facilitator to learn team skills and how to map the process of care but draw on a data expert from information services to design and implement a data collection plan.

How agents support a change process depends on the specific change, its stage of development, and the agent's knowledge and skills. The sidebar on pages 66-67 is the experience of one change agent and how she operates to be effective in her organization.

Change agents provide the following kinds of support:

- Work with sponsors to help plan the change process.

- Facilitate meetings and build an environment in which all ideas are respected and conflict is surfaced and resolved.

- Integrate ideas and feedback into the change design.

- Provide technical support, including data collection, display, and interpretation.

- Support sponsors to identify and remove barriers to change implementation.

- Ensure that those who will be making the change have the necessary skills or training.

- Listen and provide support and acknowledgment to those making the change.

- Bring positive energy and encouragement to the process.

- When their relationship with sponsors is built on mutual respect and trust, change agents can also help sponsors to be more effective by giving feedback on how well the sponsor role is being filled and by coaching on how to improve.

Lessons from a Change Agent
JANET GAFFIN

Janet Gaffin is the Quality Improvement Manager at Cincinnati Group Health Associates, an independent 120-physician multispecialty group.

It's hard to describe what I do as a change agent—I'm a bridge, a listener, a communicator, an instigator, a relationship builder, an educator, and a consultant. Our organization has been through several significant changes, including implementing a patient service guarantee and changing our physician and management compacts. The change agent role, although pretty hard to pin down, has been extremely important to the success of these changes. In reflecting on my role as a change agent, facilitating implementation of specific changes, has taught me several valuable lessons.

The support of leaders is the most important contributor to change agent success. Because there is no formal power in my role, our staff and doctors need to know that someone with authority is backing me up. If change sponsors or leaders want their change agents to be effective, they have to be willing to put some of their authority behind them. When we introduced the Service Guarantee program, the chairman of the board and top administrators helped lead the session. This sent a clear message. More important, when the Service Guarantee faced opposition down the road, top leaders were at meetings to demonstrate continued support—they didn't disappear when things got heated. Also, the support of people at the top nourishes me. Some of the changes I've worked on have stirred up controversy and emotions. Without the top saying, "We're behind you," it would have been easy to feel chewed up.

Another lesson I've learned is that it is much more important to get others to take the reins than for me to lead the change. Truly having buy-in is more important than moving quickly. I used to see my job as leading changes related to quality improvement. Now I see it differently; I go to extreme effort not to do the work that those who should lead a project need to do. As much as possible, I pass on my passion to the person who should be leading it. My job is to support that person and do whatever it takes to be successful.

I've learned that an effective agent works at two levels:

• The agent facilitates projects and supports sponsors.

Ways to Enhance the Effectiveness of Change Agents

A change agent's effectiveness depends in large part on his or her skills and credibility. To many physicians, the agent role is most "foreign." Change agents typically are not physicians, and they are therefore subject to physicians' mistrust. Their approach to supporting change is mainly through facilitation and encouragement, which some physicians misinterpret as being patronizing. To enhance their credibility with physicians in particular, agents may find it useful to demonstrate the following characteristics and behaviors:

• Show respect for all staff, clinical and nonclinical.

• Balance process with results.

• Keep commitments. Follow through when asked for information.

• Demonstrate active listening and foster understanding.

• Withhold judgment toward those with whom he or she works.

• Avoid taking personal credit for the group's work.

Sponsor support is also key to change agent effectiveness. Agents and sponsors have different responsibilities, and change implementation is most successful when the individuals in these roles understand, appreciate, and support each other's contributions. A common failing is not being clear that the roles are different. Another is assuming that an agent can move a change along without sponsorship. Recall the scenario in which the quality director is the agent leading the development and implementation of a clinical guideline for diabetes management. There is no apparent sponsorship. Appropriate sponsors are the chiefs, who are accountable for the clinical performance of their departments. The chiefs are responsible for sanctioning the change and communicating to their physicians the board's expectations and their own. The agent can facilitate meetings and bring needed expertise to the team, but only the chiefs have the authority to deal effectively with doctors' equivocation about their further involvement. The agent cannot bring about the desired change if the sponsors do not fully play their role.

The Role of the Change Champion

Champions play a very significant role by lending their credibility and support to a change. They are opinion leaders whose influence derives from their reputations or informal leadership qualities. Because many physicians are suspicious of management's motives, the views and attitudes of peers are particularly influential in creating receptivity to a change among physicians. Consider this example:

> An academic medical center introduces an initiative to increase the availability of certain specialists. It receives only lukewarm support until a senior neurologist gets actively involved, publicly supports the plan, and offers to join the first group of physicians who will work extended clinic hours. The idea of increasing physician availability had been talked about for months, and there was good sponsorship and good support from capable agents. Nevertheless, the initiative dragged along until a highly regarded and well-liked physician stepped into the champion role.

Agents or sponsors invite champions to help support a change. They seek them out at the start of an initiative or watch for the emergence of supportive individuals in the course of designing, testing, and implementing a change. Champions might be asked to serve on a planning team, take part in a pilot, or talk about the change and its benefits at meetings of their colleagues. In some cases, an individual might be invited to be a champion because he or she has knowledge or experience that could be useful in implementing change in another part of the organization. A highly respected clinical expert in diabetes, for example an endocrinologist, might be tapped to serve as the clinical champion to help primary care physicians develop a diabetes management guideline. Part of the role is to lend knowledge and expertise and to guide the implementation process across different sites in the organization. Champions can also be involved in less structured ways—for example, to take a public stand for the proposed change on a particular occasion.

An effective champion is not necessarily one who starts out a believer in the proposed change. Asking an individual with a contrary perspective to play a

- The agent works to sustain change by helping leaders deal with cultural issues.

Group Health has had a quality improvement program for many years. We took the traditional approach and put a program in place to teach quality improvement tools and methodology and form improvement teams to tackle projects. It was a good place to start, but it had limitations. It became clear that the real leverage was in getting board members to take leadership for fundamental changes in the way doctors relate to the group. I was determined to get our board to look at compact issues, because I knew that change at that level would pay off in many ways, including help us implement other needed changes. My role was to make the case for change again and again until someone at the board level took up the cause and moved it forward.

The other significant thing I've discovered about this role is that relationships are the path to getting work done. Being effective as a change agent largely depends on your ability to form relationships. Several qualities help a change agent be a relationship builder:

- **Assertive.** You need to be self-confident but not arrogant. Having a strong core belief in what you're doing gets you in the door and gets others to listen.

- **Non-threatening.** Being low-key and supportive keeps doors open. When your intention is to help, others will open up and share their issues.

- **Trustworthy.** You have to be trusted by everyone, from the top to the front line, in order to be effective.

My role has evolved from being an educator and hands-on doer to one that's a little less easy to describe but tremendously rewarding. Working through other people means that I can multiply my efforts many times over. That's extremely satisfying.

role demonstrates leaders' respect for different points of view. Moreover, individuals who initially—and perhaps publicly—express skepticism or opposition often make the most effective champions in the long run. Maximum benefits can be derived when champions are integrated into the change team. They can best support a change and speak to its benefits when they fully understand why the change is needed, how it can improve the organization's current performance, and what the plans are for its implementation.

Aligning Leadership to Drive Change
JOYCE MOBLEY, MD

Joyce Mobley is the Adult Medicine Department Chair at CIGNA Medical Group in Phoenix, Arizona. The 230-physician medical group provides care for the HMO's members. As the individual responsible for almost all primary care physicians, Joyce was one of the leaders guiding this organization's compact change process

When it comes to implementing change, step one is to align leadership. This is one of the most important lessons that came out of our organization's work to change our physician and staff compact. Our compact is our philosophy regarding how we behave and what we expect from each other. In the compact change process, an investment was made to develop agreement among all leaders regarding the need for a different compact and what the new expectations would be. This was the first time conscious attention was paid to getting every leader in the organization to understand and support significant change. Alignment was the key reason that our compact change process was effective.

The physician leadership took away from that experience a deep appreciation of how important our alignment is whenever we need to bring change to the front line. In the past, decisions would be handed down to physicians from our medical director or from just one or two department chairs. By coming to alignment around the need for a new compact and actually doing the work of drafting it, the department chairs coalesced into a functional group, making this team an essential part of the change process. This created a new and significant dynamic in the organization.

The benefits of our aligning as a leadership group have been many. Once the department chair group has worked through an issue, I can be confident that what I tell my physicians is what all department chairs are communicating. We can all count on each other to be consistent in our messages. Knowing we can count on each other to be leaders for change has helped department chairs develop a sense of being empowered. At our one-year anniversary as a group, one chair said that, in the past, physician leadership could have been represented by a tall, narrow triangle. Now, that triangle has flattened—the tip is closer to the base and the base has broadened. That's an apt metaphor for the transformation we've made.

Championing Change in Physician Organizations

Autonomy in physician organizations makes the role of champion all the more important. Because they value their autonomy, physicians give each other wide latitude to express opinions without challenge. In physician organizations, it is the norm for physicians to believe each colleague has the right to his or her opinion and not to criticize a colleagues' perspective in public. Physicians avoid communicating with one another directly when they disagree, partly from the fear of risking personal or professional relationships. It is not uncommon for the silent majority to allow a vocal minority to carry the day. Commonplace in physician organizations is the meeting in which a few physicians unleash a barrage of concerns regarding a proposed change while others say little but look uncomfortable. Afterward, physicians who support the change but were unwilling to express their sentiments publicly seek out the sponsor or change agent to communicate their views in private. This dynamic among physicians is one reason that champions are important: champions take stands and represent those who support change but are reluctant to express an opinion that appears to buck the norm. They address the need physicians have in most physician organizations for validation, reassurance, and support in doing what they know to be the right thing.

Nurturing Champions

Championing a change can be more difficult than it sounds. If a change is far-reaching or hotly contested, supporting it publicly may carry some risk. Peer pressure can be intense. A champion may put at risk the relationships he or she has with other physicians by supporting a particular change. As a result, it is essential to acknowledge and support champions and to recognize their vulnerable position. Otherwise, their willingness to champion a change will weaken or disappear.

Including champions on the change team and involving them as much as possible in planning the input and implementation stages is one way to acknowledge their value and contributions. The change team serves as another peer group for champions, one that shares their views on the benefits of the change. This support for champions can be especially important if some peers in their department or site question their motives or communicate disapproval.

Investing in champions is one way to groom future leaders. Effective champions typically communicate well and demonstrate the ability to motivate doctors to change. They have the courage to stand up for what they believe, and their peers still respect them. With mentoring and coaching, today's champions often can be tomorrow's leaders and change sponsors.

The three change roles are summarized in figure 4-1, page 70. A change team will likely include physicians and others who have knowledge about the change or who can support its implementation. Change agents are frequently not physicians, and sponsors or champions may also include nurse managers or other administrative leadership responsible for support staff involved in change implementation. Tool 4-1, page 72-73, provides an opportunity to help you build a change team for a particular change process and to ensure that all three change roles are provided for.

The Power of Alignment

Aligning Players in All Roles

Having capable, committed individuals in each role does not ensure that an effective change team is in place. The goal of alignment is to get individuals in sponsor, agent, and champion roles to work together and to ensure that all communication about a change is consistent. An aligned change team works systematically and synergistically instead of inconsistently or at cross-purposes. As in a play, it is as much the dynamic among the players that makes for success as it is the strength of each individual. Alignment needs to be consciously fostered. Given how busy the individuals in the roles are likely to be with other responsibilities, it is important to come together and develop and share the same understanding about the "what" and "why" of the change. If these individuals begin to play their roles with different understanding, potential synergy is lost. Alignment leverages individuals' efforts. The sidebar, page 68 and right, describes the benefits of aligning key physician leaders in one medical group around the need and process for physician compact change and the value of their alignment in developing cohesion as a leadership team.

Alignment means developing agreement among members of the change team regarding three important issues:

When physicians see that their leadership is coming from the same place, it has an impact. I think that, because physician leadership was on the same page, physicians got the message that there would be no place to hide, that the new compact was our philosophy, and that leaders were all behind it. After having the opportunity to engage in the compact discussions and then seeing the unity among leaders, some concluded they couldn't make the adjustment and should look elsewhere to practice.

The original work we did to get aligned behind compact change has become an engine for alignment on other changes. We now approach all changes differently; we work out our differences and get aligned as a leadership group before going public. Department chairs sponsored a recent change in communication about referrals. Before presenting in front of an all-provider meeting, a process involving the chairs led to every one of them owning the need for the change.

To get where we are today as a group of physician leaders, we've come to appreciate how important it is to tell each other what we think and are willing to support publicly. Because we're striving for alignment, we don't tolerate lip service. We all expect to challenge each other and be challenged—that's the real foundation for coming to solid agreement.

- **Why** the change is called for. The problem or opportunity that currently exists and why it needs to improve.

- **What** the change or improvement is.

- **Who** is responsible for doing what. The responsibilities of sponsor, agent, and champion in a specific change process, as well as the role and responsibilities of important others in the change, such as the board, specific councils or committees, outside experts.

When alignment is weak or lacking, efforts to promote the change, although well-intentioned, may create the impression that leaders do not know what they are doing. Consider the lost opportunities in the following scenarios:

- *Two department heads introduce the organization's new vacation policy to their respective departments. The new policy calls for a minimum number of physicians*

FIGURE 4-1. Summary of Responsibilities of Sponsors, Agents, and Champions

SPONSORS	AGENTS	CHAMPIONS
• Sanction change and hold others accountable. • Align key leaders. • Create an environment that enables change to be made. • Devote attention, energy, action to the cause. • Publicly demonstrate resolve that the change will happen. • In one-on-one and small group meetings, convey support. • Stay in touch with the effort, track and analyze progress, and give feedback to others. • Ensure that a communication strategy exists. • Make rounds and acknowledge those implementing a change. • Link the change to benefits for the organization and individuals. • Talk with those who have concerns or express resistance.	• Support sponsor(s) to be successful. • Help to plan and execute implementation of the change. • Teach new knowledge and skills. • Provide technical support and expertise. • Facilitate group work to be productive. • Through relationship skills, influence those who will be implementing a change. • Listen to concerns of those implementing a change, and support barrier removal.	• Demonstrate public and private support for an idea. • Act as role model by trying a new idea. • Reach out to colleagues who do not support a change to try to influence them. • Contribute expertise or direct experience with a change. • Answer questions about a change.

to be in the department at all times to ensure that access standards can always be met. The board mandated the change, and a team developed the new policy after engaging in a six-month participatory process. The two department heads have slightly different understandings of how the policy works and of how vacations and CME time that physicians already have scheduled will be handled. The next day, doctors who attended their department's roll-out share their reactions to the new policy and learn that two different versions were presented. No one knows for sure how it is supposed to work; many do not even understand why it is being done at all. The confusion turns many against the plan. Board members begin to receive phone calls and e-mails expressing anger over the policy and against leaders who do not seem to have their act together.

• Assigned to work with an improvement team to reduce supply costs, a quality improvement facilitator lays out a road map for a process that she estimates will take 12 weeks. She describes a high level of involvement for participants. As they leave the introductory meeting, they are enthusiastic, and everyone talks up the project to other department members. The assistant medical director joins the next meeting to kick off the process. She presents a four-week deadline, observing that the short time frame means participation will be limited. Team members all turn to the quality improvement facilitator, who seems as surprised and frustrated as they are to hear this news.

Conversations to Develop Alignment

Agreement among members of the change team around the three key alignment issues can be developed in a number of ways. The individuals might meet as a team to sort out the issues and come to agreement about what their work and messages to others will be. The sponsor might have a series of one-on-one conversations with the change agent and champion. How the needed level of agreement is reached is less important than that it is reached. Again, how complex the change is, how different it is from what is currently required of physicians and others, and what approach fits the particular needs of sponsors to use their time efficiently are all key considerations in how the conversations to achieve alignment are designed. Questions to guide these conversations include:

- What has our organization learned from past experience making change?

  - What examples are there of past change efforts' failing because the three roles were not played or were not aligned?
  - What lessons can be learned from these experiences?
  - What other past barriers to change still exist?

- Why do we need to make this change? Why focus on this problem or opportunity?

  - How well are we performing in this area today?
  - How does current performance affect our ability to achieve our vision or to meet patients' and our other customers' needs?
  - What is likely to happen if we do not improve?
  - How much better could performance in this area be? What are the benefits of performing better?

- To what extent has the idea for the change been developed or refined? How will it be further developed?

  - What do we already know about the change we are supporting? What parameters are fixed and not amenable to modification?
  - What kind of a process do we envision for involving others in the design of the change?
  - Who will take responsibility for further defining this process?

- Who is doing, or is going to do, what? Clarify expectations and make commitments to each other.

  - What will the sponsors to do? How will they demonstrate the importance of the change and make their position on it clear?
  - What will agents do to support the change?
  - How can champions most help?
  - What support will be provided to champions and to agents?

Encourage individuals to agree only to what they realistically can take on. Not over-committing eliminates frustration and disappointment later on. No one should take on more responsibility than is feasible, given the time available to devote to the specific change and other commitments.

The extent to which individuals are honest with each other makes the difference between just having these conversations and being aligned as a result of them. If individuals try to avoid conflict, for example, by failing to acknowledge "the elephants in the room," only superficial levels of alignment will result. Although creating alignment may sound straightforward, it demands honest conversation. Guidelines for honest conversations include:

- Be willing to discuss "undiscussables." Fully air all concerns about the specifics of the change, top leadership's commitment to it, and their ability to follow through and keep commitments.

- Avoid unhealthy agreement. Set ground rules that encourage everyone to speak his or her mind in the meeting, not later in the "parking lot."

- Have the tact and courage to challenge one another.

- Strive to make your thinking as clear to others as possible. Share the "why" behind comments to help others understand your reasoning and assumptions.

Tool 4-2, pages 74-75, is designed to help you align a change team for a particular change process, including clarifying team members' commitments to one another.

Staying Aligned

Alignment can slip over time as the change unfolds. As input and feedback are incorporated into plans, those supporting the change need up-to-date information. Also, other individuals might get involved as sponsors, agents, and champions as the change is further developed or is adopted in other parts of the organization. Dedicating some time to reaffirming alignment helps those in change roles optimize their support of a change.

The change team can take the following actions to ensure continued alignment:

- Meet periodically to share impressions of how the change effort is going and the kind of support needed. This is an opportunity to share what each has been doing.

- Support each other, especially if the change role involves new behaviors or means taking a positive stand in the face of skepticism or even hostility about a change.

- Discuss any gaps or slippage in commitments and action. It is very useful to acknowledge significant gaps between individuals' commitments and actions. Ignoring actions that are hampering the change effort or that are seen as unsupportive weakens the team and its potential to support change. If any change team member regularly falls short of what has been promised to other team members, re-negotiation is required. It is healthier and more productive to support someone to re-commit to expectations without judgment or anger than to try to carry on uncertain about how much support you can depend on from that team member.

The Value of the Change Team

Many changes proceed without the various change roles being sorted out or without going to the effort to coalesce individuals in these roles into a team to support the change process. In our direct experience, those responsible for guiding a change would do well to employ this change lever. An organization that develops good sponsors, utilizes the skills of agents, and grooms its change champions builds its change capability. When the team is aligned, a specific change effort is not so haphazard; it occurs faster and consumes fewer resources. Moreover, as more individuals gain mastery of the skills associated with the change roles, changes occur more efficiently, with fewer false starts and with more sustained improvement.

Tools for Taking Action

TOOL 4-1. Build a Change Team

PURPOSE: To identify individuals who will make up the change team for a specific change. To assess if all roles are being played and to consider how those not on board will be invited to play roles.

INSTRUCTIONS:

- In the table on page 73, record who is, or needs to be, on the change team. Do not limit your thinking to physicians. Consider anyone who has significant influence on whether or not the changes will happen,

  - Who is playing, or could play, each role?

  - Does this person understand the role with regard to this specific change? How do you know?

  - If an individual has not been invited to play the role, or the role has not been fully explained and clarified, who will take responsibility to invite or clarify?

- Review the chart. Is the team adequate? Who else needs to be involved? Who will invite these individuals to be a part of the team?

Role	Who is playing or could play role?	Does he or she understand the responsibilities of this role?	If not, who will invite him or her to play the role or clarify it?
Sponsors: Sanction change. Consider developing sponsorship at multiple levels.		☐ Yes ☐ No	
		☐ Yes ☐ No	
		☐ Yes ☐ No	
Agents: Support sponsors and facilitate the change. Need knowledge, skill, and credibility with physicians.		☐ Yes ☐ No	
		☐ Yes ☐ No	
		☐ Yes ☐ No	
Champions: Positively promote the change. Respected opinion leaders who are not part of management.		☐ Yes ☐ No	
		☐ Yes ☐ No	
		☐ Yes ☐ No	
		☐ Yes ☐ No	

TOOL 4-2. Align the Change Team

PURPOSE: To help a change team align by developing a common understanding of the change and coming to agreement about who will do what to support it.

INSTRUCTIONS:

- As a group, discuss your answers to each question below. Use this opportunity to share your understanding of what the change is and why it is important.

- Record key points of the conversation, in particular actions and responsibilities that each individual agrees to.

- Keep in mind that this is an initial attempt to develop agreements among team members. What individuals will be called on to do may change as the process unfolds. Some agreements may be modified and new ones added as the project moves forward.

Why has the change been proposed?

- What is the problem or opportunity that currently exists?

- Why is it important to improve now?

What is a brief description of the proposed change? (At this early stage, it may be loosely defined or well defined.)

How will sponsors support the change?

How will agents support the change?

How will champions support the change?

Involve Physicians to Enhance Change Design and Implementation

Assessing the Current State

Reflect on a time when you were asked to make a change in the way you practice or do your job. How would you describe the connection between your opportunity for meaningful input into the specifics of that change and your commitment to the change?

No connection at all ←————————————→ Very strong connection

|1|2|3|4|5|

In designing change efforts, how effectively has your organization involved physicians in order to improve the change and enhance physician commitment?

Not at all effectively ←————————————→ Extremely effectively

|1|2|3|4|5|

What has worked well to foster their involvement?

What, if any, difficulties have been encountered?

When changes have been piloted in one part of your organization, how difficult has it been to get others who were not involved in the pilot to implement the changes?

Not at all difficult ←————————————→ Extremely difficult

|1|2|3|4|5|

The Role of Physician Involvement in Successful Change

Physician involvement is critical to successful change implementation. Participation strengthens a change from two perspectives:

- When the physicians who will implement a change get to contribute their knowledge and experience to the design of the change and to the plan for implementation, the change is likely to be more workable and the implementation is likely to be better matched to other work processes. As a result,

the change is more likely to deliver the desired results and to be sustained over time.

- When physicians are involved in the design and implementation of a change, they develop deeper emotional commitment to its success. As a result, they are likely to expend more effort making the change work and building support for the change among their colleagues and staff.

Not involving those who will be asked to change leaves people feeling devalued and generates resistance. This is true for all types and levels of staff. It is especially the case for physicians. In fact, excluding them can be fatal to the change process. When physicians are shareholders in the organization, they often feel entitled to say, "Who decided that? I sure didn't, and I'm not going to go along with it." Even employed physicians expect an opportunity to influence aspects of organizational life that affect them.

Another benefit of involvement is helping doctors to get out of the victim box and to stay out of it. With so much change seemingly outside their control, many physicians see themselves as victims and experience the powerlessness and resignation associated with "being in the box." Inviting their participation in meaningful ways returns some control to physicians and supports them in taking more responsibility for the quality of their work environment. Leaving physicians out of efforts to design a change that will directly affect them gives them another reason to believe they have no influence over their environment, that someone else or some other entity has all the power.

Much of the advice in this chapter is directed to senior leaders. They are typically responsible for fundamental and large-scale changes in their organizations (e.g., compact change, developing a true customer orientation) that call for involvement from multiple levels in the organization. However, leaders at and near the top are not the only ones who need information about how best to involve others and to get input and reactions to proposed changes, as not all changes start at the top and roll down. Whenever change is proposed or initiated by local physicians and administrative leaders, it can be strengthened by appropriate involvement of those who would be implementing it.

Barriers to Effective Involvement

Leaders' Mindset

Not everyone believes that involvement leads to a better change process. Results do not always affirm that participation adds value. Many leaders have been disappointed by the usefulness of work done by committees and task forces relative to the investment of time and other resources. When involvement does not produce tangible and positive results,

leaders' skepticism about the value of participation is reinforced.

In our experience, some attitudes and beliefs commonly held by leaders serve to undermine effective involvement:

- *Seeing participation as politically correct but not truly valuing the contributions of physicians and staff.* Leaders' beliefs about why physicians and staff should help shape changes that affect them has an enormous impact on change success. When leaders use participation as a technique to get buy-in, without any real confidence that physicians and staff can make valuable contributions by sharing their knowledge and experience, their request will be seen as superficial and manipulative—and physician involvement will prove ineffective. The reasons for asking others to give their time, their thought, and their energy must go beyond political correctness to reflect respect for others and belief in the fundamental soundness of the participatory process.

- *Lack of trust and other reasons for not letting go of control.* Some leaders find it very hard to let go of controlling things themselves. When leaders are most comfortable with command and control approaches, it is unlikely that meaningful participation can become part of organizational life. It is difficult for leaders to let go of control when they assume that being the leader means being in charge and that others cannot be depended on to keep commitments, to follow through, and to offer useful ideas. Some leaders may be insecure about their ability to get work done through others. For these individuals, letting go of control is scary. They need to develop trust in others as a precursor to giving up control. Until they do, participation will feel like manipulation to those involved.

- *Leaders' not taking responsibility for past results.* If involving physicians and others consumes time, adds confusion, or creates frustration and disappointment, leaders often point to causes outside of themselves. Managing the strong egos found among the ranks of physicians is challenging. Yet the most common reasons for poor outcomes have less to do with doctors' personalities than with leaders' lack of clarity when they invite others to participate. When leaders can accept responsibility for how their own actions determine how well participation works, they are less likely to repeat mistakes that sub-optimize results.

These assumptions impair both the process of involving others and the outcomes. Getting beyond these barriers requires thoughtful reflection. If leaders are limited by these mindsets, they need to consider how they are barriers that impede creativity and commitment to change. Otherwise, all the advice about who, when, and how to involve others will be ineffective and will likely leave physicians and other staff feeling disappointed and angry about the changes they are being asked to make, their own involvement, and those in leadership positions.

Unclear Expectations and Inadequate Support

Even when leaders have the right mindset, participation can be difficult to manage and frustrating for those asked to participate and, in the end, may not significantly improve the change itself or participants' commitment to it. Consider these scenarios.

- *The medical director asks a group of physicians to come up with ways to make the referral process more efficient. After meeting for two months, the group cannot put forward a recommendation that all support. Frustrated with the lack of progress on what he perceives to be an urgent problem, the medical director steps in. After reviewing the committee's work, he unilaterally decides how the form and process will be modified. This irritates those who worked on the issue at his request. They conclude that they wasted their time and that the medical director does not respect the work they did.*

- *The board of a physician group charges a compensation task force to come up with a new income distribution formula. Every proposal forwarded to the board is deemed inadequate and sent back to the committee for more work. After more than five months of rejected proposals, the task force members are angry and hostile and ready to give up. The board is frustrated and cannot understand why the task force is unwilling to complete its work.*

- *All the primary care department heads are asked to provide input into the early stage of an electronic medical record. The department heads meet with the lead consultant on the project and offer constructive suggestions for overcoming the problems they anticipate in using this particular version. A month later, when asked to comment on the "revised" prototype, they realize few of their suggestions were incorporated. They conclude that the administration, in league with the consultant, asked for their input only as a token gesture to minimize their resistance. From administrators' perspective, however, they integrated every idea they could without going over the budget.*

- *The board asks a task force of physicians to improve the patient satisfaction instrument. Physicians' scores drive 25 percent of their bonuses. The task force meets every other week for two months and is on the verge of recommending changes. Four of the five members believe their modified form represents an improvement, but one physician thinks the changes open up Pandora's box, especially in view of the year-end bonus program. He takes a strong position against the recommendations, making his case eloquently for not changing the current form. Although the others are not swayed by his arguments, they are uncomfortable breaking the tradition of consensus decision making and prefer taking no action to moving forward on a recommendation that one of them strongly opposes.*

Poorly managed participation can undermine trust between leadership and physicians and adds little to improve a change or to develop ownership for its success. It is easy for those involved to become turned off and say they will "never do that again." Each scenario above demonstrates the consequences of inviting physicians to participate without clear expectations or with little support to ensure a healthy process. In the first scenario, the medical director took over out of frustration after failing to communicate his time frame for the task force's recommendation. In the second scenario, the board failed to clarify what it was looking for in a compensation proposal and, in the third scenario, administrators did not make the budgetary constraints clear when they asked physicians for their input. The doctors in the fourth scenario could have benefited from expert facilitation by someone able to challenge their reluctance to move ahead without complete agreement.

There are two fundamental reasons that participatory processes sometimes impede rather than promote change implementation:

- Leaders' lack of clarity about what they want to achieve and their failure to structure an effective process—not giving adequate thought to the "why" and "how" of involving physicians.

- Poor facilitation of meetings designed to solicit input or reactions—not enough support to bring out and meld different points of view into coherent recommendations or a change plan.

A change agent can often make the difference between a participatory process with a good outcome and one that fails. First, a change agent often serves as a bridge between top leadership and those involved in making change at the front line, making sure that each fully understands the other's needs and expectations. Second, a skilled facilitator helps manage group processes. The skills that make a discussion or a team interaction productive are not natural to many people. Most physicians are comfortable allowing multiple opinions about the best course of action. However, they are often less comfortable making a choice that would negatively affect colleagues. A skilled change agent, or a doctor or support staff member trained to lead discussions, can frequently prevent a stalemate and keep the change process moving forward.

Outline a Process to Involve Others

When leaders plan how a change will be developed or refined, it is crucial to define the process by which the input of others in the organization will be sought. In outlining the process, leaders think through and provide for opportunities for physicians and others to contribute in a valuable way. When asking for others' input, leaders should consider the following questions:

- Will physicians create the change or react to proposals?

- How extensive a process do we need to gather input?

- Whose input will be sought?

- Specifically, what do we want to learn or accomplish as a result of others' input?

- What mechanisms will be used to get input?

Will Physicians Create the Change or React to Proposals?

The first issue to clarify is: What are you asking others to do? Has the change already been well defined, or are those involved going to create it from scratch? Do leaders have in mind a change that is somewhat defined but needs further refinement to make it work? For example, in an access improvement initiative, leaders may already have determined some features of the change, such as patients' having e-mail access to appointment scheduling or establishing a call center to manage all appointment bookings. However, they may need help designing a method to improve access that incorporates these features and fits existing processes in various patient care settings. At the other extreme, leaders may realize that a situation needs to be improved but not have clear ideas about what should be done. In this situation, leaders must determine how much work, if any, they will do themselves to give shape to the change before involving others.

One way to decide whether to ask others to create a change or to react to an idea in draft form is to consider which approach would be most efficient and most comfortable for those involved. Given the pressure most physicians are under to see patients—and in some institutions to teach and do research—leaders must consider how best to leverage physicians' available time. In our experience, many physicians contribute more productively if they dissect and redesign a proposal rather than build a change from the ground up, especially in group settings such as task forces and quality improvement teams. This approach seems to fit their time demands and their work styles, because, for many physicians, the act of creating is more an individual endeavor. Of course, in some cases, the knowledge and the expertise of physicians is needed for the initial change planning. In these circumstances, physicians must be involved from the beginning; inviting them to participate in reacting to a clearly inadequate draft is likely to undermine their enthusiasm for participation later. In a large-scale change effort, developing a chronic disease management program, for example, more opportunities to create the change are available at the start of the process. Like a funnel that starts out wide and narrows, physicians' involvement might be more defined and less open-ended as the change moves closer to implementation. A team of physicians might, for example, design a change early on in a process, whereas, later in the process, the nature of involvement might take the form of critiquing and modifying work that colleagues have produced.

How Extensive a Process Do We Need?

The nature of the change largely determines how extensive the involvement of others needs to be. Broad input is usually called for when the change represents a fundamental shift in organizational life or affects large numbers of people or several departments or job titles. A change in scheduling systems is an example. When an operational change affects a limited number of people and locations, for example, deciding how one department will organize to administer flu shots in the upcoming flu season, the scale of input required is considerably smaller. Considering these factors should help leaders decide how many groups and rounds of feedback to include and what kind of input process to design.

Whose Input Will Be Sought?

Two considerations help determine which individuals or groups to include:

- Whose expertise adds value?

  - Who has had direct experience with the proposed change?
  - Who has demonstrated creativity in solving similar problems?
  - Who is going to implement the change and best knows the local culture and systems?

- Whose understanding and commitment is going to be important to acceptance of the change?

Sensitivity to politics might also affect the decision about whom to involve. If there are revered clinicians whose opinions physicians and others highly value, including them might help the cause. At the same time, if there is a physician who historically rails against leadership or the administration, especially one whom other physicians rally around, involving him or her might be a good idea. Physicians who are most adamantly opposed to a change can become active supporters if they are involved and their concerns get addressed in the participatory process.

What Do We Want to Learn?

Involving others is likely to be most productive when those seeking input are clear about what they want to learn from others' participation. In our experience, one key objective is to learn how to design a change so it has the best chance of making real improvement, including making life better for physicians and other staff who will be affected, and of being accepted widely. Research on the diffusion of innovations shows that five characteristics of a change influence the likelihood that it will be tried out and the speed with which it will spread.[1]

- *Observability:* the change, and the results of the change, can be studied before one has to make the change personally.

- *Relative advantage:* the change clearly offers an easier approach, better results, or both compared to current practice or other changes that could be made.

- *Understandability:* the change is not too complex; the change, and what is required for the change, can be understood.

- *Compatibility:* the change is compatible with other practices and does not require many other changes in order to work.

- *Trialability:* the change can be tested or tried out and be modified or abandoned if necessary, at a reasonable cost (economic or personal).

Those making any given change are in the best position to evaluate how well a change matches these attributes and how it can be modified to come closer. Tool 5-1, pages 90-91, helps leaders think through how a change can be designed to have as many features as possible that would make it attractive to those who must implement it.

Other important information that leaders can learn from those who will be making the change is where tailoring or personalizing it would add real benefit. Of those areas amenable to modification, where would users most appreciate being able to customize the change to local or individual needs? For example, although some features of a new scheduling system must be standardized, others could be customized to meet the different needs of small and large sites. Input from physicians and support staff at both types of sites would help leaders understand if customization is desirable and what differences are important for each group.

What Mechanisms Will Be Used to Get Input?

After clarifying who will be involved and what kind of input will add value, leaders need to identify how they will involve others. Options to get input include surveys, electronic bulletin boards, small-group meetings, interviews, and one-on-one conversations. Some factors that influence the mechanisms chosen include:

- Time constraints on those gathering and those giving input.

- The time frame for collecting and analyzing input.

- The number of people who need to be included.

- The environment and the method that will result in the best information.

In a large organization or when a change is complex, using different ways to get feedback typically builds both a better change and more support.

To outline a process for involving others, systematically think through what you hope to learn, how extensive the process has to be, who has to be involved, how the input will be gathered, and how it will be used. Using these questions as your guide will result in a process that collects essential information and at the same time builds understanding of and commitment to the change.

Clarify and Communicate Boundaries and Constraints

The other key to involving others effectively is communicating the boundaries and constraints within which they must work. Setting realistic expectations avoids much of the frustration that leads to disengagement and resentment. Three important factors to clarify and communicate are:

- What are the givens, or non-negotiables?

- How will input be used?

- What is the time frame?

What Are the Givens?

It is up to leaders to identify and communicate the "givens" when they ask for input or feedback. Budget constraints are one example. Frustration and anger can be avoided when participants understand the boundaries within which they are free to create. We are not suggesting that participation be limited to areas leaders view as safe. Rather, when leaders have boundaries in mind, they are obligated to make them explicit.

Are there budgetary limitations that physicians and others need to work within? Perhaps union issues set some boundaries. Are there specific aspects of the change that leaders have already decided on? In charging a committee to revise the compensation plan, for example, if the board is not open to any proposal in which more than 60 percent of compensation is driven by productivity, leaders should communicate that up front.

Some changes are best implemented more or less "as is" if the maximum benefits are to be derived. As with many clinical treatments, the benefits of some operational changes diminish if the changes are modified, even if the alterations are aimed at making the changes more appealing to those who must adopt them. In these cases, it is very important for leaders to communicate about the extent to which a change has to be implemented "as is" at the same time that they invite input. If there is little room to modify a change without losing the benefits, leaders should focus others' involvement on decisions that affect logistics of implementation rather than the change itself.

How Will the Input Be Used?

Physicians and staff often decide that a participatory process was a sham if their ideas are not reflected in the final change. They conclude that the leaders knew all along what they wanted to do and were only paying lip service to the importance of involvement. Leaders need to prevent this outcome by communicating up front how the input that physicians and others provide will be used in shaping the final change. If input is being sought from several sources, identify them and explain the relative weight that each will be given in the final decision process.

What Is the Time Frame?

To set a time frame for getting input from a particular group, it is important to balance process efficiency with participants' need for an adequate opportunity to participate thoughtfully. The time needed for a good process depends on the complexity of the change, the kind of input sought, the size and diversity of the groups providing input, and the specific mechanisms used. Setting a time frame provides discipline and helps everyone have realistic expectations about the deadline for making their suggestions. A time frame also suggests that leaders attach importance to the input and demonstrates their respect for contributors.

Managing the Process

A successful participatory process begins with those asking for input or reactions being clear and setting clear expectations for others. Once the process is under way, those seeking input have additional responsibilities to support the process, particularly if group or team meetings represent the principal mechanism being used.

Ensure That Adequate Attention Is Devoted to Group Dynamics

Teams of physicians and support staff in almost every health care organization are successfully designing changes that improve quality and service and reduce waste. Although such teams offer great opportunity to integrate the perspectives of those involved in a process, functioning effectively to reap the benefits of the collective experience and wisdom in the group is challenging. This is particularly true when the group comprises individuals with different professional status—different specialists or physicians, managers, and staff. (The sidebar, right and page 84, describes how one organization attempts to minimize status differences—to "level the playing field"—for quality improvement team members so that everyone on the team becomes an equal contributor.) Following are some lessons for maximizing the contributions of those asked to shape a change or react to one in a group setting.

- *Select participants with the team dynamics in mind.* A team's composition may be predetermined, as when everyone on a unit is part of the group providing feedback or input. In other cases, individuals are recruited to participate, and a new group is

Involving Physicians as Participants in Improvement Activities
CHARLES BORDEN, MBA

Charles Borden is Director of Quality Improvement at Dana-Farber Cancer Institute (Boston, Massachusetts), a comprehensive cancer center and an affiliate of Harvard Medical School. He is responsible for design and implementation of the Institute's Quality Improvement Program.

One magic moment in the course of an improvement project is when the doctors participating have an "ah-ha" experience. At the moment when they gain a real appreciation for their role in a process involving other staff, it's usually a breakthrough—for the whole team. For example, a team focused on getting encounter forms completed correctly and in a timely manner, one doctor was completely taken aback to see all the steps that happened downstream when she didn't check off the right box. In her moment of recognition, everyone else on the team could see that she had a new understanding about her own actions and the unnecessary work she had been creating for others.

It's easy to understand how this relationship between doctor and team can be challenging. As clinicians, physicians have been appropriately taught to "be the one to know, now." When it comes to participating on improvement teams, we ask them to value every person's knowledge as equal, be patient and listen, be accommodating, be team players. These two sets of expectations are not necessarily in conflict, but I believe they often *feel* conflicting. In my experience, physicians are outstanding contributors and true team players when time is invested up front to create the right team environment.

Initially, I pick projects that will affect physicians' practice life in a positive way, so they stand to gain a good deal by being involved. When considering which physicians might participate on teams, I initially try to target those who naturally pay attention to *how* the work gets done. With the interest and ability secured up front, it increases the likelihood of a good first experience. The more improvement teams produce results, the easier it is to engage other physicians. If a physician knows another group has made a meaningful improvement, that raises his or her interest.

Often, before the first meeting, I meet one-on-one with physicians who are going to participate. The primary purpose is to describe the improvement process, the various roles on the team, and how the physicians might help in keeping the team focused and productive. I explain that I can help the team work quickly to an effective solution if they will do all they can to make everyone feel comfortable and valued. The *way* they participate has a significant impact on how quickly the real issues get on the table. One way physicians can help is by holding their suggestions until others on the team have shared theirs. Their "going last" some of the time allows more room for others to put forward a different perspective. I also ask physicians if they are comfortable being called by their first names in team meetings. This is another way to start the team off on an open and productive note.

In my experience, the more level the playing field, the better the participation and results. So, at the first meeting, one of the ground rules that gets set is "leave all hats at the door." Everyone's knowledge is critical in analyzing the problem as well as in designing solutions that work. Another helpful ground rule is to "be concise." These rules help team members and the facilitator manage unhelpful moments as they occur. At the end of every meeting, an evaluation is another way to work through group process issues. Verbally commenting on what went well and what did not go well helps everyone own and improve the team's effectiveness. If there was an unproductive episode not handled during the meeting, the evaluation provides another chance to talk about it.

Teams that work well have many benefits beyond fixing processes and turning good ideas into improvements. Relationships among team members, who may be from different parts of the organization, are strengthened. The increased level of respect and appreciation among doctors and staff gets carried back to work units. The skills that doctors and support staff develop while working on improvement projects get put to use in department and unit meetings and in work groups. Improvement activities that draw on everyone's knowledge can significantly contribute to an organization's readiness for change.

formed. In selecting members, consider each person's knowledge and expertise and political contribution. Also consider how each individual will affect the overall mix of participants. Other criteria for effective team members include their willingness to listen and to contribute ideas. For example, it is useful to include physicians known to collaborate well with support staff and support staff who are assertive enough to share their opinions with physicians in a positive way. Finally, it is essential to consider the willingness of each person to attend meetings.

- *Consider the benefits of a trained facilitator.*
  Given the challenges and the potential benefits of forming teams with physicians and support staff, it is difficult, typically, for an individual who is a stakeholder with a keen interest in the group's recommendations to also facilitate discussions. An effective facilitator is one with maturity and the ability to surface and manage conflict among group members. Look for a facilitator among the organization's internal consultants, such as human resources staff and quality improvement professionals. Some organizations also have managers or other staff members who are interested in and particularly gifted at playing this role.

- *Clarify the context, the goal, and how each member contributes.*
  A heterogeneous group of professionals and support staff is most effective when they all understand why the change they are being asked to work on is important, how it fits into the organization's strategy, and how far along in the process the project is. Each individual also needs to understand the objective of his or her involvement, the work product he or she is responsible for, and the knowledge and talents other members bring to the table. An unambiguous charge helps everyone get focused. Even under this circumstance, however, it is useful to confirm that everyone has the same goal in mind by asking each person to share his or her sense of the group's objective. This conversation helps the group align behind a common aim. To develop appreciation for one another's contributions, have the group pair off and interview each other briefly so that each partner learns about the

other's expertise and potential contribution to the team. Then ask each pair to share the potential contributions of both partners with the whole group. Early in team development, such an activity can help build respect and appreciation for the different perspectives at the table.

- *Use ground rules to help ensure a healthy environment.*

Ground rules support getting work done effectively and harmoniously. To help a team work more productively, ground rules must be more than a list of rules posted on a wall. They are effective when they are used as guides to ensure participation, mutual respect, and honest dialogue and to minimize the difficulties sometimes associated with differences in professional levels. Ground rules should ensure an effective work environment and support the group in executing its charge. Examples of useful ground rules include:

- Accept responsibility to participate and to create the opportunity for others to do so.

- Demonstrate respect for other's ideas.

- Allow one person to speak at a time. Do not interrupt or engage in side conversations

- Acknowledge that each individual's perceptions are his or her reality.

- Take risks and express your thoughts and opinions in the room. Do not wait to do so "in the parking lot" after the meeting.

Some of these suggestions may seem basic and unnecessary—and they may be in some circumstances. However, particularly in groups that bring physicians together with others in the organization, investing in building a productive environment often helps a group work cooperatively and produce useful results.

- *Develop skills to overcome "unhealthy agreement."*
In *The Abilene Paradox,* Jerry Harvey identifies a common hazard when individuals work together.[2] There is a tendency to indicate agreement with a position with which one disagrees. This frequently happens to reduce conflict in teams and project groups. Sometimes, all group members will state agreement with a decision that, in reality, no one

supports. The space shuttle Challenger tragedy has been linked to this kind of "groupthink"—the inability to express a contrary opinion once group sentiment is clearly going in one direction. With a facilitator's help or by conscious awareness of its own dynamics, teams can improve their process and their outcomes by learning to avoid this pitfall of group work.

- *Implement a process to acknowledge each other's contributions.*
The power of positive feedback to energize participants and improve working relationships is often underutilized. Groups enhance their creativity and take more risks when team members feel acknowledged for their ideas and contributions. Yet, the more "natural" condition is not to overtly praise or appreciate others. In organizations in which praise and recognition are not seen as important, norms develop in which positive words for others are the exception, not the rule. A practical way to change this norm is to make acknowledgment a part of every meeting evaluation. For example, build acknowledgment into meetings by having every individual identify at least one way another group member advanced the group's work during each meeting.

- *Provide feedback about openness to individuals' contributions.*
When a task group or team is comfortable verbally evaluating its sessions and sharing what worked and did not work, encourage group members to share how well they think the group took advantage of what they had to offer. This gets to the heart of the matter of mutual respect and the group's capacity to hear all points of view. It requires a comfort level that groups with a short history of working together usually do not have. Members can also talk about what others could have done to make it easier for them to contribute their expertise. This helps develop sensitivity regarding what individuals can do to ensure that all available talent and strengths are drawn upon.

Close the Loop
A common frustration of participants is not knowing how their work ultimately affected a plan for a change or why their advice or reactions were not incorporated.

Those who seek input are responsible for closing the loop—getting back to those involved and communicating in detail about how their input was used to shape the change or why it was not.

Stay in Touch

When the process of involvement extends over time—for example, if a task force is asked to develop policies related to part-time physicians over a six-month time frame—leaders need to stay in touch with the project. Staying in touch allows whoever is taking responsibility for the change to learn what barriers those participating encounter or anticipate, the direction in which their recommendations are headed, or if additional expertise or facilitation support is needed. This kind of contact is not intended to control the process or the outcome, but rather to show support, raise issues the group might not have considered, and be sure the group is on target and not going down unproductive paths. It also demonstrates sponsors' interest in the group's work and their support of those giving their time and effort.

Tool 5-2, pages 92-93, is designed to help a leader think through the design of a process to involve others.

Pilot and Spread

Piloting a change before implementing it full scale makes a good deal of sense. It provides an opportunity to identify and work out problems, develop advocates for the change, and develop evidence regarding the efficacy of the change under local conditions. A well-executed pilot can help leaders and others assess the benefits and the complications of the new way.

Ideally, a pilot helps make a change more acceptable to others who will implement it. But just because those involved in a pilot have a successful experience is no guarantee that other physicians will be inclined to adopt the change. "Not-invented-here" is a significant barrier to wider implementation. The willingness of those not in a pilot group to implement the change can be limited. Physicians tend to believe that, unless they have had first-hand experience with a change, it is "someone else's solution" being foisted on their situation, which they perceive as unique.

Allowing every group that will need to adopt a change to do its own trial run is inefficient. Some ways to foster the spread of a change after piloting include:

- Create strong links between the specific change and the shared vision.

- Address the issue of autonomy through the physician compact. If the organization has used discussion around compact to underscore the need to balance individual prerogatives with doing what is in the organization's best interests, remind physicians of this compact expectation. When autonomy is weighed against the need to act in ways that benefit the whole enterprise, the "not-invented-here" issue becomes less charged. The organization that has open and healthy discussions of physician autonomy is more likely to implement change than one in which the concept is undiscussable.

- Align all leaders, from the board down to front-line physician managers, around key issues related to the change, including why you are doing it, what the change is, and why it is imperative to implement the change widely based on pilot results. Be direct about the reasons piloting a change cannot go on indefinitely, such as time constraints, budget limits, and the urgency of instituting a consistent practice across the organization.

- Create opportunities for direct communication between physicians involved in the pilot and others who will implement it. Learning first-hand about the experiences of colleagues is particularly effective at increasing physicians' receptivity to new ideas. Physicians relate much better to colleagues who share their training, expertise, and perspective than they do to even highly effective change agents who are not physicians. When a pilot is under way or complete, and another group is preparing to pilot the change themselves or implement it, put physicians in the communicator role. Although a change agent might be well-equipped to orient others to the change, physicians can address other physicians' concerns much more powerfully. By talking about the challenges they had to overcome in their local environment, pilot-group physicians can help ameliorate the "it-can't-work-here" attitude physicians may have and their sense that a change has to be re-created to fit their own situation.

This kind of useful communication does not need to be limited to doctors within the organization. Physicians can develop familiarity and comfort with a change by interviewing colleagues elsewhere—in person, by telephone, or by e-mail—who have had direct experience with a change.

The sidebar, right, describes some of the challenges associated with the spread of Advanced Access™ approaches to patient scheduling and the suggestions of the individuals who pioneered these approaches for maximizing the potential for this innovation to spread in an organization.

One issue leaders sometimes debate is whether a pilot should be made public or kept as quiet as possible. Keeping it low-key allows leaders to have confidence that, when the change is made public, the bugs have been worked out and it is nearly ready to implement. In our experience, there are more advantages to communicating about the pilot while it is in progress. Even if the "buzz" about the change focuses on problems, it provides an opportunity to learn what concerns are being raised before the change is implemented widely. Keeping physicians informed about the test and how it is going demonstrates the level of investment the organization is making before integrating the change organizationwide. Don Berwick has been known to recommend putting those testing an improvement in a fishbowl and making their work transparent to others in the organization. Others can be invited to visit the project team, "kick the tires," observe, and make suggestions regarding the work of the pilot group.

In planning a pilot, leaders need to decide which physicians, departments, or sites to involve. Ideally, the individuals involved at this stage are those best able to spread the change. The following guidelines can help select such a group:

- Choose physicians who have the credibility to serve as change champions for those who will later implement the change. Respected and trusted physicians with first-hand experience of a change who are willing to speak positively about it make ideal champions.

- Include physicians who are open to new ideas. The diffusion of innovation literature describes five types

Overcoming Challenges Associated with Pilots

MARK MURRAY, MD, MPA
CATHERINE TANTAU, BSN, MPA

Mark Murray and Catherine Tantau, partners in Murray, Tantau, and Associates, Sacramento, California, have pioneered a system they call Advanced Access™, which reduces delays in access to care and increases the likelihood of provider and patient continuity. They have been involved with implementation of Advanced Access™ in hundreds of health care organizations in the United States, Canada, and Europe.

Our work has given us lots of opportunity to study the value and the limitations of pilot projects in the adoption of a change. The Advanced Access™ approach has resulted in dramatic improvement in access to care, but it represents a real departure from the way in which physicians typically practice. Every patient receives an appointment the day they call—if that's what the patient wants. This approach not only improves access and increases patient satisfaction, but also creates more capacity to see patients, enhances continuity of care, and maximizes the benefits of long-term, stable doctor-patient relationships.

Pilots of Advanced Access™ are a great mechanism to work out wrinkles, showcase innovation, and develop physician champions. Once doctors learn first-hand what is involved and get the system up and running, the results are so positive they tell us a return to their previous access approaches is not an option.

But spreading the change isn't always easy, even to other primary care modules or sites. Our advice to accelerate spread relates to three key factors:

- **Leadership.** Without sponsors who foster interest in the innovation and support it, and communicate its results, the pilot will go nowhere. Vigilant leadership makes all the difference. Too often, physician leaders are not helpful because they won't set standards or hold doctors accountable. Leadership is the most important reason some pilots spread and others don't.

- **Pilot selection.** Considerations in selecting a pilot group include:

  ▪ The pilot group must be credible—have a high likelihood of success and a positive attitude about the change.

- The pilot group environment should be similar to other parts of the organizations so its results are not discounted or seen as related to the pilot's unique circumstances.

- The impact of the innovation must be substantial. Improving access at a site where it's not a significant problem is much less impressive than making dramatic improvement at a site where access has been a chronic source of patient dissatisfaction.

- **Critical mass.** When multiple pilots are used, the differences in practice settings and style become marginalized as a reason the change won't work elsewhere.

There are some challenges in spreading Advanced Access™ improvements piloted in a primary care site or a specific specialty area to another specialty area. In our experience, vigilant support is required for successful spread under these circumstances. One urology department we worked with reduced its wait time for an appointment from 340 days to seven days, an astounding achievement. However, when the doctors in the pilot tried to interest cardiologists in Advanced Access™, the specialty languages spoken by the two departments were so foreign that one department's success made no impression on the doctors in the other department. Two things work against spread in such cases. First, pilot physicians learn how Advanced Access™ principles apply in their own setting but don't fully understand the underlying principles required for spread to other areas. Second, pilot physicians are not familiar enough with the world of other specialties to be able to fully communicate the underlying principles in terms the other specialists can relate to. In this example, the urologists could not think in cardiologists' terms.

The key to spread across specialties seems to be translating the change and how it works into terms meaningful to other physicians. Either the pilot doctors must develop the skill to translate the change into terms their colleagues in other specialties can relate to or outside experts must continue to shepherd the process of spread and facilitate that translation for others in the organization.

of change adopters, from innovators to laggards, based on their receptivity to untried ideas.[3] The ideal individuals to include in a pilot are innovators and early adopters, individuals who are attracted to trying out new ideas.

- Identify sites or teams whose settings and practices are typical—not viewed as out of the ordinary with regard to resources, staffing levels, physical facility or equipment, opulence of setting, or any other feature that might affect the credibility of the pilot results. In one medical group, staff members referred to a new branch location as "Fantasy Island" because of its opulence and amenities. Physicians and staff are likely to discount the transferability of any change tested at a site they view as dramatically different from their own.

- Choose physicians who have a track record for follow-through—physicians you know you can count on to do what they commit to doing.

Tool 5-3, page 94, helps leaders evaluate potential pilot groups in terms of how likely they are to help make a change more transferable, and Tool 5-4, page 95, helps to plan communication to others in the organization about a pilot and its results.

Mastering Physician Involvement: Is It Worth the Effort?

Developing expertise in designing and optimizing opportunities for participation has a win-win outcome: Changes that leaders and others propose are improved, and, when these changes are ready to be implemented, they are as user-friendly as possible. Getting input that is useful is a complex process and one that often is not managed well. If physicians believe that their ideas are sought only to minimize their resistance, they feel manipulated and angry. These feelings reinforce whatever cynicism already exists in the organization about how much physicians are valued. When physicians do not trust leaders and administrators, they are much less willing to engage in change efforts. Even when leaders have only the best intentions, mishandling any step in the participatory process gives physicians reason to doubt their sincerity in wanting to hear their concerns or suggestions regarding a change.

Mastering participation by physicians is fundamental to improving the change capability in physician organizations. Foundational changes, such as vision development and compact change, cannot occur without physician participation. Their involvement is helpful, if not essential, for many smaller changes. When the ideas of physicians and support staff drive what a change looks like and how it gets implemented, everyone benefits—physicians and staff members themselves, leaders and the organization, and patients and other customers the organization exists to serve. Nevertheless, one of the most frequent complaints we hear from physicians, in almost every setting, involves their not being included in decisions that affect their daily work. Given the pace of change in health care organizations today, leaders must learn how to collect useful data from physicians and support staff efficiently and appropriately. Involving them does not require a process spread out over months; e-mail and voice mail ensure quick turnaround even with a large group. Whatever the mechanism, a thoughtful and well-designed process adds value to the specific change implementation and builds trust between leaders and others in the organization that promotes readiness for more change.

Tools for Taking Action

TOOL 5-1. Gather Input to Make a Change Attractive

PURPOSE: To create a change so that it has as many features as possible that would make it attractive to those who must implement it.

INSTRUCTIONS:

- This exercise can help those designing a change—if they are the implementers or if they are a change team overseeing the process—consider ways to make the change as attractive as possible.

  - Identify a change and fill in the form below.

  - Share your answers if you are working on this as part of a group.

  - Consider if there are ways that the change as it is currently formulated can be modified to be more attractive.

Observability: To what extent can the change be seen or studied by those who will be implementing it before they personally have to make the change?

Relative Advantage: To what extent does the change offer an easier approach, better results, or both compared to current practice or other changes that could be made?

Understandability: To what extent is the change and what is required to make it happen easily understood?

Compatibility: To what extent:

- Is the change compatible with other practices and does not require many other changes in order to work?

- Does the change mesh with the self-image or identity of those implementing it, or does it take something away from how they see themselves or their profession?

Trialability: To what extent can the change be tested or tried out and modified or abandoned if necessary, at a reasonable economic or personal cost?

Looking at the change relative to the five attributes, in what ways can it be designed or modified to be more attractive, easier to implement, or more likely to be sustained?

TOOL 5-2. Plan to Involve Others

PURPOSE: To help a leader think through a process for effectively involving physicians and others in designing a change.

INSTRUCTIONS:

- Answer these questions to clarify your thinking and to set expectations for those who will be involved in providing input into a change.

Clarify fixed parameters

- What are the "givens" or non-negotiables—that is, factors not open to modification?

- What is the time frame for getting input?

- What process will be used to make final decisions?

Consider the why, who, and how of the input process.

• What do I want to learn or accomplish by involving others? What am I going to do with the input I get?

• Which individuals or groups will be invited to participate? Consider who has useful knowledge, experience, and influence, as well as who might, by participating, move from being opposed to the change to supporting it.

• What mechanisms best suit this input process?

• How will I close the loop and get back to those involved?

TOOL 5-3: Plan a Pilot That Will Spread

PURPOSE: To evaluate characteristics of potential pilot groups or sites that can help make a change more transferable after piloting.

INSTRUCTIONS:

• Identify the change to be piloted.

• Identify groups or sites that seem appropriate to pilot the change.

• Consider each potential pilot group or site in terms of the four criteria listed below. Rate each group or site relative to the criteria as: H (high), M (medium), or L (low).

• Discuss the reasons for comments about each group or site and use this information to inform your choice.

Potential pilot group or site	Openess of these individuals to new ideas	Credibility of individuals in the group	Representativeness of the setting	Track record of local leader(s) regarding follow-through
	H M L	H M L	H M L	H M L
	H M L	H M L	H M L	H M L
	H M L	H M L	H M L	H M L

TOOL 5-4. Plan Communication about a Pilot

PURPOSE: To begin developing a plan to communicate to the rest of the organization about a test of a change and its results.

INSTRUCTIONS:
- Identify the change to be piloted.

- Answer the questions below to begin a plan to communicate about the pilot to the broader organization.

How is the pilot linked to the vision?
What communication will take place during the pilot to showcase it—to let others know it is happening and give them the opportunity to check it out?
After the test, how will results be communicated? Who will be involved in sharing the results with others? What opportunities for dialogue or two-way communication can be created?

Develop Tension for Change

Assessing the Current State

To what extent do physicians in the organization believe that they personally need to change?

Very little ←—————————————————————————→ Very much

1	2	3	4	5

What effect, if any, have physicians' perceptions of the need to change had on leaders' ability to implement changes?

Consider your own personal readiness to change. In the absence of any threat, or when there's no price to be paid for continuing with your current way of doing things, how likely are you to adopt a change?

Not at all likely ←—————————————————————————→ Extremely likely

1	2	3	4	5

A Solution in Search of a Problem

A better idea is not sufficient to motivate change. The messages carried by advocates of improvements and innovations fall on deaf ears if physicians do not believe they need to change. Sometimes, physicians do not perceive a problem or, if they acknowledge one, do not see it as serious enough to warrant the risk and the inconvenience associated with change. Integration of clinical quality improvement methods into physician organizations offers a case in point. As powerful and beneficial as the results are, when physicians do not perceive that improvement is necessary, as has been the case in many organizations, care does not improve much. When physicians consider the status quo good enough, or as good as it is likely to get, what leaders or change advocates regard as improvements turn out to be solutions in search of problems.

A basic requirement for change is tension. This tension can come from discontent with the current situation; from attraction, or pull, toward a new way that offers something better for those willing to change; or from both. Leaders play two critical roles in developing the tension required for change. First, they work to minimize the level of complacency toward change in general. Then they generate a sense of need and/or desire to engage in implementing specific changes.

Physician Complacency in the Midst of Turmoil

When it comes to change, complacency acts like gravity to anchor the status quo. Overcoming the effect of gravity takes considerable force. The space shuttle breaks through the pull of gravity powered by two rocket boosters that each generate 3,300,000 pounds of thrust at launch. To many leaders, it seems that a comparable amount of force is needed to move physicians out of the comfort of the status quo so that they are ready to adopt change.

Complacency among physicians is complex. Some physicians are content. Many others are not happy but consider the current state to be as good as it ever will be for them. Some are suffering from change fatigue; others have little time to do anything beyond seeing patients. Overall, these physicians have little energy to put toward change, and few reasons to be concerned about changing. This is what we mean by "complacent."

To help physicians become receptive to change, leaders need to calculate the level of complacency that exists, understand what contributes to it, and identify what they can do to reduce it. In our work, we frequently deal with situations in which physicians do not believe, or even sense, that they have to change, even though their local health care market is being transformed. Complacency in physician organizations is the result of a number of factors:

- *Poor communication about the extent or seriousness of problems.* Leaders usually have more direct knowledge of organizational performance and external threats and opportunities than front-line physicians do. Although leaders often cite poor attendance at meetings or physicians' lack of interest in the business side of the practice as reasons for complacency, many leaders fail to communicate why change is needed. They worry that the message will upset physicians or cause an extreme reaction among them. While we were helping one medical group plan for a retreat, the board candidly discussed its concerns for the group's survival if performance did not turn around. As we discussed how to make the case for change and educate the physicians about the seriousness of the situation, one board member said, "Let's think twice about this. Let's not upset the doctors; we don't want them to think there's a chance we won't make it."

- *"Make nice" messages undermine urgency for change.* For most leaders, signaling that change is needed while conveying that there is a light at the end of the tunnel—that tomorrow will be a better day—is a communication challenge. One of the cardinal reasons physicians fail to perceive any real urgency for change is that, in introducing the need to change, leaders all too often engage in "make nice" conversations. On the one hand, leaders point out how shortfalls hurt the organization and make the case for change, while, on the other, they reinforce doctors' sense that all is well by reassuring them, "We are the best doctors in town, and we will always be the best." Most often, "make nice" conversation is an attempt to soften the blow of bad news or to assuage concerns. Such comments, however, encourage complacency and counter the change message. As part of the human condition, we are inclined to remember the "make nice" message that allows us to rationalize current behaviors.

- *Past success breeds a sense of invulnerability.* Many physician organizations have had long and successful histories, filled with accomplishments and growth. It is easy to drift into complacency if your organization has not been threatened. Even if there are strong signals in the industry or the marketplace that change is called for, a reputation for "getting it right" or being seen as an industry leader reinforces a positive self-perception and diminishes urgency for change. Past successes and a stellar reputation can infuse passion for greatness into physicians, but they can also, if not managed well, contribute to a sense of invulnerability that makes it hard to acknowledge that change is needed.

- *Past experience of rabbits pulled out of hats.* Many physicians have experienced the following pattern often enough for it to become an expectation: Administrators or physician leaders announce the equivalent of "the sky is falling"; at the last minute some fix is found to put the situation right. For example, the talk for months is about how tight the budget is and how unlikely physicians are to get their customary bonus. At the eleventh hour, a rabbit is pulled from the hat in the form of an unexpected settlement check from an insurance company, a better-than-expected last quarter, or some other solution that is not sound in the long term but succeeds in the short term in funding the anticipated bonuses.

When figurative rabbits materialize on a regular basis, physicians expect that, whatever the crisis, leadership will find a way to make the situation work out. One of the downsides of this pattern is physicians' conviction that, when leaders call a situation urgent, they are just overreacting—again. After all, leaders have always come through in the past.

- *Infrequent use of external benchmarks.* Physician organizations tend to compare current performance to their own past performance or to rate departments or sites relative to one another. Although useful, these comparisons do not provide a complete picture; they do not capture how an organization compares to the best-in-class or to local competition. Looking only internally can give physicians a false sense that everything is on target and change is not needed.

- *Denial is human, especially when you're busy.* Physicians experience a disconnect between the message that change is needed and their current busy schedules. Physicians find it hard to buy the need to change when they are as busy as they are, although, in some cases, they are busier to offset falling reimbursement rates. Physicians who are booked well in advance can be blind to the shifts taking place in the market. They may be oblivious to fundamental change in what customers want and expect and to the emerging truth that doing "more and better" versions of what they have always done is not a recipe for success going forward.

- *Externalization of responsibility for fixing problems.* Internally, a physician organization may not be tranquil. The turmoil in the external environment may translate into a keen sense that the organization needs to transform itself. It is easy for physicians to look outside of themselves, however, for the source of problems—to other parts of the system or to the marketplace—and hold "them" responsible for changing. When they can point fingers at others who need to change, physicians can maintain a high comfort level with their own performance.

Reduce Complacency

Mobilizing energy to change is difficult when complacency is high. Leaders play a pivotal role in reducing complacency. The first step is to assess honestly the extent of complacency among the organization's physicians and how leaders' own decisions and actions add to complacency. Once leaders understand how complacency is created and reinforced in their organizations, they can take actions to minimize it. Some ways in which leaders reduce complacency are:

- Be direct when sharing bad news. Communicate from your heart why a concern is keeping you up at night.

- Take the time to enhance physicians' business literacy so they can achieve a better balance between pride in their organization and concern over its future.

- Stop "making nice" when it undercuts urgency for change.

- Dialogue with departments and individual physicians about how their behavior is threatening the organization or sub-optimizing performance.

- Share external benchmarks with physicians to educate them about how their organization compares to others on performance dimensions that the market says are important.

- Help physicians break the "busyness" trap. Educate them about how just increasing patient volume to make up for lowered reimbursement is not a sustainable strategy.

- Avoid the temptation to pull rabbits from your hat if such fixes potentially threaten the organization's future or reinforce perceptions that relief is always forthcoming when leaders describe a situation as urgent.

Tool 6-1, pages 106-107, is designed to help leaders understand how they contribute to complacency.

Pain and Pull Approaches to Change

When there is less of a sense of complacency overall, an organization is more receptive to change. Still, when introducing specific changes, leaders need to generate some tension to make the proposed change more appealing than the status quo. The potency of combined "pull" and "pain" strategies is usually needed. Pull strategies link the change to personal or group aspirations to draw individuals away from the comfort of the status quo and toward the change. Pain approaches focus on making the status quo more uncomfortable and less secure than the perceived threat and risk associated with the change. Physicians are often drawn toward a change when they believe it will build a better tomorrow, but they tend not to adopt a change until they are convinced they have to.

In our early days consulting to medical groups, we believed that physicians would want to implement change once they personally connected with it or understood how it would advance the shared vision. We thought that making a change appealing and relevant to physicians would be leaders' greatest challenge. Our experiences over the years, however, have taught us the key role of "pain" in engaging physicians in change. Some individuals are motivated intrinsically to initiate changes or modify the way they practice. For example, there are physicians who are deeply committed to clinical quality improvement; they work with colleagues on tests of changes and integrate best practices into daily work because of their conviction that improvement is the right thing to do. We find that, for large-scale or organization-wide change, which needs the support of the vast majority of physicians, leaders cannot rely on this kind of intrinsic motivation. Some level of urgency to change based on pain or discomfort is also needed.

Pain Strategies

Make the Cost of the Status Quo Clear

Allied Signal's CEO, Lawrence Bossidy, uses the burning platform as a metaphor to describe what it takes to get people to change.[1] An organization is on a burning platform when the cost and the risk of maintaining the status quo outweigh the risks and the uncertainty of making changes—when, for survival, change is the only viable option. This metaphor conveys the level of intensity often needed to get physicians and others to change.

Two forces create the burning platform dynamic: the risks and pain associated with the status quo and the risk of abandoning the current state. For most of us, the threats associated with changing are more compelling than the risks we perceive in the status quo. When physicians contemplate giving up the status quo, they readily connect with the fear and the perceived cost of change, including loss of control, loss of income, and more work. Even if they cannot precisely articulate all their concerns, their emotional response to a change is typically visceral and negative. The dangers of not changing, of staying on the platform, can seem theoretical or less compelling. In many physician organizations, however, there is a significant threat to business success lurking in the status quo. Hazards are present, even though they may not be as obvious as the perceived drawbacks associated with making a change.

It is leaders' responsibility to help physicians come to terms with the cost of not changing and to help them understand how that cost stacks up against the real and the perceived costs of changing. Once physicians are uncomfortable with the current state, the change becomes the "fix" or the way to reduce tension. Not having a change proposal to follow up with can lead to panic. Leaders can leverage the "unfrozen" state by offering an alternative or an invitation to help create the new way.

Two key strategies to help physicians appreciate the threat inherent in the status quo are:

- *Use data and other means to educate.* Educational strategies alone typically do not generate sufficient urgency to prompt change, but they play an important role and should be incorporated into your change plan. The purpose in educating physicians is not to beat up on them; generating negativity does not help implement a change. The aim is to help physicians become more business literate and appreciate what they risk by not changing. Share data with physicians regarding market trends, information about the competition, and the organization's performance relative to targets or benchmarks. Some organizations have stimulated change by sharing unblinded data that compare physicians on key performance dimensions.

  Another strategy is to invite physicians from organizations that faced similar circumstances but did not act in time to learn from their experiences about the price paid for not changing. Still another strategy is to distribute articles about national and local trends or about organizations that failed to recognize the need to change and the consequences they suffered. All these ways to enlighten physicians can be used together as part of a strategy to develop discomfort with the status quo.

  The educational approach only works when the information is credible to physicians. Data, speakers, and articles need to connect to the experience of physicians in the organization in order to create uneasiness or discontent. Otherwise, physicians are likely to dismiss the information as inaccurate or irrelevant.

- *Remove buffers to experiencing the pain of the status quo.* Educational strategies help get physicians ready for change, but, when it comes to stepping off the platform, most human beings need more motivation than hearing about others' experiences or pouring over data. They need to feel the heat of the burning platform—that is, the pain of business as usual.

The use of pain to motivate change is illustrated in the following scenarios:

- *An IPA board set a 15 percent increase over the previous year's HEDIS scores as a target for financial bonuses for primary care physicians. After the numbers were crunched, very few doctors qualified for the bonus. In the past, the board would have lowered the threshold to increase the number of bonus-eligible physicians. This time, it agreed to let the threshold stand and discussed with each physician who fell short what he or she needed to do to earn it.*

- *In a multispecialty group practice, physicians in one department were allowed to decide among themselves when they would take time off. When several physicians chose to take the same week off, the others pitched in. Being swamped occasionally was a fair trade-off for the flexibility in scheduling. This system worked because the patients who could not be accommodated were sent to urgent care. When the chief and medical director decided physicians could no longer send patients to urgent care under these circumstances, the physicians had to accept the consequences of their scheduling practices. This approach got physicians to change the way they scheduled their vacations.*

The pain approach is most effective when exposure to consequences is coupled with education. Just relying on education results in "change lite" at best, a watered-down version of what is really called for. To precipitate pain without first giving information or demonstrating how and why an alternative is better increases resistance and anger.

A meaningful motivator to many physicians is loss of income, threatened or real. As much as one would like to think that appeals to do the "right" thing would unfreeze the current state, experience suggests that nothing focuses physicians' attention as quickly as loss of income. This kind of pain can fuel change when leaders do not try to cover over it and if they offer ways to involve physicians in fixes that reverse the situation.

If change could be implemented and sustained with little sense of urgency, leaders could afford to use a purely educational approach. In our experience, however, there is no guarantee that physicians will embrace a change just because it makes intellectual sense. Proposals to improve quality of care, service, or even financial performance are unlikely to move physicians unless they first feel a need to change.

Using the pain approach, leaders help physicians experience the problems and costs of the status quo and understand the steps they can take to reduce the discomfort. It does not call for fabricating threats in the status quo when none exist. If there is no short- or long-term risk associated with the way physicians are currently doing something, do not make this a focus of change. Concentrate efforts on aspects of the practice that do threaten the organization's health or future viability unless they change.

Leaders' Willingness to Use Pain Strategies

Actively taking steps to make physicians uncomfortable can be challenging for many leaders who have seen their role as protecting physicians. As counter-intuitive as it seems, allowing physicians to have some discomfort, psychologically or experientially, is exactly what leaders need to do if they are convinced that change is a necessity. This is not just counter-intuitive; it is extremely difficult. Given the mental models common among physician leaders, when there is pressure for doctors to change, leaders often take action that is equivalent to passing out asbestos booties or building stronger firewalls. Their actions are geared toward protecting physicians from the heat or pain. Regardless of whether they are elected or appointed, physician leaders are typically reluctant to give bad news or send an unequivocal message that change is needed. Other physicians do not want to hear this kind of news, and, in practical terms, it could cost a leader political support or even his or her position. When they try to lead and make the case for change, leaders face the possibility of loss or cooling of friendships.

One approach to gain greater comfort using pain strategies to motivate change is for leaders to discuss their concerns with other leaders. Useful questions for discussion include:

- If you are convinced that there is a need to change—the platform is smoldering or ablaze—why do physicians not see it the same way?

- In what ways might you be shielding physicians, and how does this eventually affect physicians' overall motivation to change?

Strategies to Engage Physicians

WILLIAM GOLD, MD

Bill Gold is Chief Medical Officer and Vice President at Blue Cross/Blue Shield of Minnesota. Reporting directly to the CEO, he leads the effort to improve health for two million Minnesotans.

In my experience, the central challenge in any strategy to improve or significantly change the organization's direction is getting physicians intellectually and emotionally engaged in the change. In many situations, there is no perceived urgency around the need to change and yet significant change is needed.

Despite market forces that have shaken the very core of the profession, many physicians are fundamentally fulfilling the fruits of their educational journey. They are busy seeing patients and making an income that provides substantial security, and the immediate future does not seem that scary. Some are still reeling from the last change process. The chaos of major consolidation activities has left a growing number of physicians disheartened about facing more change. The slow and painful process of true integration has left these physicians frustrated. This situation does not provide fertile ground for getting physicians to explore and commit to changes such as significant care improvement.

Over the years, I've come to rely more on strategies other than those that depend on doctors' experiencing the pain of the status quo. Engaging physicians in quality issues seems to require different thinking.

- Get leadership, not one leader, to commit to improvement. Any change that has only one key sponsor at the top is vulnerable. Getting most major changes, such as clinical quality improvement, embedded in an organization takes years. Relying on one leader is high-risk, because distractions and other critical issues present themselves. Getting many leaders to see what role they need to play takes time but is a worthwhile investment as change is planned. Having the CEO "on board" is necessary, but much more is needed from the broader leadership group.

- Peg something meaningful to physicians' willingness to take on a change project. For example, as a department is negotiating to replace its computer systems, raise the issue of the difficulty patients are having getting into the clinic in a timely manner.

- What personally concerns you about using any of the "pain" strategies?

- For specific changes or improvements that the organization is committed to making, what opportunities exist to take away buffers and allow direct experience of the status quo to motivate change?

- As leaders, what, if any, price might you pay for applying any pain strategies?

Pull Strategies

While pain increases discomfort with the status quo, pull approaches create tension by connecting a change to personal aspirations or the organization's vision. Pull approaches are best used as an adjunct to those that make the current state uncomfortable. For pull to work as a motivator, the attraction toward the change or its benefits has to surpass the inertia of the status quo. The experience of one insurance company's medical director in using pull strategies to interest physicians in improvement activities is described in the sidebar, left and page 103.

Leaders can most productively employ pull approaches when the change is seen as a way to advance a shared vision or when there is personal benefit to implementing it.

- *A change helps achieve a shared vision.* When a specific change and the vision are clearly connected, less effort needs to be expended to create discomfort with the status quo. The tension needed to move beyond the status quo comes from wanting to move the vision forward. For example, if physicians are committed to a vision of outstanding service, changes that improve access or make scheduling more convenient for patients can be positioned as a means to achieve their shared vision.

- *Physicians see personal benefits in the change.* When a change reduces steps in a process or makes daily work easier, it has a strong pull built in. Pull is also a powerful motivator when the change can be linked to physicians' needs, aspirations, or interests. The change then becomes a means to an end that is important and personally relevant. The end could be to earn the maximum bonus, to excel in one's specialty, or to advance one's proficiency in an area of personal interest. A change could also help individuals meet latent human needs, such as the need for security or a measure of control over business outcomes, for recognition and feeling important, for making a contribution, and for the pride that comes from being part of a cutting-edge organization.

To effectively "piggy-back" a change onto what is personally important to physicians, tailor the change message. No single message is likely to tap into the needs of a majority of the physicians in the organization. For example, if a leader is trying to implement clinical quality improvement, it would be important to understand the benefits of making the change from physicians' perspectives. Then it would be possible to target specific communications to physician segments or sub-groups. Messages that are tailored are better at generating pull because individuals can appreciate the benefit of a change in terms that resonate with them.

To tailor communication usually means that leaders need to spend some one-on-one time with physicians. Although labor-intensive, this approach to engaging physicians can be very powerful. To some, this may sound like manipulation. On the contrary, leaders whose organizations need to implement significant change have a responsibility to understand what is important to individuals. Leaders are responsible collectively for the organization's future. Helping physicians to appreciate how implementing a specific change can be a win-win is one of the tools that leaders use to help their organizations succeed.

Orchestrating Pain and Pull Strategies

Pain and pull strategies are additive; they move individuals away from the status quo and toward the change (figure 6-1, page 104). It is useful to develop a plan that integrates the two approaches. Pain gets physicians' attention. Pull approaches are generally more personal and require leaders to invest more of their time. Because reliance on making the status quo uncomfortable as a way to motivate change can wear people down, developing ways to pull physicians toward the change makes sense. Tool 6-2, pages 108-109, is an opportunity to identify both pain and pull strategies that could be employed to further a change your organization needs to implement.

When this linkage is successful, it's a real win-win. We are working with one organization that needs to expand its clinic space. We are helping the clinic secure favorable funding while, at the same time, asking them to reconsider how care is delivered. We are asking them to help us convey to the market—employers—how care in the expanded clinic will be better. This dialogue has resulted in formulation of an aggressive care improvement plan with appropriate investments.

- Tap into physicians' competitiveness and professionalism. Some of the rural clinics associated with Blue Cross/Blue Shield of Minnesota experience little competition and have good patient volume and good reimbursement—basically no "burning platform." Using statewide data, we are able to profile clinic performance, which may reveal significant differences between clinic systems. Suggesting that they can be as good as any clinic in the state around quality and cost appeals to their competitiveness and professionalism to do the very best job possible. This approach has begun to engage these clinics in improvement activities that otherwise would not have been a priority.

- Focus on developing physician champions. I learned when I was quality improvement director in another organization that I didn't have to be the one to change the practice of the internal medicine department. I had to find and nurture physician champions in that department. It's easier and more satisfying to ignite the passion for quality in one or two people who show interest, and then continue to support them, than it is to convince a whole department it should want to improve.

- Ask questions. Once I found the champions in a department who believed that things could be better, I would engage them through questions, not data presentations. What is the best care? What kind of care does this department or this clinic stand for? Can we explain the variation that shows up today? Where do you think the variation contributes to patient care and where does it only add cost and complexity? How can we start taking out some of the unnecessary variation?

The key to engaging physicians in change is to be tuned in to what is important to them. You have to be flexible and able to tailor your approach so that it resonates with at least a few who can carry the message deeper into the organization.

FIGURE 6-1. Pain and Pull are Synergistic Strategies

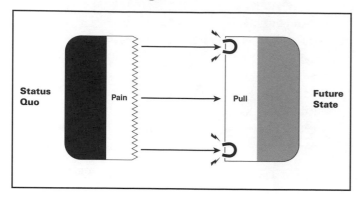

Leadership alignment plays an important role in creating tension for change. Leaders need to agree about the legitimacy of creating urgency as part of the change process. Otherwise, the efforts any one leader makes in this regard will be diluted. Leaders also need to be aligned around the need to use both pain and pull strategies. All must be willing to give up protecting physicians when maintaining the status quo risks the organization's future. Finally, leaders will have the greatest success if they actively support one another when they feel stretched beyond their personal comfort zones.

When a Crisis Provides Tension for Change

In a crisis, the case for change is transparent and urgent. Everyone knows the platform has ignited, and not changing is not an option. A crisis for a medical group might be learning that the local hospital with which it has had a long-term relationship is building its own physician group. For an IPA, a crisis might be precipitated when reimbursement is drastically and suddenly lowered because a managed care company that covers a vast majority of its patients is on the verge of bankruptcy. Such circumstances provide a natural opportunity to change daily work life.

Because a crisis can cause paralysis and dysfunction as well as unfreeze an organization and prime it for change, leaders need to leverage the situation and energize individuals while minimizing dysfunctional anxiety. Some guidelines for productively using a crisis as an opportunity to drive changes that improve organizational or departmental performance include:

- *Have a plan.* During a crisis, everyone in the organization wants to believe that senior leadership knows what to do and has a turnaround plan. Communicate as clearly as possible how the organization is going to work its way out of the current situation and the role physicians, support staff, and management are going to have to play in the turnaround.

- *Translate your plan into actionable items.* Help everyone to understand what they need to do to stabilize the situation and improve performance.

- *Set clear targets and provide regular feedback to everyone regarding progress toward meeting the targets.*

- *Be straightforward with information.* Do not downplay the reality the organization is facing. Communicate the change message often and through a variety of channels. Do not depend on memos or newsletters. Be visible and hold as many large- and small-group meetings as possible, especially meetings that permit two-way communication.

- *Get directly involved in removing barriers.* Work with other leaders to ensure that physicians and staff have what they need to do what is expected. Address barriers that keep them from contributing to the turnaround effort.

- *Express confidence in the ability of physicians and staff to make the changes that are needed.* The core of the most important message is that there is a light at the end of the tunnel that can be reached *if* changes are implemented and everyone does his or her part.

- *Stay aligned as leaders.* Consistent messages about progress and the effect of changes are essential.

- *Plan communication so that it motivates positive change.* Communication professionals can help leaders take advantage of the window of opportunity a crisis offers for implementing change. There is a special art to crafting messages that can rally everyone to action without creating undue panic or raising the level of insecurity to a point where it is dysfunctional.

The crisis one group practice faced and how the senior executive used it to motivate large-scale change is described in the sidebar on page 105.

There Is No One Right Way

The basic principle conveyed in this chapter is that physicians need to be engaged in a change for it to be successful. If you find you are pushing a change, stop what you are doing and try a different approach; pushing is only going to generate resistance. If you fail to interest physicians in a change by sharing information, connect the change to a deeply felt personal interest or need. There is no one right way, and no one way works for all physicians. However, no amount of effort or exhortation will result in successful change if physicians do not feel a deep sense of the need for change.

Leading Out Of Crisis

MARTIN HICKEY, MD, MS, FACP, FACPE

Martin Hickey is a practicing internist and President and Chief Executive Officer of Lovelace Health Systems, a wholly owned subsidiary of CIGNA Healthcare. The integrated system in Albuquerque, New Mexico, includes a medical group with 270 physicians, a tertiary care hospital, and a health plan with 250,000 members and 3,000 IPA physicians.

There had been an undercurrent of anger at Lovelace directed toward CIGNA, our for-profit owner. But those sentiments were also the rumblings of a group of doctors being pulled out of complacency. They did not see that the outside environment had changed, so they did not understand why life couldn't go on as before. We were being lauded nationally for our reputation in disease management and health status improvement; why wasn't that enough for CIGNA and everyone else? Well, the market told us that it wasn't enough and that, to remain competitive, we had to lower our premiums.

Then, one day in 1997, crisis showed up at our door. We had a loss of $22 million on $350 million in revenue. This situation was clearly not sustainable. We were on a platform that had burst into flames. Our response had to be immediate and dramatic.

First, we came clean to everyone in the organization. We made the seriousness of the financial situation absolutely clear. Second, we communicated that losses of this magnitude were not sustainable. Third, we charged task groups to look at every facet of our business for reengineering. We gave them two months to present recommendations. Nothing was considered sacred. We eliminated services and programs. Twenty-three physicians were let go. By moving quickly, we created optimism about the future. My message was that we would find the holes and plug them. It would cost us, but our ship would stay afloat and 95 percent of us would be going together into the future.

Moving quickly, while it hurt, was less demoralizing than dragging it out would have been. We knew we would make some mistakes. We didn't try to get it perfect. We had to save the organization. People feared that their jobs would be eliminated. The sooner we moved to cut losses, the faster people could heal. After two months, we had a plan, and people felt we were rebuilding.

At that point, I wished I could have said that the job was done, but all I could say was that the large, low-hanging fruit had been harvested. We would keep looking for further opportunities in little places and address those if it meant keeping us on our course financially.

We're not out of the woods yet. Leading this organization to financial health is more like taking care of a chronic diabetic than performing surgery. We made $12 million in 1998 and lost $6 million in 1999. But morale is getting better. A lot of us are learning to live with unrelenting challenges.

Doctors have to be business literate. We've opened up our books, and we communicate monthly about our finances. I believe that the more people know about the business the more likely it is they'll do the right thing. I tell our physicians that information is like blood and that money is like air—basic to our survival. We've got to take care of these two items or nothing else is going to matter. A good deal of my time is spent in the field to drive this message home; three times a year, I visit every department to give the 50,000-foot view of where we are as an organization.

A crisis can be a good teacher. To help me lead through this crisis, I got help in strategy and communication. This experience taught me that the organization craves honest information. Leaders need to be straightforward and admit mistakes if they've made them. Leaders have to have a vision for getting the ship back on course. The other lesson for me was the importance of surrounding myself with good people. I couldn't do this alone. I was able to do what I had to do because I had people around me who can communicate, execute, and hold others accountable.

In our medical group culture, one of the painful lessons we have to learn is that success is about results, not relationships. We need to get beyond the guilt of not keeping everyone in the race. Our eyes have to be on the well-being of the whole organization.

Tools For Taking Action

TOOL 6-1. Take Action to Reduce Complacency

PURPOSE: To reflect on actions leaders take that contribute to complacency in their organizations and identify what they will do to reduce their contributions to this dynamic.

INSTRUCTIONS:
This tool can be used as a personal exercise or as a group activity with leaders who wish to examine their collective role in creating complacency.

- Assess complacency by rating every item listed in the left column below in terms of its contribution to the current state of complacency in the organization.

- If you are working as a group, stop at this point and share your ratings.

- Then select up to three items that you all agree are significant contributors, and, for each one, discuss how leaders contribute. Consider what you do and say as well as what you ignore or do not say. If you are working alone, reflect on how your own actions contribute to complacency.

- Identify what leaders individually and collectively will do differently to help reduce complacency.

Actions that contribute to complacency	To what extent does this contribute to complacency in my organization?	What do I do that contributes?	What will I do differently?
Providing little communication about the extent or seriousness of problems.	High Medium Low		
Engaging in "make nice" messages	High Medium Low		

Reinforcing a sense of invulnerability.	High Medium Low		
Pulling rabbits out of hats.	High Medium Low		
Providing inadequate balance of internal and external benchmarks.	High Medium Low		
Reinforcing that increasing productivity is an adequate strategy to address the pressures to change.	High Medium Low		
Actively or passively agreeing with physicians when they externalize responsibility for problems.	High Medium Low		

TOOL 6-2. Build Tension for Change through Pain and Pull Strategies

PURPOSE: To identify and coordinate strategies to develop tension for a specific change, including strategies that expose physicians to the pain of the status quo and strategies that offer benefits.

GENERATE PAIN
INSTRUCTIONS:

- Identify a change you are responsible for implementing.

- As a group, identify all the strategies you could use to help get physicians ready for this change. Do not limit your thinking to what seems clearly doable or practical. Consider:

  - Educational strategies that rely on data or information.

  - Strategies that remove buffers and expose physicians to the consequences of business as usual.

- After completing the idea-generating phase, review the lists and pick out a couple of ideas that you will use, based on their power to motivate change and their feasibility.

- Discuss how the change team will move forward and implement the strategies.

Educational strategies based on data and information	Strategies that remove buffers and expose individuals to the consequences of current behavior

GENERATE PULL
INSTRUCTIONS:

Generate a list of pull messages for this change based on how the change benefits the organization overall and the individuals making the change.

After completing the idea-generating phase, review the lists and pick out a couple of ideas that you will use, based on their power to motivate change and their feasibility.

Discuss how the change team will move forward and implement the strategies, appreciating that personal benefits are more powerful than organizational benefits as a source of pull.

The benefits of the change for the organization	The benefits for those who will implement the change

Given the opportunities to use pain and pull strategies that you identified, how can you coordinate the use of both to create tension for change?

CHAPTER 7   Address Resistance

Assessing the Current State

In general, what emotional responses have you observed when physicians have been asked to change something that affects their practice?

How does your organization handle physicians' emotional reactions to change?
- Who helps them work through their reactions?
- What approaches or methods are used?

Recall a time when you were expected to implement a change. How much communication did you get about the change and the part you were supposed to play in it? What effect did getting that much (or that little) communication have on your response to what you were asked to do?

In a meeting of a medical group's leadership, the following conversation is taking place:

"The first time I heard of this Health Accountability Project, I thought I must have missed something. How can a business coalition think they know what it takes to run an ICU? Board-certified intensivists to staff every hospital ICU? That just shows how little they know. They've set up standards, and there are not enough doctors in the country to meet them—even if somebody could pay their

salaries. And the same for putting in computers for medication orders. It might be a good idea some day, but by 2002? No way."

"It sounds outrageous, doesn't it? Just where do they think the money is going to come from to meet their demands?"

"At the plan, they say that the coalition is going to enforce the standards through contracts, and that's why we have to get on board. If you ask me, they're playing hardball with us, and personally I find it offensive. After all, just look at

what happens when any manufacturer is mandated to put in safety equipment—they don't absorb that cost, they pass it on to their customers. Well, maybe we should charge extra for having Dr. Thompson in our ICU."

"Dr. Black, I'm offended, too. That's why I say we send back a memo with our own timetable for improvement. We've already bent over backward to work with the plan on immunizations and beta blockers. And we're actually doing pretty well relative to last year."

"Let's just tell them we don't do business this way."

"I don't know…remember that the businesses in the coalition are also the plan's biggest customers. That makes them important for us too. Can we afford to ignore their Health Accountability deal?"

"I said it once, and I'll say it again. We provide health care. We don't produce widgets. What about that don't they understand?"

The Emotional Environment Sets the Context For Change

Implementing change is not easy in the best of times. Today, the emotional environment in most physician organizations makes it more challenging. The forces reshaping the health care delivery system leave many physicians feeling powerless and victimized. Physicians' interest in unionization is indicative of the anger and frustration many of them experience. In general, physician morale can be related to a number of factors:

- **Changing societal views of physicians.** Today's patients are less inclined than previous generations to see physicians as gods in white coats whose advice is not to be questioned or challenged. Patients and families are increasingly bent on litigation when outcomes are less than positive. Negative publicity surrounding managed care plans leads some patients to suspect that physicians are acting in their own financial interests when a referral or a test request is denied. This strains the intimacy and trust in the doctor-patient relationship and leaves many physicians feeling devalued.

- **Loss of power in the doctor-patient relationship.** The information explosion is shifting power in the doctor-patient relationship in a way that is unsettling to many physicians. Patients come to appointments armed with information from the Internet, direct advertising from pharmaceutical companies, and other sources. They expect their physicians to help them evaluate volumes of material, some of it unsubstantiated or from questionable sources. The baby-boom generation, now reaching middle age, is inclined to look to physicians to be partners in health care. Some physicians welcome patients' involvement in this way, but many more sense a loss when patients put themselves in the driver's seat in the relationship.

- **Mainstream acceptance of alternative medicine.** Health consumers are increasingly looking to alternative care for prevention and treatment. In 1997, visits to alternative providers exceeded visits to primary care physicians.[1] Many patients do not even inform their physicians that they visit alternative therapists, because they believe, rightly or wrongly, that their physicians would not support or would even criticize their decisions.

- **Restrictions on physicians' clinical authority.** Preauthorization processes and other cost containment procedures have put some limits on physicians' professional autonomy. Even following clinical guidelines developed by physicians can leave many feeling that their judgment is being restricted.

- **The financial rewards are declining for many.** In most parts of the country, physicians are, or fear that they are, working harder—seeing more patients, going to more locations, putting in longer hours, doing more paperwork—for the same or less money.

- **Lack of optimism about the future.** Even where market forces have not substantially eroded physicians' incomes and authority, physicians' uncertainty about the future diminishes their ability to take pleasure and satisfaction in what they are doing today.

The magnitude of these influences on physician morale and professional satisfaction are beyond individual leaders or physicians to reverse. However, leaders can help physicians to understand where some of the pressures have come from and to take some responsibility for their role in today's situation. Although physicians rail against what they perceive as threats to their authority and economic security, they often overlook the antecedents to today's reality. The rise in health care costs outpaced inflation, and quality of care has been, and still is, widely variable across, and even within, institutions. Patients have been treated paternalistically by the medical profession, and doctors, by and large, have shown little interest in unconventional treatments. Engaging physicians in discussion about the broader context that is bringing on so much of the change they do not like can help put some of the pressures in perspective. When physicians can take some collective responsibility for the present reality, they take steps out of the victim box and toward finding ways to provide value to consumers while taking advantage of opportunities in the market.

Declining professional satisfaction among physicians in general is one source of poor physician morale. Another important factor is the unique emotional environment of the organizations in which they practice. This environment is influenced by several related factors:

- **The financial success of the organization and of each physician's practice.** If physicians are taking pay cuts or working a lot harder for very little gain, it is unlikely they have high morale.

- **The extent to which leadership is capable and inspiring.** When an organization has effective leadership that has developed strategies and positioned physicians for success, the esprit and internal environment are far healthier than in organizations competitively disadvantaged by inadequate leadership and direction.

- **Efforts made to acknowledge and honor physicians and to help them feel positive about their future.** Some environments are more acknowledging than others. Organizations that do not take their physicians for granted but recognize their need for acknowledgment are more satisfying places to practice.

- **The amount and kind of change physicians have had to make.** When expectations to change are unrelenting or the changes are numerous and seemingly disconnected, most physicians get worn down and experience change fatigue.

- **The extent to which processes and systems support physician practices.** Basic processes such as getting access to a patient's chart or to laboratory results need to support physicians to practice efficiently and productively. If processes are barriers to meeting targets or providing care, frustration runs high.

- **Physician involvement in their organizations.** Given all the influences on professional satisfaction that are beyond physicians' control, it is especially important that they are able to influence their own work environment. In some organizations, physicians perceive that administrators have the control and do not value their input. The sidebar on pages 114-115 describes steps one system took to give physicians more influence over their practices and to support them to take greater responsibility for their own and the system's success.

- **The match between expectations and what the organization can realistically promise and deliver given market realities.** A significant influence on morale is the extent to which physicians' expectations of their organizational life are realistic. When expectations are inappropriate, given what the organization has to do to remain competitive, and efforts are not made to help physicians develop different expectations, they are bound to be constantly frustrated by new demands to change. (Chapter 3 addresses ways to understand and modify physician expectations of what they are required to give the organization and what they should expect to get in return.)

Given the strength of the relationship between an organization's emotional environment and physicians' readiness to engage in change, dealing with morale issues is important to building change capability. When reasons for low morale are well defined—lack of acknowledgment, processes that are not physician-friendly, the compact out of step with reality—leaders should address these issues. Change efforts do not succeed in positive environments only, but leaders can be more effective when they recognize how low morale exaggerates resistance to new ideas and makes it more difficult to rally physicians.

Resistance to Change

A commonly understood truth is that resistance is the natural, universal, inevitable human response to

From Resistance to Responsibility

FREDRICK TITZE, MHA

Fred Titze is President and CEO of Health Midwest Medical Group, a primary care network owned by the Health Midwest system, with approximately 130 physicians practicing at more than 30 locations in Kansas City, Missouri, and the surrounding area.

Physicians in our network have been through what most others in hospital-acquired practices around the country are dealing with. Physicians who sold or merged their practices saw being relieved of business issues as a benefit. In time, however, they experienced themselves as powerless because they did not have a way to affect change at the system level or even at the level of their practices.

When I joined Health Midwest as COO in 1997, the doctors' lack of meaningful influence while under pressure to improve performance was eroding morale. The system had gone through an amalgamation stage, adding hospitals and practices, but operational issues in the practices had not been systematically addressed. The practices were challenging the system financially and, when pressure on the system increased—from managed care, downward pricing, BBA, and so on—this became less palatable. The system made it absolutely clear that the practices needed to improve. The challenge was making that happen against a backdrop of frustration and mistrust that had developed in this organization as well as in like organizations nationwide over the years.

Some of the steps we took to help doctors make a transition from feeling victimized and angry to taking responsibility included:

- **Listen and follow up.** Early on, we spent a lot of time listening to physicians express anger about being held responsible for what was not in their control, for example, improving the financials when they were saddled with a billing service that performed poorly and that they did not have any authority over. Because I was new and not associated with the past, it was easy for me to listen to and acknowledge their feelings and try to get things done for them. Sometimes I could get issues resolved in physicians' favor and other times I couldn't. But getting back with a resolution began building their belief that administration cared. At the same time, we tried hard to exhibit leading, not advocating for any one side. We

change that someone else thinks is a good idea. When people resist change, Peter Senge says, they are fighting to preserve something they care about, something they know, something they are good at and enjoy.[2] Viewing resistance this way opens up new levels of understanding. Physicians who resist change or improvement are not bad or narrow-minded. They may see change as a threat to current practices and respond, from where they stand, appropriately. Being able to "hold" resistance as a natural and understandable response empowers leaders to address it positively, in ways that do not cause further entrenchment.

Not all change provokes resistance. We all seek change and freely choose to change when it pleases us. Let's take the example of Lindsay Smythe, a doctor who decides to get in shape by swimming three mornings a week. She is making a change, but the impetus is internal. She may not relish starting the day extra early on those mornings, but her emotional state could not be labeled "resistance." When she tries to enroll her spouse in the new routine, the response, "Leave me alone and let me sleep," suggests resistance. A change at work that is not of her own choosing, on the other hand, triggers resistance. When Dr. Smythe learns that, instead of pairing each physician with a nurse, administration is proposing that the five physicians on the doctor's unit share three nurses and two new assistants, the doctor feels angry, frustrated, and let down. Determined not to let this happen without a fight, Dr. Smythe e-mails the medical director demanding a meeting. The doctor is outraged at what is happening, despite the fact that cost-cutting, and the plan to take the cost out of physician salaries if it cannot be saved elsewhere, have been talked about for months.

Those leading change need to be attuned to all manifestations of resistance, from nuances to the obvious. While anger and complaints are obvious expressions of resistance, some symptoms are subtler but just as important to recognize and address, including:

- Superficial agreement with a change with little or no commitment to follow-through.

- Slow progress.

- Apathy.

- Excuses for lack of engagement or lack of progress.

Not recognizing resistance leads to missteps and to taking actions that backfire. If leaders continue to move forward when there is little support for a change, they increase the risk that the change will fail.

It is also important to appreciate that individuals will be in different places in response to the pressures leading to change or created by undertaking specific changes. Elizabeth Kübler-Ross[3] identified the following mechanisms that help us to cope with loss:

- Denial.
- Anger.
- Bargaining.
- Depression.
- Acceptance.

In almost any physician organization, there are individuals in every stage of grief. When leaders proactively deal with physicians' reactions to the losses they are experiencing, physicians move faster to acceptance of change. Not acknowledging physicians' emotional state slows change implementation.

Physicians' Reactions to Proposed Changes

The resistance triggered by a change can be minor or seismic, depending on the nature of the change, how disruptive it is, and how it fits with physicians' self-identity. Asking physicians to order office furniture from a new vendor is far different from asking them to extend office hours. The changes that go against physicians' self-identity provoke the fiercest resistance and prove the most challenging to implement. Disease management guidelines are a case in point. Many practices find that formulating a guideline is the easy part; actually achieving consistent adherence is extremely challenging. Some physicians view guidelines as eroding their freedom to exercise clinical judgment. The closer a change comes to threatening strongly valued and deeply held aspects of self-identity, the more emotional the reaction to it is likely to be.

Sometimes, the resistance expressed toward a specific change seems out of proportion to its impact on physicians' practices or to what it requires of them. Take the earlier example of the physician responding to changed unit staffing. We know the doctor had been given a lot of information about the financial

wanted the doctors to develop a different mindset about what leaders do.

- **Create a new model of leadership.** Historically, leaders were "site champions" who negotiated the loudest and could get what others in their site wanted. Moving away from leader-as-advocate was essential to everything else we did. This was not accomplished overnight but through a lot of dialogue. Changes in the external environment, specifically systems inside and outside Kansas City cutting doctors loose, helped the newly formed Physician Advisory Committee (PAC) and many doctors understand the need for different leadership. Now, the 12 appointed physicians on PAC are rising to the leadership challenge. This group has created a market-driven, productivity-based compensation plan; negotiated group managed care agreements; and improved business office and general operations. As a direct result, the network's financial performance has improved.

- **Provide data and make it actionable.** Doctors did not get enough information from the traditional profit and loss statements to be able to improve. Now we give them tools comparing each practice to targets. Any shortfalls between actual performance and targets are obvious. Knowing where the gaps are and the size of the gaps, PAC is considering greater standardization to improve results. Now that it sees the need, PAC is pulling for standards with administration—we're not pushing it on them.

- **Give doctors some control.** In my own life, when a lot was happening beyond my control, being able to make and act on some decisions—even if they dealt with minutiae—helped me get through tough times. We're putting more control back in the practices with the new metrics providing the guidance. Another avenue is putting actionable items on every PAC agenda. When physician leaders are given legitimate authority, they are very good decision makers and take the leadership challenge to heart.

Feeling victimized breeds paralysis that cannot support improvement. In our organization, it has taken attention to both the "soft" and the "hard" dimensions of leadership. We've listened to physicians' feelings and made changes that give them back some meaningful influence over what they're held accountable for, and we have asked them to join us in leading the changes that are necessary.

pressure the organization is under. If the doctor continues to agitate for one nurse per doctor staffing in the face of this reality, the reaction could be considered extreme. Most physician leaders have faced physicians whose reactions on the surface seem overblown. When this is the case, chances are that the change has unleashed emotional reactions related to much more than that one change. The most effective strategy is to listen without defensiveness and without criticizing the other person's perceptions.

Not all resistance is an affective response to change that leaders need to manage. If leaders automatically interpret resistance as evidence physicians do not like the change, how they try to address the resistance might be well-intentioned but off the point. In some cases, a proposed change is poorly thought out or unlikely to yield real improvement, and physicians' concerns about it merit thoughtful attention. When an organization has a poor track record implementing change, physicians' skepticism of leaders' ability to make a change that pays off in a positive way for them can be understandable. Physicians who have been asked to implement change with inadequate planning and sponsorship are likely to have legitimate reservations about how things will be different this time around. Their reaction to a change could have less to do with the specifics of it than with their lack of faith that leaders and managers will provide adequate support to make it happen. If the change is a bad idea or if the underlying concerns are about leaders' abilities, deal with these real issues; do not rely on listening alone as a strategy to help physicians work through their reactions and get on with change.

Strategies to Address Resistance

Because resistance is a typical response to change, leaders need strategies and skills to deal with it effectively. Basic physics teaches that for every action there is an equal and opposite reaction. Despite knowing this, many leaders still "push" a change in the face of opposition or concerns. They may plow ahead when others express apathy or hostility. For example, change sponsors might decide to have yet another round of meetings with reluctant physicians to make sure they fully understand why a particular change is called for. Pushing harder predictably generates more pushback. The alternative is to break out of the

dynamic that fuels resistance and use an approach that focuses on understanding and reducing resistance.

Strategies leaders can employ to minimize resistance include:

- Cross the bridge first by coming to terms with their own reluctance or concerns.

- Help physicians let go of expectations of their practice life that cannot be met.

- Communicate about change:
  - Get out the news.
  - Leverage the power of storytelling to engage others in the change.
  - Ensure that communication flows to the front line.
  - Listen to and honor resistance.

Leaders Cross the Bridge First

Leaders need to come to grips with their own emotional reactions before they can help others work through their resistance to a change. At times, leaders are asked to lead a change with which they do not agree or for which they lack enthusiasm. They may react in this way because of genuine concern about whether the change really will be an improvement. Reticence may also reflect a leader's own resistance to what might otherwise be a very good idea. The leader's discomfort could relate to personally having to get used to a new process or to sponsoring a change he or she knows will upset colleagues. Leaders have the responsibility to work through their resistance by using personal reflection and talking to other leaders. When leaders do not work through their own uneasiness about a change, the ambivalence they carry gets communicated to others. Because leadership commitment is such a critical ingredient in change, anything less than total commitment can signal to others that the change is not all that important. Leaders who have not done so themselves are less able to help other physicians cross the bridge and engage with change.

Help Physicians to Let Go of Expectations

A prerequisite to getting on with change is letting go of attachment to the current situation. There are times when embracing a change means that physicians have to give up a finely tuned or predictable process or behavior that they have mastered and at which they excel. The reluctance to give up what currently works is compounded when the new way is less convenient and more demanding, involves new skills, or conflicts with physicians' self-perceptions.

Openly Acknowledge the Loss Associated with a Change

William Bridges[4] uses the term "transition" to identify the psychological process that individuals go through to come to terms with a new situation. He distinguishes this internal emotional processing of a change from the actual situation itself, such as a new vacation schedule, a different basis for determining compensation, having to go to multiple sites to see patients, not just one.

As part of processing change, Bridges asserts, individuals need to let go of the "old way." Something has to end—closure has to be brought to the way something had been done—before individuals will be open to trying the change. In some changes, for some people, letting go happens instantly and without angst or even consciousness. One physician can look at access data and quickly conclude he or she needs to put in more hours. The data are so compelling that the physician considers the change being proposed a "no-brainer" and turns attention to adjusting his or her schedule and finding activities to drop or ways to streamline his or her schedule to find the extra hours. The physician may never experience any difficulty either adjusting his or her personal expectations or actually making the changes in his or her daily routine and family life in order to put in more time at work. Another physician may have a harder time and a prolonged transition process. This physician may resent having to extend patient care time because of the disruption in his or her routine and the value he or she puts on time with family. This physician prefers the old way, and, to the extent he or she clings to a deep belief that "this is the way it should be," is not open to what could be positive about the change in clinic hours. Physicians unable to bring closure to or let go of current reality tend to focus energy on denying change is needed or fending it off for as long as possible.

Bridges offers leaders guidance in helping physicians get beyond resistance to change. In his model, the work that needs to be done is psychological. However, this is an uncomfortable realm for many physician leaders—indeed, one that many give short shrift. As a result, conversations that could help physicians process their anger and loss rarely happen or are unproductive. In general, disappointments physicians have but never fully articulate and work through block their willingness to get on with a change. Not identifying what will have to end when a change is implemented, or glossing over, soft selling, or minimizing what is no longer workable, stymies successful implementation.

It is up to leaders to help physicians work through the letting go and grieving that is required. Although it may seem that physicians are capable of endless grousing and complaining, when supported to express their concerns and disappointments constructively and to identify what is within their control, most move on and engage with change efforts. Leaders can be helpful, but they first need to accept the premise that successful change involves a psychological process. They also need to be comfortable dealing with and talking about emotions, particularly loss and anger, and have the skill to move conversations from venting to constructive discussion. A medical director at an HMO shares his work on helping physicians let go of the past and move on with change in the sidebar on page 118-119.

In addition to listening, specific actions leaders can take to help physicians to develop a readiness to engage in a proposed improvement include:

- Clarify what the change is and why it is being made.

- Do not underplay what will be different and what will stay the same. When his hospital was folded into a larger system, one chief executive officer stressed to the staff doctors and employees that the only thing that was changing was who signed their paychecks. His intention to minimize the trauma of the hospital losing independent status was honorable. But downplaying the implications of the change robbed doctors and employees of the opportunity to grieve what they valued and were losing. As a consequence, three years after they were formally integrated, this hospital still had difficulties collaborating with other parts of the system.

- Change is often experienced as criticism of the old way. Give appropriate acknowledgment to the

Acknowledging Transitions
GREGG BROFFMAN, MD

Gregg Broffman is Medical Director of Univera Healthcare, a mixed-model HMO in Buffalo and Syracuse, New York. Univera has changed from a staff to a mixed model, transforming employed physicians into an independent, at-risk medical group.

As we were forming our independent medical group, the organizational structure, by-laws, and compensation system were changed so that they would support the medical group as a whole, not individual physicians. One example was including a rigorous non-compete clause in physician contracts. Physicians' responses were typical of grief: denial, bargaining, anger, depression, and finally acceptance. Moving to acceptance happened over a number of monthly meetings. It was during this process that the leadership of our organization learned it was about grief and not morale!

The hardest transitions for physicians to deal with are all proxies for a loss of a sense of autonomy. These include having to work harder for the same money (or for less in some cases), having someone in the group define standards for productivity or quality, being told a portion of compensation depends on achieving these goals, and having to follow clinical algorithms. All these changes are about letting go of autonomy. Our physicians had to come to terms with the reality that being allowed to practice with complete independence as a member of a large organization was coming to an end.

In order to help physicians let go, we held didactic sessions on transition management that gave them at least an intellectual understanding of the connection between change, transition, and how they were feeling. We also had workshops that allowed doctors to participate in transition management. These sessions included an intellectual overview of the transition process and had physicians participate in a series of exercises, such as listing what is really changing, what real losses are occurring as a result of the change, and what continuities remain in their professional and personal lives.

This kind of exercise allows us to see that not all is changing and not all is lost! Another simple exercise asks physicians to categorize their losses, or at least what they perceive they have lost. Some losses can be replaced, reinvented, or perhaps reframed. This also allowed our physicians to identify something they truly

past by reinforcing that it is what makes the future possible.

- Stress how the change is in step with individuals' interests and what the organization needs to do to ensure future success

Tool 7-1, page 126, is an opportunity to consider how leaders can help those implementing a change to let go of what might block their openness to the change.

Communicate about Change

Communication can make or break a change effort. When executed effectively, it helps physicians feel respected, included, and supported to move through their feelings. Sharing information is vital but is not sufficient to engage most physicians to make change. A number of mechanisms can be used to communicate, including memos, electronic bulletin boards, large-group and small-group meetings, and one-on-one conversations.

The approach used should be based on the objectives to be accomplished. Sharing information when there is no need for give-and-take can be done through a memo, e-mail, or in a large-group meeting. When one goal of the communication effort is to field questions or get all concerns on the table, smaller meetings and one-on-one conversations work better. Although one-on-one meetings are time-consuming, they represent the most powerful way to understand where physicians are coming from when they have a good deal of concern about a change. Many physicians appreciate leaders' taking time to have personal conversations with them. It communicates concern, respect, and a desire to be helpful. When the objective is to help physicians process emotions or come to terms with transitions, opportunities for two-way dialogue have to be included. Two-way communication allows physicians to feel heard and leaders to learn what they can do to effectively address resistance.

Four tactics are key to communicating about change:

- Get out the news to those who will be affected by a change.
- Leverage the power of storytelling to engage others in the change.
- Ensure that communication is flowing to the front line.
- Listen to and honor resistance.

Get out the News

When information about a change is inadequate, rumors and distortions undermine implementation. Leaders who are juggling many priorities often fail to appreciate how much communicating they need to do. One axiom is to communicate 10 times more than you think is necessary. Attempting to quantify how much communication is enough may seem frivolous; in reality, however, significant change is often undercommunicated, and the result is an increase in concerns, doubts, and resistance. One rule of thumb is to consider communication inadequate until those who are involved, and ultimately need to make the change, can accurately describe:

- What the change is supposed to accomplish.

- Why the change is being implemented.

- What the plan is for moving forward.

- What their role is in the change process.

Because there are advantages to clear and consistent communication, leaders can best leverage their investment of time by having a thoughtful plan. Planning for getting the news out will help ensure that all stakeholders are identified and will lead to a logical sequence for communication. A communication plan should address these issues:

- Who needs to know what about this change? It will be important to consider others besides physicians. Who else will need to know so that the change can be implemented smoothly?

- Do some individuals need to learn sooner than others? Consider what sequence makes sense. As a generalization, it is important to get the word out to physicians early in the process. Learning about a change that will affect their practices from their support staff or through rumors rather than from their leadership tends to increase physicians' resistance and undermine trust in leadership. Local or site leaders who will be expected to be sponsors for a change clearly should be informed before others are.

- How much detail about the change do various individuals and groups need to get?

- What are the most effective mechanisms to get the information out to each intended audience? What

had to let go of, and ceremoniously "send it off" in a Federal Express box.

In a recent exercise, it became apparent to the participating doctors that their ability to care for people, which is the most important factor at the conscious level that led individuals into medicine, has not been lost. The manner by which we cared for people in the past is no longer an option. After bidding that pathway good-bye, there was energy in the group to consider new and creative ways to accomplish this mission.

In another discussion I facilitated, the physicians shared their original reasons for going into medicine. In reconnecting with their original goals, they discovered that the changes they were struggling with did not necessarily lead to abandoning their goals, only the pathways to achieve them. This was a powerful tool to help them let go.

As we engage in this challenging work, we must remember that leaders are in transition too! We must understand our specific losses, grief responses, and behaviors. Perhaps the greatest loss is the loss of our peer group when we become a "suit" or administrator. Physicians see leaders—even physician leaders—as different: Although they pay lip service to the importance of managerial work, in their hearts they believe that providing clinical care is the only "real" work for physicians.

is the objective of the communication—is it to inform and educate or to engage?

- Who will take responsibility for communicating to the various audiences?

Tool 7-2, pages 127, is an opportunity for leaders to put together a plan to communicate about a change.

The Power of Stories

A picture may be worth a thousand words, but a story told well has a uniquely powerful sway over listeners—even no-nonsense physicians. Great leaders studied by Harvard psychologist Howard Gardner,[5] including Eleanor Roosevelt, Martin Luther King, Jr., and Alfred Sloan, Jr., all drew on stories instinctively to relate to their followers. Increasingly, corporate leaders are using the power of stories to communicate about change and transformation in their businesses.[6] Noel Tichy, in *The Leadership Engine*, writes: "Winning leaders personalize their visions and ideas by telling stories that touch people's emotions as well as their intellects."[7]

The Power of Storytelling

JOHN G. O'BRIEN

John G. O'Brien serves as Chief Executive Officer of the Cambridge Health Alliance. A safety net health system that comprises two hospitals, a skilled nursing facility, the City of Cambridge Public Health Department, a Medicaid managed care plan, and more than 20 primary care sites, the Alliance is a Harvard Medical School affiliate. Mr. O'Brien also serves as Commissioner of Public Health for the City of Cambridge.

Before I see resistance, I see fear. When I talk to a physician leader about making a significant change, fear is the first reaction I often see in his or her eyes; fear of the unknown or of how the change might upset the status quo with peers. More often than not, the question flashing through the physician's mind is, "Will this put me in a tough spot? Will my brothers and sisters in the department see me as aligning with the CEO at their expense?"

In the past, I'd move the conversation forward with something along these lines: "So, that's where we're headed; get with the program." I'd try to kick the other person out of the present. And he or she would very understandably get more anxious. Now I turn to a story—one that pulls the other person into the future. I know the story I'm telling is the one that's likely to get repeated back in the physician's department. The story could be about how our present condition is letting patients down. Or it could paint a future for our institution that's in line with the doctor's personal values.

Because many of the physician managers I deal with are in my age cohort and beginning to think about the 10 to 15 years left in their careers, I often set the stories in a 10-year time frame. The story is frequently about the day I retire. Part of that story is what I'll tell my children. I want to be able to say this institution did everything we could to serve this community, not ourselves, and we never compromised on key values. After telling it, I often ask the physician leader to tell me his or her story, what the physician would like to leave behind and what's possible for him or her to accomplish. This engages most people and helps them move out of the present. Then they have their own stories to tell as a way to talk about change in the institution.

Recently, to celebrate the success of our Birthing Center, I met with OB nurses and shared a very specific incident

Stories are effective because they fill a basic human need. We grow up listening to fables, parables, and myths, and the need to hear and rehear stories stays with us all our lives. Of all recent American presidents, Ronald Reagan knew best how to use the power of stories. He peppered his speeches and press conferences with folksy parables, and his new-day-in-America re-election campaign resonated deeply with people from all walks of life. It was a story that people wanted to believe; it made people feel good about their country and about Reagan as a candidate.

In physician organizations, stories can serve multiple purposes:

- Explain marketplace competitive pressures.
- Describe what a true customer orientation looks and sounds like.
- Reinforce the identity and mission of the organization.
- Ennoble what people do.
- Explain how the pieces of a system fit together and the power of synergy.
- Help learn from failures and successes.

Stories can be an effective way to make the case for change. Noel Tichy describes stories as a way to familiarize people with terrain that is new to them. Leaders make the unknown familiar and desirable "by taking them there first in their imaginations. Winning leaders create and use future stories to help people break away from the familiar present and venture boldly ahead to create a better future."[7] Stories can bring life to data and reports and make them more powerful and convincing. An effective way for leaders to get others' attention is to share what led them to the conviction that significant change or transformation, although painful, is in everyone's and the organization's best interest. Stories shared from the heart connect with others' emotions and intellect. One system CEO's experience with using stories to motivate change is described in the sidebar, left and page 121.

Story Sources

Telling a story to illustrate a change objective or the specifics of a change can have tremendous impact. Stories personalize the change message and are often the best-remembered part of a talk or presentation.

Some individuals are natural storytellers; others may have less familiarity with this communication technique, but they can practice and learn it.[8] Given the potency of stories to drive a point home, it is worth leaders' time to experiment with and develop comfort with storytelling. Tool 7-3, page 128, describes a way in which leaders can start to experiment and incorporate stories into their communication about change. Here are two tips for the leader who is a neophyte storyteller:

- *Look for opportunities to experiment.* The start of a speech or the opening to a presentation is a natural opportunity to share observations or personal stories.

- *Listen and look for stories to share.* Dig deep into your own personal experiences for inspiration. Figure 7-1, below, lists some other story sources.

Ensure Communication Flows to the Front Line

In many organizations a sizable gap exists between what is communicated to middle managers and what they in turn communicate to the front line. This can happen in physician organizations, too. Managers, including chiefs and site leaders, are sometimes referred to as "the frozen middle." The chief executive officer, chief medical officer, top administrator, and board members all might assume that what they have communicated to managers is passed on, with little if any distortion, to the front line. Unfortunately, that is often not the case for several reasons. Some managers

FIGURE 7-1. Inspirations for Stories about Change

- An observation you made, or conversation or experience you had in the organization (positive or negative).
- A story told to you or written correspondence from a physician or staff member or a patient, family member, or other customer.
- Your personal picture of the organization's future.
- An experience you had in another organization (e.g., on a vacation, visiting another business).
- A personal story of overcoming adversity or having to change.
- Literature.
- Mythology.

that had happened to me. At a community meeting, I met a woman who had given birth at our center recently. She told me it was the best medical experience she had ever had. When I conveyed the details of this woman's experience and her name, the nurses remembered her. Hearing how the patient had perceived them meant a good deal to those nurses. Communicating stories is such a powerful way to connect with people that we shouldn't shy away from doing it. Not every story has to glorify the organization. We shouldn't be afraid to talk about what's not going well. The celebratory stories are enjoyed more when we're also willing to openly share examples of disappointment and missed opportunities.

Sometimes a lesson can be woven into a story. I addressed the medical staff recently and began with, "I want to tell you a story about a patient who wanted to see me, and when any patient asks to see me I always make the time," and then I shared the relevant details of that conversation. Making the time for the patient wasn't the main point of the story, but it was an opportunity for me to communicate about values in a non-preachy way.

If the storyteller's not credible, the story is just a fantasy. Walking the talk is the storyteller's foundation—a leader who does this on a regular basis garners a lot of observations and experiences that are source material for his or her stories. And, the stories you share are more powerful because they are your truth. When a story moves me, it moves others. I don't hold back my own feelings and I'm sure this makes some of my communication more powerful. As long as a story is told from the heart, it makes an impact.

Not long ago, I was in Oklahoma City with other executives listening to a hospital CEO describe his institution's response to the bombing of the federal building. He told about his doctors and staff and how they cared for and treated the victims, some of them knowing they had family who worked near the bomb site. This man was a business person—not particularly emotional, but the power of his story moved everybody in that room and will probably stay with me for the rest of my life.

use information as power, believing that the more information they control, the greater their influence is over resource allocation or daily operations. Sometimes, the expectation to communicate is not clear. Physician managers may fail to communicate when they are not clear what is inappropriate or premature to communicate widely. Lack of time, real or perceived, is another reason physician managers do not get word out about impending change. Communication requires an investment of time and, given physicians' full schedules, the logistics of scheduling a meeting that they will attend can be overwhelming. If a change puts physician leaders in the hot seat with colleagues, they might be particularly reticent to communicate much about it. Not having confidence in their ability to handle the resistance or disappointment of colleagues is another reason leaders might avoid communicating about a change.

Senior leaders can take several steps to help ensure that communication gets to the front line:

- *Clarify expectations around communication.* For example, unless told otherwise, managers and front-line supervisors should assume they are expected to communicate to the front line.

- *Clarify when it is not appropriate for leaders to share information.* Generally speaking, information that should not be shared includes that which is proprietary in nature, jeopardizes competitiveness, or is sensitive, such as information about a personnel issue. Other information that might not be appropriate to share is that which concerns legal or regulatory matters. To help leaders be effective communicators, develop and disseminate clear guidelines for what is appropriate and inappropriate to pass on routinely to others.

- *Support physicians managers in communicating by providing talking points and visuals, such as handouts and overheads, if having these aids would facilitate consistent information getting out to all physicians.*

- *Help physician leaders develop skills for sharing information and dealing with pushback in large and small groups and in one-on-one interactions.*

- *Review and provide feedback to physician managers regarding their communication plans.* The effort you put in demonstrates the priority of communication, and it creates an opportunity to improve the plan and to coach managers.

- *Be visible and be in touch with physicians directly.* This gives you the chance to learn first-hand what physicians know and believe about change initiatives and thus to gauge how effectively your messages are getting through. It also provides opportunities to directly communicate essential messages or to reinforce what managers have already shared.

Listen to and Honor Resistance

One of the most effective ways to address resistance is to probe for it and listen to it. Although it may seem counterintuitive, encouraging physicians to express all their doubts or negative feelings about a change is one of the most helpful actions a change sponsor or agent can take. Physician leaders often back off when their efforts meet with resistance. Their instincts tell them that, if physicians are that upset, pressing for a particular change is probably not the right thing to do. Leaders need to accept and plan for such reactions and develop the skills to help others move beyond their doubts and negativity. To be effective, leaders need to see such reactions as normal and not develop negative perceptions of those whose point of view about a change is different from theirs.

Some reactions to expressions of resistance help diffuse it, while others reinforce it. When physicians challenge the need to change, one response is a reasoned explanation of the new way, its advantages, or the consequences of not changing. A person who is stressed or seething with emotions is not interested in more data. In well-meaning attempts to respond to feelings, the behavior leaders often engage in is the equivalent of pouring water into an already full glass. As a result, the physician does not get a chance to ventilate and digs in further, while the leader grows impatient that his or her explanations haven't helped the other person to get on board. In the early stage of the emotional transition process, reason and logic are not effective antidotes to resistance. Rational dialogue can only take place after all sentiments have been fully expressed, heard, and respected.

Developing tact and knowing when to listen and encourage talking it out and when to step in with

FIGURE 7-2 Examples of Active Listening Responses

PHYSICIAN COMMENTS	ACTIVE LISTENING RESPONSE
• "This is craziness. Every time we turn around we're being asked to change."	• "You're frustrated by all the changes we've been through."
• "I have serious reservations about how the new error reduction program is going to be introduced. From what I heard, it sounds totally unrealistic and is going to be a huge burden for every one of us."	• "You don't think the implementation protocol is well thought out."
• "What you're saying may have worked in other practices but that does not mean it will work here. I could tick off a number of reason why it won't."	• "You don't see us being able to do this."

logic, reason, and data to make a case is an essential skill for addressing resistance. Listening communicates the validity of the other person's perspective, allows for ventilation of emotions, and facilitates transitions. To listen to and encourage full expression of concern or negativity does not come naturally to most people. In their clinical practice, however, physicians know that a patient who is angry or afraid cannot also absorb information. This lesson can be very usefully transferred to dealing effectively with resistance.

Active listening is a powerful tool for helping others to express their concerns and feelings. Based on the work of psychotherapist Carl Rogers and popularized in the 1970s by Thomas Gordon in his workshops and books for parents[9] and leaders,[10] active listening calls for listening with empathy and creating space for the other person to air his or her concerns. The person listening makes only a brief statement to reflect what he or she hears, without interjecting opinion or other comments. If the speaker has more to say, he or she will say it. Being able to "just" listen is the equivalent of tipping the full glass of water to create space and receptivity to another point of view.

The power of active listening to lessen resistance does not depend on choice of words but on being able to empathize. To use active listening effectively requires the ability to hear the emotional content, as well as the literal meaning, of another person's words. When those who express their concerns understand that you appreciate their perspective, they in turn become more open to yours. The core skill is being able to put yourself in the other person's shoes and have empathy for that position. Carl Rogers wrote, "Before presenting your own point of view, it would be necessary for you to achieve the other speaker's frame of reference, to understand his thoughts and feelings so well that you could summarize them for him. Sounds simple. Try it, and you will discover that it is one of the most difficult things you have ever tried to do."[11] (See figure 7-2, above, for illustrations of active listening responses.) Active listening is a core skill for helping others communicate all their concerns, fears, and disappointments. It is not a manipulative technique or psychological jujitsu. It is a way to learn what is fueling resistance so that you can take it into account in planning and in further communication. Listening without judgment and without pressuring or convincing the speaker of anything is a powerful way to support another person to move through the transition process.

For most leaders, this is not an instinctive skill, so practice and coaching can be very helpful. One of the challenges for leaders is expressing acknowledgment that the other person's concerns were heard without giving the impression that the leader agrees with the point of view expressed. Potentially helpful resources for developing competence in this skill include trained facilitators and mental health professions.

Figure 7-3, page 124, lists a four-step approach to honoring resistance in which active listening plays a key role. These steps are meant as a guide to a conversation that opens up receptivity to a change. It is also an opportunity for leaders to learn what the resistance is all about. This information might lead to a change in course or redoubled efforts on leaders' parts to correct misperceptions. This conversation might be the first of a couple that a leader has with an

FIGURE 7-3. Four Steps to Honoring Resistance

1. Bring the resistance to the surface. Although never easy, it is better to hear all the resistance than to try to work through the situation without understanding the other person's real feelings or concerns.

- Make it safe to express resistance.

  - "I'm here to listen."
  - "I'd like to hear your thoughts about this."

- Use active listening—that is, feed back the main message communicated—in order to encourage full expression of what is on the other person's mind.

  - "You're saying this seems unworkable."
  - "You're resentful of how things are turning out."

- Ask directly for all of the reasons why this is a concern for the other person.

  - "Tell me what concerns you about this idea."

2. Honor the resistance. At this stage, do not reinforce your point of view or in any way imply the other person should not feel the way he or she does. Just listen.

- Acknowledge the resistance. This does not mean that you agree with the other's point of view.

  - "I see how that could be a problem for you."
  - "You're right that this is going to mean some inconvenience in the short term."

- Periodically reinforce that you want to hear all concerns.

  - "Is there anything else that you see as a problem?"

3. Go deeper, and explore the resistance and possible options.

- As best you can, try to understand as much as possible about why the other person sees the situation the way he or she does.

  - "I want to understand your assumptions about this change and how it will affect you."

- Help the other person take on a proactive stance or suggest alternative approaches.

  - "What would you prefer?"
  - "How can this be made to work from your point of view?"

4. Check out your understanding of what you have heard.

- Summarize what you heard.

  - "Let me summarize the ground we've covered."
  - "Here's what I heard you say."

- Ask how the other person feels about the conversation and his or her current feelings about the change proposed.

individual to hear and address concerns. In this interaction, the focus is on supporting the other person to fully express his or her reactions to a change and to begin to think proactively about how his or her issues might be addressed. This approach does not lead to convincing anyone. It allows for discovery of barriers and concerns that can be addressed in subsequent conversations oriented toward problem solving.

The approach outlined in figure 7-3 leads to a conversation that can diffuse negativity toward a change. However, it feels unnatural to many individuals. The impulse toward immediate problem-solving needs to be put aside in favor of the diagnostic process to learn as much as possible about the other person's perspective. For all leaders, developing familiarity and comfort with this approach is a worthwhile investment.

When Leaders Create Resistance

Addressing resistance is not necessarily easy work. It is time-consuming, takes skills physician leaders might have to learn, and calls for leaders to be vulnerable and really listen to what physicians are saying. Few people are naturally "wired" for the kind of dialogue that helps others make the psychological transition. Most people need to work on these skills. The temptation, when confronted by a physician who wants to know why yet another change is considered essential, is to educate or inform—not to listen and learn. Developing the capacity to address resistance is key. Rushing toward implementation in the face of resistance ends up costing more time and energy in the long run.

The hardest kind of resistance for leaders to own up to is that which they themselves cause. When a change gets bogged down or when resistance is spiking, leaders would do well to consider how much they might be contributing by not listening, by not taking concerns to heart, or by pushing ahead or being driven by a timetable when signs of resistance were abundant. Leaders need to stop engaging in behavior that slows or sabotages change efforts.

Tools for Taking Action

TOOL 7-1. Consider the "Letting Go" Process

PURPOSE: To identify what a leader or change team can do to help those implementing a change let go of what might block receptivity to the change.

INSTRUCTIONS:

- Identify a change you have some responsibility to implement.

- Give thoughtful consideration to the questions below. It might help to put yourself in the shoes of those who will be making the change and look at it from their perspective.

How does this particular change fit in with or go against the self-perception or professional identity of those who need to implement it?

What parts of professional identity or expectations might those implementing the change need to let go of in order to be receptive to this change? What would be ending for them?

Given your role in supporting this change, what actions can you take or what conversations can you have that would facilitate others to let go of what blocks their receptivity to the change?

TOOL 7-2. Develop a Communication Plan

PURPOSE: To help a leader or members of a change team to develop a plan to communicate about a change.

INSTRUCTIONS:

• Identify a change you have some responsibility to implement.

• Identify one specific audience that needs to understand what the change is and their role in it. In the space provided, write down the audience you will answer the questions for.

Take each communication issue listed below and answer the related question for the audience you identified.

AUDIENCE:

Message: What needs to be communicated?

Timing: When should they be informed?

Channels: What are the best mechanisms? Consider how much two-way and one-on-one communication is needed.

Communicator: Who should inform them or engage them in a conversation?

TOOL 7-3. Create New Stories

PURPOSE: To experiment with storytelling as an additional way in which you can communicate and engage those who need to change.

INSTRUCTIONS:

- Identify one or two colleagues who you think would be willing to experiment with stories as a way to communicate. These individuals can help you craft a good story, react to your drafts, or give you feedback on your presentation style.

- Create an outline of a story that illustrates an important point regarding a change you will be implementing. You can use a hero and/or a villain to make your points or make reference to another fable or allegory. You can draw on a recent experience you had or an observation you made.

- Be creative and begin to craft a story that would move others. You might want to start with a dramatic event and go back and give background or history. Other elements you might include, but not necessarily in this order, are:

  - The heritage and accomplishments of your organization or your part of the system.
  - Where the organization is at the present time. Factors contributing to the current state, such as competition in the marketplace and declining reimbursement. Why the old way of doing things will no longer support success.
  - What the new way is and why it would make a difference.
  - The role of the individual in the success of the change.
  - What it looks like when your change is fully implemented.
  - Parallels that exist between the challenges your organization faces and another organization and how it responded to the situation.

- Make the story compelling. Build in some tension or drama. Put human emotion into it.

- Begin to experiment, and share the story to get reactions.

CHAPTER 8

Build Consistency

Assessing the Current State

To what extent would physicians you work with or lead agree that they get the resources, tools, staffing, equipment, education, and training they need to implement the changes they are expected to adopt?

Very little ◄——————————————————► Greatly

| 1 | 2 | 3 | 4 | 5 |

In your experience, what impact does the relative absence or presence of these kinds of supports have on change implementation?

Overall, how effectively has the physician organization aligned incentives with changes or behaviors that are important to organizational performance and success?

Not at all effectively ◄——————————————► Extremely effectively

| 1 | 2 | 3 | 4 | 5 |

What kinds of performance data does your organization routinely share with physicians?

How do the physicians typically respond to data and what accounts for these reactions?

The Power of Consistency

Leaders are responsible for creating a matrix of supports that are consistent with one another and that help those implementing a change to incorporate it into their routines. There are four principal mechanisms leaders can use to create a consistent environment that supports a change:

• Provide the capacity so that those making the change are enabled to do so. Space, equipment, staffing, work design, and time all affect capacity.

• Align financial and nonfinancial incentives and human resource policies with the change.

• Design and deliver feedback so individuals and teams involved in a change know how well they are performing.

• Seek feedback from the front line so that consistency can be strengthened and deepened.

When leaders align all these supports, everyone involved recognizes leaders' commitment to the success of the change and feels enabled and accountable to make it happen. When leaders do not take responsibility to address the supports needed for change, physicians and staff are apt to let themselves "off the hook" as well by concluding that the change is optional or by putting forth only minimal effort. In our experience, although building a consistent environment to support change is extremely important, the environments around significant change are typically inconsistent. And the impact on the pace of change and the sustainability of change is substantial. When promised resources do not materialize or support is inconsistent, the impact is not neutral; it actually creates drag on the change effort, slows momentum, and leads physicians to conclude that leadership is engaging in double-speak. They hear, "Change. But you're not getting any resources to help you change" or "You will not be paid or acknowledged any differently" or "You'll have to make it work within current policies, even if they are a barrier to implementation." In today's complex and rapidly changing organizations, achieving total consistency and support might not be possible, but the more consistent and supportive the environment is, the better, faster, and longer-lasting the improvements are likely to be.

Provide Capacity

Even a change that makes delivering care to patients easier and that physicians are highly motivated to implement will not be successful if those involved do not have the capacity to carry through and make it happen. Capacity includes tangible resources, such as capital, facilities, equipment, and staff. For us the term also refers to those critical but intangible factors in the work environment that profoundly affect change implementation, including knowledge and skills, the way work and jobs are designed, and the ideas and plans of leaders and others for changing the way in which care is delivered.

Capacity sets a change up for success and is a key part of developing a consistent context for change. Implementing a disease management program, a typical change under way in many physicians organizations today, can be used to illustrate the kinds of capacity issues that leaders need to recognize.

In the following hypothetical example, the Highland Medical Clinic leadership commits to implement a hypertension disease management program. Early in the process, they charged a task group with identifying capacity issues involved in setting up a successful program. A partial list generated by the task group included:

- A process to develop guidelines for managing hypertension.

- Education about the guidelines for physicians and support staff.

- A software program that would give physicians critical real-time information about the hypertensive patients in their panels and support for managing them—provide pertinent health status information; identify those out of control or overdue for follow up; and print lists or labels with names, addresses, and phone numbers to facilitate patient contact.

- Adequate support staff to contact and appoint patients as appropriate. Training for this staff.

- A method to redesign the frequency and the format of doctor-patient interactions—for example, group appointments for chronic medical patients—to create needed appointment availability.

- Conference room space, an appointment system, and staff training to support group appointments.

- A plan to integrate health educators and nutritionists into physicians' clinical practices.

Given the number and level of details that need to be taken into consideration, it is not surprising that many change efforts fail because of inadequate capacity. Even an intense effort to identify and provide the capacity to support a change does not always turn up all, or even the most important, factors related to effective implementation. We were impressed to learn from a colleague of the effort her organization put into designing a diabetes management program. The organization had devoted significant resources to build capacity for this change. A sophisticated software program linked to the electronic medical record allowed physicians to access critical information for disease management from their computers. They could learn which diabetic patients in their panel were not in control and generate contact lists for follow up. They could also see how their own performance in managing diabetes compared to the performance of peers in their department, to all other doctors in the group, and to national norms. It was an innovation with the potential to have a significant impact on patients' health with just a couple of mouse clicks. However, many physicians failed to use the system with any regularity because of an overlooked capacity issue. Even though the information was available on desk-top terminals in the clinic, physicians had to exit the electronic medical record program they routinely used in patient care in order to access it. Given the pressures of daily work and the time required to move from one program to the other, only the most motivated physicians ended up looking at the data outside of regular office hours. In this case, failing to address fully physicians' typical work routine had a negative impact on implementation of the change.

It is not uncommon for leaders and those implementing a change to disagree about how much time, money, training, planning, or adjustment for fit is enough. Although fiscal limitations might ultimately determine how much is enough, leaders have the responsibility to consider carefully the requisite capacity for all the changes they expect others to carry out. To be sure a change has needed support, a leader does not always have to provide more resources. If a particular resource is limited, it might be available elsewhere in the system and could be transferred. In other cases, resources might be adequate, for example, the number of staff, but they may need to be deployed differently. Often, human resource staff can provide helpful guidance to leaders or an improvement team on how work and jobs can be redesigned for more efficient use of available resources. If no creative way can be found to deal with a resource shortage, the options to consider include scaling back the change objective or extending the time frame for change implementation. It is also useful to reexamine the planned sequence for other change initiatives and advance those expected to generate more capacity. Group appointments or use of e-mail for patient consultation are two examples of capacity-generating changes.

Physicians will see any gap between the capacity at their disposal and what they perceive they need as evidence that leaders are not serious about a change. When leaders respond to real and perceived disparities in capacity with, "Sorry, but it's not in the budget," they undermine others' commitment to the change and confidence in them. When physicians do not believe they can navigate the change with the capacity they have, leaders need to pay attention and listen. There may be a real lack of capacity that needs to be dealt with in creative ways. On the other hand, physicians may be casting themselves as victims, in which case they need to be engaged and supported out of the victim box, not dismissed. Either way, leaders are the ones responsible for recognizing the importance of the capacity issue and understanding it in order to determine which condition is true.

Align Incentives and Policies

Incentives and policies are significant contributors to consistency around a change because of their power to shape behavior. Incentives, including both money and nonfinancial rewards, are high-level governors of behavior that are often overlooked in introducing change.

Physicians, Money, and Change

Financial incentives cannot replace leaders' visibility and individuals' commitment to the organization's vision and values in sustaining change. However, it is appropriate for leaders to ask what role financial incentives should play in conjunction with other strategies to support individuals to incorporate a change into daily work.

There is a considerable literature that argues against tying pay to performance.[1-3] W. Edwards Deming, the figure most often associated with the management philosophy and methods of organizational quality improvement, took a strong stand against merit pay. Deming called compensation systems that reward individual performance "the most powerful inhibitor to quality and productivity in the Western world."[4] In *Punished by Rewards*, Alfie Kohn makes an eloquent and solidly researched case against pay for performance: "Whenever people are led to think about what they will get for engaging in a task, they will do only what is absolutely necessary to get it."[5] Much research suggests that extrinsic rewards undermine and weaken intrinsic interest in and motivation for a behavior.[6-8]

Yet, pay for performance is as American as apple pie, and belief in its power as a motivator is deeply embedded in most physician organizations. Medicine in the fee-for-service era connected income with patient volume and the number of procedures performed. This has led to an almost piecework mentality among some physicians. Remuneration based on productivity remains a paradigm in medicine, even in settings in which most patients are enrolled in managed care plans. There are hazards in using financial incentives in physician organizations, but, given their prevalence, it is likely they will continue to be an important mechanism for supporting physicians to adopt and sustain change.

The power of compensation to reinforce a change largely depends on an organization's traditions around the role of money. Broadly speaking, there are two very different approaches to compensating physicians. Some organizations compensate physicians largely or entirely on production or other measures of individual work effort. At the other end of the spectrum are some groups with a fee-for-service model as well as those that come out of a prepaid tradition in which physicians are largely salaried. In these organizations, financial incentives are often perceived as undermining collegiality and teamwork and being inconsistent with the organization's original values. Unless they choose to revise their philosophy about money as a reward, these organizations are better off looking at alternative ways to support change.

Where compensation is based on a pay-for-performance philosophy, physicians expect pay for any work that takes time away from seeing patients. Asked to join a quality improvement team working on reducing hospital length of stay, the physicians are likely to expect compensation to offset any reductions in productivity. Similarly, if an organization's emphasis on HEDIS scores requires the time and attention of physicians to help design a community outreach health promotion program, they will likely feel that the compensation formula should include a factor for HEDIS performance. In such environments, financial rewards would seem to be important in sending a message about the importance of a change.

However, whenever money is linked to change, leaders should consider the hazards:

- Rewarding every behavior important to organizational success leads to complex compensation systems that are ineffective to motivate change. Formulas intended to make compensation both fair and accurate end up being so complicated that they work against, not in favor of, their intended purpose. Physicians distrust a compensation formula they cannot easily understand and lose motivation to improve when it is not clear what they need to do to increase their income.

- Tying financial rewards directly to a change reinforces a piecework mentality and undermines commitment to broader organizational goals. When a piecework mentality is ingrained in an organization, every request for change is met with, "What will I be paid to do this?" Feeding into the expectation of pay-for-effort extinguishes willingness to contribute to the enterprise's success.

- Pay for performance means the compensation formula is constantly being re-worked. The formula has to change to keep pace with the changes physicians are expected to implement.

Organizations at both ends of the spectrum have important work to do to use money effectively to support change implementation. Many physician organizations in which money has not been considered an appropriate incentive are crippled in the marketplace by low productivity and cost structures that are out of line with those of competitors. Leaders could take steps to help ensure the organization's viability by linking financial rewards with a small number of behaviors that are fundamental to the organization's vision, such as some standard of productivity and patient satisfaction.

The leaders in pay-for-performance organizations also might want to reconsider their use of financial incentives in the context of their vision. When physicians share little in the way of vision beyond each maximizing his or her income, they will likely want to be paid for each additional responsibility. Decoupling willingness to adopt changes and compensation is possible only when physicians are committed to a collective vision for the organization. The work to move toward a truly shared vision might need to precede any effort to change the compensation philosophy and how financial rewards are used in conjunction with change implementation. In the sidebar at right and page 134, a physician leader offers guidance on how to design, and what to expect from, an incentive compensation plan.

Providing Incentives for Support Staff

Another consideration is whether some part of support staff compensation should be tied to performance if the physicians they work with are so compensated. This is particularly important when physicians and support staff are jointly responsible for an outcome, such as access or patient satisfaction. Team incentives can be more difficult in unionized environments, but, whenever possible, they deserve consideration, for several reasons. If staff attitudes, skills, and commitment are an essential part of patients' overall experience, and if physicians bear some downside risk when performance is not high, the system is not entirely fair to physicians. In a sense, physicians are being penalized for performance over which they do not have control. Likewise, the system is unfair to support staff if their efforts and commitment contribute to high patient satisfaction but only physicians receive direct rewards. Given the difficulty in separating the influences on patient satisfaction, and the likely effect of separate and individually based rewards on the willingness of physicians and support staff to work as partners, wise leaders will consider ways to provide incentives for the team.

Nonmonetary Rewards

Nonmonetary rewards are an important part of the matrix of supports for change. The most powerful and meaningful rewards tend not to be tangible; they are those that respond to physicians' need to be recognized, valued, and appreciated by peers and respected leaders. Celebrations of success or of what is working well are, in our experience, far too rare in physician organizations.

There are many sources of frustration in physicians' lives, including paperwork, approval processes, regulatory issues, and multiple demands on their time beyond patient care responsibilities. At day's end, many go home feeling under-appreciated. It has great meaning to physicians engaged in a change when their leaders seek them out to acknowledge their success to date, demonstrate interest in and understanding of challenges, discuss difficulties encountered, and offer sincere thanks.

Compensation in Perspective
WILLIAM CONWAY, MD

Bill Conway is Vice President, Henry Ford Medical Group, an 850-physician group practice that is part of the Henry Ford Health System. As director of medical staff compensation and personnel affairs, he led design and implementation of the Henry Ford Medical Group incentive compensation plan.

Experience has taught me that it's best to keep the formula for physician compensation as simple as possible. At Henry Ford, we try to avoid the illusion that compensation is the principal way to accelerate change. I don't believe you can solve everything by manipulating compensation. I would say that changing culture, providing data, and using performance reviews effectively are just as powerful and have fewer toxic side effects, than using money. Compensation surely plays a role in influencing physician behavior, but the key to optimizing the power of money is to not over-rely on it. It is a powerful tool that can cut both ways—it can help make change happen, and it can become a dysfunctional motivator if it's all that's used.

The basic approach I believe in is tying compensation to a few "mega" issues that directly affect the group's viability. The issue that is most appropriate to link compensation to is "work effort," or productivity. Data or performance reviews alone aren't as effective in promoting change in work effort. At the Henry Ford Medical Group, we found compensation to be a very helpful tool in moving from a seniority-based value system to one that is more productive and entrepreneurial. In changing to production as the base for compensation, we anticipated losing staff. About 10 percent of the 300 primary care doctors affected decided to leave—almost all would have seen their incomes negatively affected by the new formula. Second, we factor patient satisfaction scores into the formula, which reinforces behaviors that help the group to be competitive in the market. The third basic factor is citizenship. We've put about 5-10 percent of a physician's incentive in the hands of local leaders. This communicates that these are leaders with authority.

There are two keys to using compensation effectively to reinforce behaviors that make the business successful. One is linking it only to those measures that are 100 percent in physicians' control. A few years ago, the medical group did a study of drivers of productivity in primary care to see how much of their work effort physicians did control. We found that individual practice style, decisions such as whether to work over lunch, and the way physicians handled added patients were the key drivers. Productivity wasn't as strongly correlated with the number of support staff and examination rooms as I would have predicted.

Second, when pay is linked to performance on a number of parameters, all the measures you use need to be accurate, and the data have to be high-quality. If the data are suspect, physicians will challenge every point. And if the data used are flawed, how can you respond to their challenges?

Beyond the big issues important to the organization's success, it is very challenging to apply compensation to specific physicians' clinical decision making, such as pharmacy and hospital utilization. These, in my estimation, are best managed in other ways—by linking them to a shared vision, using performance feedback, and sharing comparative data.

It isn't possible to design a scheme that rewards every dimension of professional performance. Years ago, I believed, or at least hoped, that there was a magic bullet—a formula that perfectly aligned financial rewards and physician behavior. But there's not, or at least I haven't found it. The only real solution to motivating and rewarding excellence is multi-factorial—leadership, reward system, goal setting, regular competitive performance data, and the performance review process. You can't rely on a compensation formula to inspire physicians. I believe complicated formulas evolved because, in the past, medical leaders weren't comfortable having difficult conversations. While compensation has a role, it can't take the place of having the courage to set clear expectations for physicians and then engaging in real conversations about how well they are performing.

One very effective physician leader we know makes a point of sending e-mail and handwritten notes to physicians to acknowledge their accomplishments, such as publishing a paper, taking part in a pilot project for a change, or running a marathon. He visits every one of his organization's sites several times a year. These personal visits and the other expressions of acknowledgment are highly meaningful to other physicians.

Physicians also feel acknowledged when asked to share their experience, ideas, and wisdom. In our experience, most physicians want to have a say in any change affecting their practices; they take involvement as a sign of respect. All too often, physicians feel out of the loop—the victims of change, not the drivers. Without being conscious of how their actions contribute to low morale, many leaders move ahead without giving those affected by a change adequate opportunity to influence it. Reluctance to invite physicians to participate may stem from previously botched efforts to involve them. Participation can be designed to produce win-win outcomes. Including and respecting physicians' contributions meets deep-seated human needs and is therefore an important way to demonstrate appreciation. (Chapter 5 is devoted to the importance of involving physicians and to strategies for doing so effectively.)

When physicians feel respected and acknowledgement is expressed in various ways, tangible tokens of appreciation, including tickets to a movie or sporting event, gift certificates, and even a small personal gift, can have meaning and be used to support change. If the emotional environment is devoid of encouragement and appreciation, tangible rewards typically do not contribute in any significant way to creating an environment that supports change—in fact, they may reinforce existing cynicism. If tangible rewards are used, it is important for the token to have some meaning to the individual receiving it and for the person giving it to show sincere appreciation.

Align Human Resource Policies with Important Changes

When leaders seriously attempt to build a consistent environment to support a change, they are likely to discover policies that work against it. A vacation policy that does not address the minimum number of physicians available in a department can be a serious barrier to access improvements. In many organizations, winter flu season coincides with the most popular time for physician vacations, and access between January and March is unsatisfactory. One medical group's attempts to improve access failed to have any significant impact until leadership, in conjunction with the pediatricians, developed a new policy that called for the rotation of winter vacations.

In planning for significant changes that will call for new behaviors, it is useful to consider if any human resource policies might be barriers and how they might need to be changed. Consistency is key. If the policy is for physicians to be able to go home by seven o'clock in the evening, a plan to improve access by extending hours is destined to fail. Policies around part-time practice can conflict with strategies to build doctor-patient relationships. A policy for part-timers that does not require physicians to enter into a shared practice arrangement can compromise continuity of care for their patients. Part-time practice and related human resource policies become more of an issue in academic settings where physicians have part-time teaching and research responsibilities and, with some regularity, move in and out of their own clinical practices. It is worthwhile to sort through how policies related to those who teach and do research part-time can best support the organization's vision and change capability. As specific changes are planned, leaders need to address the potential for organizational policies to support or thwart their implementation.

Beyond reviewing policies for their fit with specific changes, it is very useful to consider them in light of how well they build the kind of workforce that can help the organization achieve its vision and strategies. Begin this assessment with a review of the physician compact to understand the appropriateness of the expectations it creates. Then, consider how the organization recruits, selects, develops, rewards, and acculturates physicians. Assess the impact of current policies on professional satisfaction. Are there written policies on enriching physicians' practice lives by providing opportunities to teach, conduct research, and develop new clinical skills?

Design And Deliver Feedback

Performance feedback is another powerful mechanism for building consistency in the environment to support change. If a change is extolled as critical, measures of its impact need to be designed and the information shared in an understandable and actionable way with those making the change. Without feedback, those involved may question whether they are on the right track, assume they are when they are not, or even wonder if their effort is all that important.

Problems with Data

Using data with physicians to build consistency around a change is fraught with difficulties. Sometimes, talking about a physician's performance on the basis of measures and data is like walking into a hornets' nest.

Physicians almost always challenge data, and rarely if ever do they accept negative data about their own performance. When they do not like the results, and particularly when the data are used to hold them accountable, they will often respond angrily and point to the inadequacies of the data. Some leaders find that physicians are capable of endless debate over the merits and flaws of a data set and have trouble using it to find opportunities for improvement.

Hostility toward data can, in part, be attributed to physicians' beliefs and previous experience with data and in part to the quality of data used. Physicians tend by nature to be analytic and expect a high level of precision in data related to their own performance. Data that do not mesh with how physicians see themselves are likely to make them defensive. Throughout medical school and residency, data are viewed as one part of a whole picture. If laboratory results are not consistent with clinical manifestations, the data immediately are suspect. If physicians get data about their performance that do not fit with their own perceptions, again, they see the data as flawed. In addition, physicians commonly believe that their own practice is different from the norm, in that their patients are older, have more chronic diseases, or are more demanding. Convinced of the uniqueness of their practice, physicians become uneasy when compared to others.

Physicians' concerns about data are compounded by the reality that the data used for feedback are often far from ideal. Common problems include:

- *Poor fit with the change being evaluated.* Sometimes the data do not provide feedback about the specific change physicians have been asked to make. When it is not possible to provide data that directly indicate the success of a change effort, proxy measures may be used. Sometimes these proxies make little sense to physicians. In one case, physicians were asked to reduce pharmacy costs in the ambulatory setting but were provided only with data about their inpatient drug use.

- *Flaws in measurement.* Sometimes the data used in giving feedback are flawed. That is, they are based on a poor or an inadequate sample of patients. Sometimes an assessment is based on a composite

Simple, Obvious, and Wrong!

DAVIS BALESTRACCI, MS

Davis Balestracci is Principal Research Analyst at Blue Cross/Blue Shield of Minnesota. He lectures widely on the use of statistics in quality improvement and, with Jeanine Barlow, co-authored Quality Improvement: Practical Applications for Medical Group Practice.*

With the intense current pressures to "reduce costs," we are seeing a tendency for performance goals to be imposed from external sources. The way in which data about performance are displayed often contributes to improvement efforts' floundering. The following are a few illustrations of feedback that doesn't help the cause of performance improvement:

- Report cards are presented in aggregated row-and-column formats, complete with variances and rankings.

- Perceived trends are acted on to reward and punish, even when too few data points are available to be called a trend.

- Labels such as "above average" and "below average" get attached to individuals/institutions.

- People are "outraged" by certain results and impose even "tougher" goals and standards.

Good statistical analysis is the backbone of understanding quality, but merely applying statistics to a data set does not make it a statistical analysis. Similarly, a good statistical analysis of a bad set of data is worthless. Any statistical analysis must be appropriate for the way the data were collected. Another problem is that data that were not necessarily collected *specifically* for the current purpose can usually be "tortured" to confess to a "hidden agenda."

Without data being seen as accurate or valid, improvement efforts go nowhere. To influence physicians to improve, it's imperative to use good data, to collect them explicitly for the purpose to which they will be put, and to perform appropriate analysis.

Physicians' exposure to statistics is generally taught as the research model. Carefully controlled conditions are created to keep the influence of outside variation at a minimum, which is why formal research is so expensive.

Quality improvement requires a different statistical mindset. The statistics used need to expose the variation that compromises predictable, desirable outcomes and points out questions that have to be asked to reduce

score derived from individual measures that physicians do not trust.

- *Data that distort or oversimplify reality.* Performance or work effort may be captured in a way that oversimplifies reality to the point of distorting it. Physicians reject the data's conclusion because "my patients are different." In one case, physicians given data about their patient panels without adjustments for acuity and age concluded that management completely failed to understand key differences and complexities in the populations for which they cared. In another example, the organization compared the productivity of women primary care physicians with their male peers without taking into account the fact that their panels were up to 85 percent female patients. Many of the women physicians felt that the data failed to reflect the extra effort and time required to address the needs and expectations of female patients.

Improve Data Usefulness and Credibility

Measurement and feedback are critical supports for a change. Because of their potential impact on the course of a change and on how individuals are evaluated, the information captured needs to be seen as useful and accurate. Those who design the ways in which data will be collected, analyzed, and shared are responsible for avoiding the common pitfalls described and helping to make the data credible and useful. Some simple strategies to enhance data credibility and usefulness include:

- *Get expert advice.* In planning for a change, identify the measures that will provide the best feedback about the effectiveness of the change and about the performance of those involved. It can be extremely useful to involve a data expert or analyst for guidance as the approach to collecting and using data is designed.

- *Seek input about the plan for measurement.* When identifying measures, it can be helpful to solicit input from those who will be receiving the data. When feedback reflects what doctors and staff want to know, the measures are more likely to be seen as useful. Involving physicians and staff also is an opportunity to educate them about how to use data. Physicians are much more likely to accept the plan for measurement, even if it has limitations, if they have had a chance to react and provide feedback. While seeking physician input requires an investment of time and may require additional planning as well as facilitation, it pays off in terms of the usefulness of data and physicians' ownership of them.

- *Acknowledge limitations in the data up front.* Data collected around change almost always fall short of what everyone involved would find ideal. Acknowledge areas in which data are less than optimal. Once limitations have been acknowledged, those giving and getting the feedback can come to some level of agreement regarding how the imperfect data can still be useful. One medical director we know uses admittedly less than ideal data by focusing on their directionality. In conversations with physicians, his goal is often to focus the physicians less on the specific numbers he is sharing and more on the direction in which they are pointing.

- *Build understanding of statistical methods used to measure the impact of improvements in daily practice life.* Physicians are most familiar with statistical methods used in clinical trials and large-scale research projects, where outside influences are controlled. They tend to be less well acquainted with a body of knowledge that draws on the work of Walter Shewhart, Joseph Juran, and others regarding statistical process control. This approach assesses whether a change is an improvement through a series of small-scale tests done in real time.[9,10] Educating physicians about the power of these methods to measure the impact of a change in everyday practice can help minimize their inclination to discount such findings as not being rigorous or scientific enough to be credible.

In the sidebar on page 136 and at right, a statistician describes what to do, and what not to do, when using data to determine if a change is an improvement.

Make Feedback Delivery Effective
The feedback about the effect of a change can be shared in a number of formats and ways. Team members might collect and monitor the results of a change by collecting and analyzing data themselves and posting run charts in their clinic. Physicians might get reports of their prescribing practices from a central information services

inappropriate and unintended variation. Problems arise when well-intentioned change leaders analyze and present data as if they were produced by rigorous research where variations are tightly controlled or, worse yet, produce cursory summary tables, bar graphs, or graphs with inappropriate trend lines drawn in. Many erroneous conclusions are drawn about what needs to change, the effectiveness of a change, or who (if anyone) is "at fault." The methods that improvement requires are quite simple—although initially counterintuitive—and create a common language to depersonalize issues.

Contrast the display of data for C-section rates in the typical bar graph with the same data plotted in naturally occurring time order (see figure on page 140). Displays such as this bar graph are simple, obvious, and statistically inappropriate. In other words, *wrong*… and very damaging to both physician morale and administration credibility.

Looking at the simple plot of points, known as a run chart (a time plot of data with the median of the data drawn in as a reference), one immediately notices a distinct break in the data occurring at November 1998. There is also statistical evidence of a change because of the sequence of eight consecutive points above the median from March 1998 through October 1998. This pattern is not one that could be expected randomly.

This indicates the presence of more than one "average" during the course of this data set and, visually, it seems obvious that the process average has decreased. This pattern alone should raise some interesting questions for those involved in the process, and productive dialogue could ensue. Was there a formal intervention during November-December 1998, or does there need to be an investigation? If this change is seen as beneficial, one would begin another run chart, constructing it using the data from December 1998 onward. This would help to make sure that the "gains" were held and could even detect further improvement.

If I could give just one piece of advice for data display and analysis, it would be this—"Plot the dots!" One should not draw any conclusions from a data summary that one would not also make by "plotting the dots" in their naturally occurring time order.

*Balestracci, D., and Barlow, J. *Quality Improvement: Practical Applications for Medical Group Practice.* Englewood, Colo.: Medical Group Management Association, 1996.

or utilization management department. Leaders give physicians face-to-face feedback in performance reviews. Increasingly, physicians get information electronically about the make-up and health status of their panels and about the effectiveness of their panel management.

Leaders can increase receptivity to feedback by being cognizant of the emotions that feedback situations and the feedback itself can provoke. Even positive or supportive feedback is sometimes hard to take in. Physicians, in particular, are socialized to expect that they will always do the right thing; in medical practice there is little room for error. Feedback that threatens that self-image can be very difficult to absorb and process. In addition, data are too often used to identify poor performance, not to find out why a process is not working. This practice reinforces physicians' fear that data will be used against them. When physicians argue over the relevance or quality of data, they might be venting their anxiety and defensiveness. A leader who senses that these deeper concerns are at the root of a physician's objection to a report will move faster to resolution by surfacing and addressing the underlying perceptions. A conversation at this level can be more fruitful than a debate about the exact percentage by which the data are skewed. (Chapter 7 describes sources of resistance and strategies to address resistance, including how to practice active listening in order to invite physicians to express their concerns or fears.)

In addition to being sensitive to the "charge" that data sometimes carry, leaders can ensure that information will reinforce what's going well and identify areas for improvement by:

- Sharing information in a way that is useful and actionable.

- Sharing unblinded data.

- Providing ongoing feedback.

- Integrating feedback about change into performance reviews.

Share Information in a Way That Is Useful and Actionable

Whether information is conveyed in hard copy or electronically, the reports that organize and interpret the data need to be clear and readable. Physicians typically want straightforward information. Overloading a report with information that is not directly relevant only creates complications for those trying to use it.

Data reports should also indicate whether a change is an improvement or is explainable by random variation. When this is not clear, it's easy to conclude that performance is better or worse when in fact the difference reported is not meaningful. Those generating reports need to use the appropriate statistical methods and present the information in such a way that those reading the reports will readily understand whether or not improvement has been made.

Reports are most useful when targeted to the appropriate audience, the individual or the team, depending on who has the capacity to influence results. Patient satisfaction data can be reported for teams or individual physicians depending on what specifically is being measured. Responses to questions related to physician behavior—e.g., my physician listens to me—are best reported on an individual basis. Issues that are within the team's purview to control, such as keeping patients informed about wait time after arriving for an appointment or ease of access to information after leaving the physician's office, are best reported on a team basis.

Reporting data on multiple levels can be helpful and can contribute to consistency that supports change. For efforts that are integral to the organization's strategy—for example, patient access data or HEDIS measures—it can be very useful for doctors and staff to see how their organization compares to others, how their unit compares to others in the organization, and how individuals compare to peers.

Most important, data about a change or performance have to be actionable. That was not the case for Dr. Edmunds, who learned his patient satisfaction scores were the lowest in the department by 15 percentage points. He sees himself as sensitive and caring and sincerely believes his patients find him easy to talk to. Neither the report he was sent as an e-mail attachment nor his conversation with his site chief gives him guidance as to what he can do to improve. Feedback that does not also point out the path to improvement ultimately is not useful. Moreover, it can be frustrating and dampen a physician's drive to succeed. If the organization believes something is important enough to measure, it should provide support to deal with shortfalls the data identify.

Use Unblinded Data

Physicians are highly competitive and have a strong drive to succeed; wise leaders use these traits to leverage improvement. When only blinded data are used, so that individual physician identities are obscured, the positive effect of peer pressure is muted. Blinding data at the beginning of a change effort may be appropriate in order to avoid any stigma or embarrassment as performance gaps are discussed and improvement opportunities are identified. Over time, when physicians have developed competence in the new way of doing things, sharing results with doctors identified by name can be a powerful motivator and can facilitate their seeking advice from peers whose performance is at or near the benchmark.

Provide Ongoing Feedback

Another way leaders build consistency is giving feedback to colleagues outside of scheduled reviews. Frequent, informal feedback can be very supportive when physicians are adopting a change. Not sharing an observation until a scheduled review has several drawbacks, as illustrated by the experience of Dr. Gardner, an internist in a group practice. The module leader, Dr. Boucher, who works alongside Dr. Gardner, has noticed that she is not making the changes in her schedule everyone in the module agreed to make to improve access. Rather than communicate his observations and why they concern him, Dr. Boucher waits until the monthly access report is available. He reasons that the discussion is best put off until he has the "black and white" evidence regarding her scheduling. He believes having the data in hand will make the communication easier to deliver and easier for her to hear.

Dr. Boucher's reluctance to share his feedback in real time represents a missed opportunity. It gives permission for behavior that is inconsistent with the team's agreement. Not getting any information to the contrary, Dr. Gardner's believes that it is permissible to stick to the old scheduling system. By not participating in a change others on the module are trying to adjust to, her actions undercut their commitment. Paradoxically, delaying the conversation until there is "hard" evidence does not necessarily make the

Giving Doctors Feedback
LOUISE LIANG, MD

Louise Liang is Medical Director of Group Health Cooperative, the nation's largest consumer-governed health care organization, serving 600,000 people in Washington and northern Idaho. She is also President of Group Health Permanente, a professional corporation of more than 1,000 health professionals that contracts with Group Health Cooperative.

Because doctors are competitive by nature, data are very useful for motivating and reinforcing change. The hard part is getting to the point where a doctor looks at the data and says, "Yes, this is about me." To achieve that, data need to be specific, actionable, and credible. To talk about poor overall patient satisfaction scores is not particularly useful. If data are not relevant and understandable, change will not occur.

Actionable data require enough information to point to solutions. When a doctor agrees that the data identify an unacceptable situation and asks, "How do I improve? What can you do to help me?" you need data that identify the nature of the problem. You need to be able to point to specific questions on a patient satisfaction report, for example, that indicate what is behind the overall score and what behaviors the doctor should change.

It isn't easy getting to the point where data are this accurate and specific, so we often have to deal with "less than perfect" data. When doctors take issue with the data, I sometimes don't even try to get agreement on finite targets but aim for directional improvement. My goal is to get agreement on two basic points:

- This is not where we want to be.

- This is the direction we need to be headed in.

When I deal with outliers who dispute the accuracy of the data, I don't argue. I ask them how inaccurate they think the data are. If they say they're off by 15 percent, I double it. My point is, even if the data are off by 30 percent, there's still a problem. That's been effective in helping some doctors to develop acceptance.

Under certain conditions, data alone can be sufficient to drive change. For example, patient satisfaction data promote change when a doctor has not had feedback before. If the perception is "I'm doing just fine" and that's not the case, data can really open eyes. Even in group practices, doctors tend to practice "alone together," with little sense of how they're doing relative to others until they see comparative data. So, data are most powerful when the discrepancy between reality and perception has been unknown, when the data indicate what has to change, and when these variables are within the doctor's control to improve.

In many situations in which we need change, however, what's required is more than recognition of the problem and willingness to change. We need to be prepared to provide coaching, training, and ongoing feedback for personal change. To drive organizational change, I find that making the right thing to do the easiest thing to do is most effective. Otherwise, even with understanding and support of the desired change, good intentions are frequently overwhelmed in the day-to-day rush.

conversation easier. When Dr. Boucher reviews the module data and shows her how she is the outlier, Dr. Gardner reacts strongly, not as much to her access statistics as to what appears to her to be a set-up. She claims she would have adjusted the way she schedules patients if only she had known earlier. The fact that Dr. Boucher had an impression that he did not communicate left her feeling betrayed.

Integrate Feedback about Change into Performance Reviews

The performance review is another opportunity to create a consistent environment for change. Ideally, both positive and negative feedback aimed at improvement is given throughout the year, so a physician should not be hearing about a performance concern

FIGURE 8-1. Alternative Displays of the Same Data

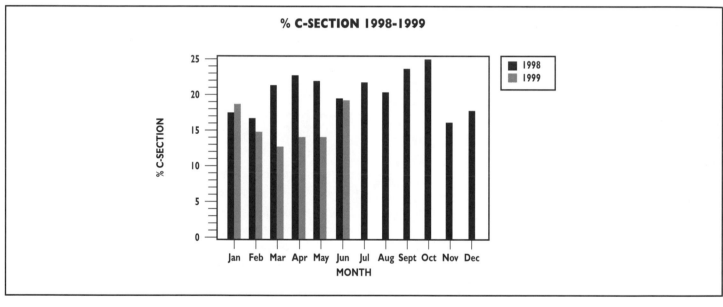

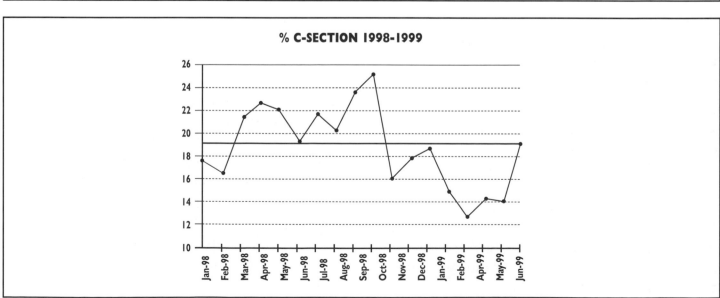

for the first time at the annual review. The review is an excellent opportunity to reinforce the importance of improvement and physicians' commitment to change. As discussed earlier, no incentive plan can possibly reward every change without collapsing under its own weight. The performance review provides an opportunity to acknowledge behaviors and results that are important to the organization's success—for example, improving pharmacy utilization, hospital days, and outside referrals—but that are not covered by incentives in the compensation plan.

The sidebar on pages 139-140, describes how one physician leader uses data with physicians to drive improvement.

Beyond Feedback—Accountability for Performance

Creating capacity for a change, aligning incentives, and delivering useful information are all forms of positive support for change. Despite efforts to help them, not all individuals succeed. Accountability is an important way to build consistency.

Physicians need to be given ample opportunity and support to improve. When performance does not improve, there needs to be some accountability. No physician organization should condone "got'cha" practices; however, it is important to ensure some consequences for poor performance. Consequences might be a talk with the board, coaching, attendance at a course, a financial penalty, or dismissal. It is important to set clear expectations and a timetable for improvement. Stepping up the consequences when the needed performance improvement is not forthcoming after support has been provided is a useful approach. The process for holding physicians accountable should be known to all and should be applied even-handedly and consistently.

When not changing carries no consequences, physicians get the message that implementing the change is elective. This mixed message is detrimental to those who make the transition and incorporate new behaviors, for they are certain to ask themselves, "Why am I doing it?" Some see the only reward for doing the right thing as additional work or taking on the stress associated with the change. They resent leadership for tolerating an unfair situation.

Leaders Seek Feedback to Deepen Consistency

Ensuring a consistent message and context for a change requires ongoing work. Sponsors, agents, and other leaders need to be visible in the field, learning how the change is going and what leadership can do to align available support. Informal conversations can be more productive than meetings organized to give leaders feedback. When leaders are in the field regularly, physicians are more likely to share their experiences and observations of inconsistencies that work against their efforts to change. When leaders receive feedback about mixed messages that they or the organization send, it is important to not get defensive or angry in response. This is particularly hard if you think what you are doing as a leader to be positive and supportive has not been noticed. Learning not to get defensive when you get feedback about your own behavior or other leaders' behavior is important.

Collecting information about inconsistencies in the environment is the first step. Leaders need to use the information to deepen consistency. Tool 8-1, pages 142-143, is designed to help identify specific actions to build consistency to support effective implementation of a change. Many physician organizations overflow with cynicism because leadership appears to be out of touch or not to care about the inconsistencies physicians experience in daily work life. We have consulted to many leaders who lamented the inability of their organizations to successfully implement change. In our interviews with physicians, we have learned that a significant reason for physicians' inflexibility is their lack of trust in leaders who do not acknowledge the gap between what they ask physicians to do and what they give them to get there. It is sad when leadership needs to get this message from a consultant. Organizations would be better off if leaders made themselves vulnerable enough to learn first-hand what is going on at the front line. Their willingness to face physicians and engage in dialogue about the changes the organization needs to make can go a long way toward reducing cynicism. In the process, they will gather valuable information to use to build consistency and support needed for effective change implementation.

Tools for Taking Action

TOOL 8-1. Build Consistency

PURPOSE: To identify specific actions to build consistency for a change

INSTRUCTIONS:

- Identify the change for which you will be developing a plan to build consistency.

- For the specific change, consider each item in the left-hand column, and identify what currently exists (or is planned for) to support the change and what currently exists (or is planned for) that will undermine the change.

- Next, consider what actions might be taken to build consistency and increase support for the change—during design, piloting, implementation, and spread.

- Review your answers and select up to three actions you will take to increase consistency and support for the change.

Factors that can build consistency	What exists to support the change?	What undermines the change?	What actions could we take to build consistency
Equipment			
Staffing			
Physical space			
Knowledge and skills			
Design features that make a change more or less useful or compatible with how work gets done			

Plans for transitioning to and implementing the new way			
Financial and non-financial incentives			
Human resource policies			
Meaningful, actionable feedback			
Feedback from the front line to assess the perceived level of consistency			

Actions we will take:

1.

2.

3.

PART III   **Moving to Action**

CHAPTER 9

Application of Change Levers to Compact Change

Background

In this chapter, Beth Briere, MD, Medical Director at CIGNA Medical Group, Phoenix, Arizona, shares her experience in applying the levers of the change management framework to implement a new staff and physician compact. An overview of the new compact implemented in this organization is shown in figure 9-1, below.

This is the story of what *one* organization accomplished. It is included as an illustration of what is possible, not to represent the definitive approach. How leaders in any other organization use the levers to map out a strategy and implement a change in compact could look very different. The commentary related to each lever is the authors' perspective and provides the reader with general take-aways.

The organization is a staff-model HMO that has been in existence since 1972 and is fully owned by CIGNA HealthCare. Care is provided almost exclusively to patients with CIGNA insurance by approximately 1,500 employees and 230 physicians in 16 health care centers. The organization has a strong local reputation and has achieved some national recognition for its quality initiatives. In general, physicians work here because of the promise of a good lifestyle and because of the organization's commitment to quality.

For a number of years before the beginning of this journey, the organization had made an effort to engage the physicians and staff in the business of health care. They were given information about the costs of care and the impact these costs had on employers and their patients. They were also given information on members' expectations. Variable compensation was linked, although not always clearly, to the results that the group achieved on quality, service, and cost measures as well as individual measures of performance. Incremental improvements were achieved each year but were insufficient to sustain a competitive market position. This was evidenced by shrinking membership.

FIGURE 9-1. Overview of New Compact Implemented at CIGNA Medical Group, Phoenix, Arizona

The new compact describes expectations of physicians and support staff in the areas of: quality, work ethic, teamwork, customer focus, and business focus. It also spells out what physicians and support staff can expect from the organization.

Under each section are multiple, specific manifestations of the underlying principle. Some expectations set forth in this compact are:

From the quality section…"I will follow established policies and procedures, departmental clinical standards, and guidelines to ensure consistency and quality."

From work ethic…"I am responsible to work toward solutions to problems with the team" and "I participate with management to establish clear expectations for my performance."

From teamwork…" I recognize that my team consists of the entire group practice with multiple locations (centers), departments and staff at different levels."

From customer-focus…"My focus is meeting patient/customer needs and expectations for quality and service."

From business-focus…"I recognize that I am part of a medical group that I regard as partners and colleagues and will make decisions that serve the greater good of the group versus my own personal needs."

Some examples of what physicians and support staff can expect from the organization are clear job expectations, a fair and just work environment, and honest communication regarding organizational status.

The driving force behind the compact change was Beth Briere, together with three other senior leaders, Sally Dimond, the Administrative Director; Dorothy Coleman, Chief Financial Officer; and Sylvia Bushell, the Organizational Development Specialist. These four led the 12-member guidance team that included two of the five department chairs. These two chairs were involved because they were responsible for most of primary care and for all medical specialty and surgical care. The other members of the guidance team were key administrative leaders of sites and support functions. This group largely led and managed the compact change process. The entire group of department chairs crafted the new compact and helped drive the process with physicians. Dr. Jack Silversin provided advice, education, and support during six visits over the course of one year.

What follows is Dr. Briere's first-person account of the process used to change the physician and staff compacts. Tool 9-1, pages 156-57, helps identify how your organization's change foundation supports a specific change you need to make. Tool 9-2, page 158, is an opportunity to develop a work plan and time line that incorporate all appropriate change levers to move a specific change forward.

Why Change?

To me, the compact is the explicit statement that defines how we relate to one another. It is the foundation of our relationships with one another. It defines what we need to do for one another and what the organization's responsibility is to each doctor and staff member. Our old compact was holding us back as an organization. As a staff-model HMO, we had promised our physicians and staff a variation of the protection-entitlement-autonomy compact. Predictable hours and freedom to do things their own way were a part of what people saw as the promise. Having to cope with a lot of change was not an expectation built into our old compact. Nor was it an expectation that we needed to work together as a team to maximize our value. There were significant issues between departments that had not been fully aired and resolved. By early 1999, it became clear that, from a number of perspectives, our business had to change:

- A business such as ours requires a large investment and is considered high-risk, based on the performance of other staff models around the country. Every year, we made an annual plan and historically accomplished only about 50 percent of what we committed to do. Even when we, as leaders, thought we were aligned and believed the targets were important to meet, we couldn't get beyond 50 percent. We needed to do better.

- The environment in which we practiced was undergoing dramatic change. Consumers were becoming more knowledgeable and had higher expectations. At the same time, our state legislature was getting more involved with health care regulation. We were under increasing scrutiny from purchasers who were looking for more accountability on costs and outcomes.

- Our physicians were feeling that their professional lives were out of their control. We, as leaders, were asking physicians to make changes without having the basic conversation about their expectations of the organization or about what the organization needed and expected from them. So, we were trying to get physicians to behave differently without explicitly changing the compact. This approach often resulted in limited success.

- Support staff were reflecting many of physicians' attitudes and behaviors, which made it difficult to address cost structure and service issues.

Changing the compact was a basic business decision. As part of a for-profit system, we have to innovate and improve continually. We weren't losing money, but we had to get better. Also, I believe that the only way in which physicians and the organization can have control over our future is to meet the needs of our stakeholders; the old compact did not set us up to do this.

In early 1999, we identified the largest gaps in our performance and initiated two significant operational changes: customer-focused access and increased capacity—caring for more patients without adding physicians or staff. Sally, Sylvia, Dorothy, and I deeply believed that the old compact expectations would limit the success of both these changes. We also saw a great opportunity in doing all three at the same time. The compact can seem like a nebulous concept if discussed in isolation. These two operational changes gave us something concrete to which to link our compact work.

The four of us were very clear about why we needed to change and about what we needed to do. But it became clear after our first meeting with Jack Silversin that, in spite of all of our efforts to get this information out to others in our organization, they did not share our sense of the need for change. In his assessment of our current state, he was able to demonstrate to us that staff did not understand and/or believe in why we needed to change and what we needed to do. Although painful at first, holding up the mirror for us as a team, and ensuring our commitment to clearly defining the need for change so that it was understood, was a very significant first step toward gaining alignment in our change process.

Align Leadership

General Approach

The most critical step we took was to develop alignment among leaders. This began with the four of us—Sylvia, Dorothy, Sally, and me. We invested four months in aligning leadership and drafting the compact before going public. One of the profound insights we had out of this work was that a sponsor is different from a messenger. Before compact change, the closer to the front line, the more likely it was that the manager or supervisor saw his or her role as a messenger, not as a sponsor of change. We could not have gotten where we are today if we still had leaders who could not embrace what sponsorship entails—being visible, talking about the changes, holding their staffs accountable, and engaging with them in defining the details of the change.

Crossing the bridge is a metaphor Jack shared with us that we locked onto as a shorthand way to talk about an individual's commitment to lead compact change. We consciously began incorporating the phrase into our everyday language. At meetings that focused on leaders' taking responsibility, we used a graphic of a bridge to remind us of our goal—having every leader emotionally cross to a place where he or she felt confident as a sponsor of the change.

We made it the responsibility of the department chairs and the administrative leaders to keep track of where their direct reports were—of who had crossed the bridge and who needed additional help. We also communicated that it was everyone's responsibility to honestly express reactions and feelings. If any of them had

difficulty with the compact change process or with what they were asked to do, we wanted to hear from them. We knew we could not go forward with a fundamental organizational change if we did not have all leaders believing in what they were being asked to do.

One way we tested alignment was to play out "what if" scenarios at every level of leadership. We hashed out what we would say, for example, if someone threatened to leave rather than get on board the new compact. We knew our responses to the challenges we encountered would have to be consistent.

Specific Actions

We incorporated a lot of leadership development into the alignment activities. So, a number of the activities we undertook to get aligned included training and reflection on the role of leaders. The steps we took once we four senior leaders were committed were:

- The guidance team participated in a day and a half of education on change management and compact change with Jack to kick off the process. This meeting set the context for all the other activities. It was the first step to getting the team on the same page.

- Senior leaders had off-line conversations with guidance team members after the kickoff session to process their reactions and strengthen their commitment to compact and other changes they were going to be helping to lead.

- The first draft of the new compact was written by the department chairs group, supported by Sylvia. The guidance team was the first group to react to this early draft.

- Jack provided on-site consultation and training on two occasions, a month apart, with a focus on individuals crossing the bridge. On each of these visits, he facilitated one meeting for senior management (department chairs with their administrative colleagues, department heads, and health care center administrators) and a separate meeting for front-line leadership (lead clinicians, center managers, supervisors, and nurse managers). The theme of these sessions was helping individuals work through their commitment to being change sponsors. Specific topics addressed included: why change is needed, what a compact is and why it is important, what our compact was and its implications for performance, input into the draft of the new compact, and individuals' role and willingness to play their role in the change.

- The consultant was on site during the alignment process on two additional days. On each of these visits, he facilitated half-day meetings for all levels of management (the groups that previously had met separately, met together on these occasions). To foster discussion among senior leaders, managers, and front-line supervisors, participants sat in mixed groups at round tables. The goal was to develop alignment throughout leadership ranks. By alignment, we meant that everyone understood why change was needed, what the new compact was (how it was different), and the role of compact change in the other changes we were implementing simultaneously. Education and practice in listening to resistance and responding appropriately was an important part of these sessions.

- Between these large-group meetings, we focused on reviewing and assessing our progress in these areas in all of our management team meetings. The guidance team met weekly, the department chairs met monthly, and various other functional teams met on a regular basis to talk about operational issues and about progress toward our goals, and in general to test and enhance the alignment we were developing.

Commentary

- The up-front investment on alignment in this situation was extraordinary. Leaders did not take the compact out until there was comfort that alignment was real.

- Leaders used the skills and expertise of their internal change agent well, for example, by asking her to facilitate meetings, support those who drafted the compact, and provide change management expertise. By the same token, they did not ask her to do what only sponsors should do.

- The process was not consultant-driven—senior leadership asked for and took advice from the consultant, but the guidance team and department chairs owned the process at every stage and drew up the plans for next steps.

- Leaders demonstrated deep understanding of the importance of the sponsor role and used a common language for the complex transition process that accepting leadership called for—specifically, moving from messenger to sponsor.

- The plan for compact change in this case seamlessly combined alignment activities with activities that built greater leadership capacity in the organization.

Develop Tension for Change
General Approach

We focused next on creating a compelling case for change. The leadership group—Sally, Dorothy, Sylvia, and I—was very aware that:

- In the near future, the organization would have to perform much better, and we were fully aware that it would take time to turn ourselves around.

- Because we were still making money and physicians were busy, those on the front line had much less reason than we did to feel any need for change. Without any education, they would not realize the platform was beginning to smoke.

- Getting reactions to the compact from everyone in the organization would be important to ownership. We committed to get wide participation because we knew that ownership would be critical to living by the new rules.

Taken together, these factors led us to focus on creating a "why change" message that would be credible and compelling to everyone in the organization. We asked the guidance team to draft a message that would set the context for the compact and for other operational changes. The team's members thought the key points to communicate to set context were: Membership was shrinking and employee morale was not where it needed to be, although we were financially successful and recognized by many for excellent quality of care. They then tested their message in what we called challenge groups. They asked for critical reactions and used the feedback to refine the "why change" message. The challenge groups led to minor revisions in the message.

The "why change" message was shared next with all levels of management at the alignment sessions. The strategy for taking the message to the front lines involved senior leaders' making presentations at local meetings, but we knew that, once we left, doctors would likely turn to their lead clinician and staff would turn to their supervisor and ask, "Is this for real?" We believed it was imperative that alignment around the need to change go all the way down to the front-line supervisors.

When it came time to go public with the first round of meetings that set the context for change, teams of senior leaders, with Sylvia's support, went to every site. We made it a point to have more than one physician leader at every meeting to demonstrate our solidarity around the key messages. To help communicate about where we were headed, Sylvia created what we called our road map—a graphic depiction of how the compact change and operational changes fit together and moved us toward a particular vision for the group. The road map was used as a prop to focus the presentation on the case for change.

These case-for-change sessions prepared doctors and staff members for change by making clear how the status quo was a barrier to our success. The "why change" messages began to resonate with our doctors and staff. They gradually understood and accepted that, more than ever, we had to meet our stakeholders' needs. We were unable to serve patients in the way we all said we wanted to because of murky or outdated expectations. Given how health systems are disintegrating, we talked about the need to provide value to our owner.

We also built in messages about the positives of compact change. Many were unhappy with the way people were treating one another. And a lot were frustrated because they felt the organization was not keeping up its end of the bargain; although they had never clearly articulated what they expected, they felt let down. So clarifying what the organization would do was seen as a positive. Some people got excited and could easily see that life would be better if the new compact were a reality. That doesn't mean they saw themselves behaving differently; their enthusiasm sometimes related to the fact that the new compact meant others would treat them differently. In any event, doctors and staff could look at current reality and at the new compact and understand that there was gap in how we treated one another that had to be closed.

Specific Actions

Our process to help our physicians and staff feel less complacent and get ready for change included the following actions:

- The senior leadership got clear that a two-step approach to introduce the changes would be needed, one to set the context for change and a second to present the specific changes and to solicit feedback.

- The guidance team drafted and tested a series of messages that conveyed the danger to the organization and to individuals of not changing and the benefits of change.

- We conducted three challenge groups to test the messages for clarity and salience. Participants in the groups were invited to push back and challenge the logic of the case for change. We did not want the case for change to be seen as overblown, nor did we want anyone to doubt that there were compelling reasons we had to change. The guidance team listened to and considered all feedback and prepared the presentation that would be used to set the context for change.

- The "why change" message was further tested with all managers during the alignment sessions. We strove to get their commitment to the need for change and to the messages that would be conveyed to the rest of the organization.

- Senior leaders took the case-for-change presentation to every site. At smaller sites, doctors and staff met together; at other sites there were two meetings—one for staff and one for physicians.

- At the case-for-change meetings, full discussion of staff and doctors' reactions and concerns about change was encouraged.

Commentary

- Making the case for change was especially critical in this organization because there was little felt pressure by the front line to change. The leadership group made personal visits and participated in group discussions, which sent an incredibly important message throughout the organization.

- In this organization, there was not an impeding crisis. The case for improvement was made from many different angles, however, and it was made solidly enough that doctors and staff came to acknowledge the need for them to change.

- Going to the effort to test the message proved very worthwhile. By the time the leadership group was ready to set the context for change, it knew that the communication it was delivering would be on target for those who needed to buy into the change.

Involve Physicians and Staff
General Approach
After the case-for-change meetings, we were ready to move forward and introduce the new compact. The health center managers, supervisors, and lead clinicians had the responsibility to run the meetings at which the new compact was introduced. Their visible leadership of these meetings was part of their sponsorship role and, for the most part, local leaders had high credibility with their people. They were supported in their efforts by their managers.

One objective of the meetings was to collect feedback about the statements in the compact. We wanted people to tell us what each statement meant to them. We fostered a lot of discussion because we wanted every person to own the compact. Even with all these opportunities for doctors and staff to make changes in the compact, the process never got out of control. Suggestions were made, some of which were incorporated in the final compact. As leaders, we had decided that we would ask for input, but we gave final decision-making authority about what to include to department chairs. This was explained up front at every site meeting so that no one would have misperceptions about how their suggestions would be used.

With the context set, everyone understood why the new compact was needed. The quality of discussion around the compact was constructive, in large part because of the level of preparation of managers, lead clinicians, and supervisors and their comfort in explaining what the compact was and why it was needed. Being a sponsor, not a messenger, was new to some of these people. To help them be successful, we provided a communication guide that supported all leaders to make consistent points and be prepared to respond appropriately to challenges and suggestions.

Specific Actions
- Because the compact had been refined by managers through the alignment process, they had a chance to add input early in the process.

- Over two months, the leaders closest to the front line all met with their staffs and went over the compact draft. Local leaders were backed up by their managers who were also at the meeting to provide support and lend credibility to their efforts.

- Everyone who was leading a discussion was provided with a comprehensive communication guide with detailed information to help them prepare for their meetings and to facilitate the compact conversation.

- The modifications physicians and staff suggested were all given to the department chair group, which used the input to shape the final version of the compact.

Commentary
- The process to define what would be included in the new compact began during the alignment phase, but it was not complete until the draft had been shared at every level in the organization. The input was sincerely sought and carefully considered.

- Taking the compact to the front lines and asking for feedback was effective and efficient because the case for change had already been made.

- Senior leaders, supported by Sylvia, communicated the need for change, but the compact was communicated by local supervisors with support from managers. This was important to further solidify the sponsor role. The effort spent to support every leader to cross the bridge paid off in having a committed cadre of leaders, and it supported their personal effectiveness in introducing the compact to their people.

Address Resistance
General Approach
There was not a lot of hostility or negativity in the roll-out stage, in spite of how much change we were asking our doctors and staff to undertake, for several reasons:

- Leaders definitely believed in what they were doing. There was solid agreement that the new compact was needed by the time we were ready to go public with the change.

- Tying compact change to other innovations in delivering care seemed to proactively minimize resistance. We built the case for change and showed how old expectations would not support the other specific changes.

- We aimed for genuine discussion about the compact at every level. We tried hard to foster open dialogue. Managers and supervisors went into the compact meetings with an honest respect for others' ideas

A compact is a reciprocal agreement; we have our end to keep up. When we've had difficulty delivering on what we said we, as leaders, would do, it gives people a reason to resist. If you go to the effort of defining a compact and involving the whole organization, be sure you keep your commitments; that sets a tone that helps to minimize resistance.

In some areas, we are meeting all the agreed-to expectations but aren't communicating what we're doing. We need to do a better job communicating how we're keeping our commitments. You cannot forget that management puts itself under the microscope with the compact process and that you are entering into a contract to be accountable. You proactively reduce resistance when you look at what you promise, do it, measure it, and communicate what you've done.

Specific Actions

We anticipated resistance and so we prepared from the start of the process to address it. Steps we took were:

- Not going public until we were confident leaders, managers, and front-line supervisors were equipped to be true sponsors for this change. Any indication from these individuals that this was going to be a fruitless exercise would have made the change process much harder.

- In sessions with Jack, we allowed all levels of management to have and express their own emotional reaction to what we were asking them to do. We were aware that the new compact had implications for everyone in leadership roles. We made an effort to surface feelings and reactions of those whom we were counting on to be leaders for the process. Again, this helps individuals cross the bridge.

- Those who were leading sessions were supported with communication skills training and a practical communication guide. While we provided some skill training in communicating and dealing with resistance, we could have done more.

- We made clear to all leaders, down to supervisors, that their job is to help people cross the bridge, not to announce this change and say that's the way it is—take it or leave it. When leaders have a good feeling for how to listen and can make a reasonable case for change, they are very effective in keeping resistance from reaching the point where it overwhelms the process.

- Making the case for change before introducing the new compact helped it be more readily accepted. We have been extremely conscious of keeping the commitments we made to physicians and staff and of communicating about how we are doing that. In actuality, we haven't done this enough. This is a real opportunity for improvement that we are currently working on.

Commentary

- This is an outstanding example of working proactively to minimize resistance. Here again, the investment in aligning and preparing leaders to help others cross the bridge paid off.

- The case for developing proficiency in the basic skill of listening and not pushing your point of view on someone who is emotionally not ready to hear it cannot be overstated. It is on our short list of skills that every leader, from the front line through executive ranks, should develop

- The importance of walking the talk cannot be overstated when you have committed your organization to compact change.

Build Consistency

General Approach

People won't invest in any initiative they see as transient. We wanted to communicate that the new compact isn't going to go away. We built in measures, feedback, and rewards so that everyone understood we were serious about making the words in the compact live. Our goal is to be the employer of choice, and a significant contributor to achieving this goal was to make the compact explicit and to build it into our core identity.

Our performance review is now based on the compact, and we're using 360-degree feedback to assess all the physicians and staff. I call our approach objective subjectivity. We get data from a number of people and look for patterns. The department chairs have developed a tool that allows them to directly tie these data to bonus distribution. As they gave feedback on performance this year, this information was shared with each clinician.

Putting the new compact to use to implement the access and capacity projects made it real very soon after it was finalized for those individuals involved in those two projects. Reinforcement came from tying the compact to the other changes and from the immediacy of the application.

The most potent reinforcement of all is leaders aligning the compact with decisions or, as happened recently, being called to task by others when our decisions are inconsistent. In one site where our patient base did not support two pediatricians, leadership gave the tenured doctor at the site the option to relocate to another site of his choosing. This deference to a senior physician had been a part of how we used to operate. But this doctor's first choice of a new location had a couple of drawbacks. He would be bouncing a more junior physician from the site, and we would be disrupting a highly functional team and one additional panel of patients. When the inconsistency between the new compact and our decision was pointed out, the decision was changed. The doctor was told he would be relocated in a way that was in our members' best interests and therefore in the organizations' best interests and that would, we hoped, be acceptable to him. A rational decision based on a number of factors was made with regard to his new practice location.

Specific Actions

- For a significant number of our physicians and staff, the new compact was put to the test by their involvement in the access and capacity projects. For example, in the customer-focused access model, the end of the day for providers and staff is much less predictable.

- We interpreted 360-degree feedback about physicians' performance in the context of compact expectations.

- We are rewriting our performance assessment tools for all staff so they more clearly and explicitly solicit input on the new compact. The tools will continue to be tied to the performance management process and to bonus distribution.

- We are redefining our compensation system and will incorporate compact behaviors into the new compensation system for all staff. As part of this project, we will rewrite all job descriptions.

- We are beginning to tell stories of how individuals in our organization have made changes around compact behaviors, and we are recognizing them for this in public ways.

Commentary

- With compact change, which calls for a whole new set of expectations and behaviors, leadership has to build consistency and provide needed support. Beth Briere and her colleagues are lining up a lot of reinforcement to sustain the new compact.

Lessons Learned and Looking Ahead

The process of gaining total ownership of the compact is still in progress more than a year after we started. On one hand, I'm disappointed it hasn't gone further faster. On the other hand, I see our pace as positive. Words are cheap. I am absolutely clear that it's not about the words in the compact documents. The important outcome is that every person who works or practices here tries it on and knows that these expectations are different from the ones the organization set up for them and reinforced in the past.

My first lesson relates to how much effort on leaders' parts this process takes. If you are convinced you need to rewrite your compact, a few key leaders will need to be prepared to invest an extraordinary amount of time in the process if it's going to work. You really need to believe that you are going to get a return on your investment to be willing to put the time into this.

We undertook this complex change at the same time we were starting two other changes. That meant managers had to focus on three very important changes at once. That's a lot to juggle. But I firmly believe that doing the compact work in conjunction with another significant change was the right thing to do. Anyone could look at the compact change and the access change and see how they related, how the compact change would support our patient-centered access initiative. There is also the efficiency of communication when you tie all the changes together and tell one story about how the changes are connected and all support one goal. The value of linking compact to other changes and presenting one integrated message is a key lesson others could take away from our experience.

Our approach was to change the staff and physician compacts at the same time and to try to develop one universal set of expectations. The new compacts are basically the same document, with some additional issues for doctors. This worked well for us because of our need to reinforce how linked all of our staff are and that our real differentiation in the marketplace is around the integration that can be achieved in a multispecialty group practice.

On Jack's last visit, we talked about compact revisions. We understand that, as our market changes and we have to change processes and systems internally in response, our compact may need to be revised. Our intention is to review our strategic vision and operation plan annually and hold up our compact to one test: Will these expectations support us in getting to where our strategy and annual plan indicate we need to go? At this point, we feel that we did such a broad-based participatory process to develop buy-in to the new compact that any future efforts to revise it can be more leader-led. As long as we continually update our people on the state of our market and on how we are doing as a business, we believe their buy-in to new or changed expectations will be easier to achieve.

There is still a lot of work to be done to get us to live by the new expectations. But I also sense we have work of a different kind to take on. Our managers have never been so energized, but our front-line people aren't having the same experience. Given the amount and kind of change we've asked them to make, their spirits aren't as high. Our new goal has to be to communicate how valued every doctor and staff member is. We've got to do better at expressing and demonstrating acknowledgment. I know that, if we don't encourage people and appreciate them, the compact won't be sustained.

This has been an incredible learning process for me personally and for our entire team. We are beginning to demonstrate that, by using a systematic approach to change and by attending to the details of each component of the change model, we can ensure success in change efforts. In fact, it is a critical commitment that our organization and leaders must make to each employee so that we can continue to make our new compact a living and valued part of our organization. We can successfully implement customer-focused care and the capacity model, and we will be able to implement a systematic way of recognizing and acknowledging people for the incredible work that is being done. Without the compact and the application of the change model, we could not be nearly as successful in all of our efforts.

Tools For Taking Action

TOOL 9-1. Build a Foundation for Change

PURPOSE: To evaluate the strength of the organization's change foundation and identify actions to address weaknesses.

INSTRUCTIONS:
- Fill out Table A: Current State of Change Foundation.
  - Identify a significant change that the organization needs to implement—for example, a change that would involve many or most physicians and that represents fundamental change in how they do something. Write this in the space provided.
  - Consider each of the three "building blocks" in the change foundation. For each one, describe how that building block currently would support the change and how it might impede it.

- Go to Table B: Ways to Compensate for Weaknesses in Change Foundation. For any foundation area that currently is weak or does not support the change you are trying to make, consider actions you can take to compensate for the weakness.
  - For each building block, review the suggestions for compensating for weaknesses in the change foundation in column two.
  - In the third column, identify actions you and other leaders will take. Focus on the application to the specific change so that your decisions about what actions to take remain clearly connected to "real" issues, to a change you think the organization has to make to succeed.

A. Current State of Change Foundation
The change:

Change foundation building block	How this part of foundation currently supports the change	How this part of the change foundation currently impedes the change
Leadership		
Vision		
Physician compact		

B. Ways to Compensate for Weaknesses in Change Foundation

Change foundation building block	Ways to compensate for weaknesses	What I will do
Leadership	• Develop leadership for this change. • Get the change team aligned. • Engage sponsors in a discussion of their mental models of leadership and of what mental models would best support this change. • Get other leaders who need to be involved to "cross the bridge" and own a leadership role.	
Vision	• Build a solid case for this change and communicate it clearly—consider stories, visual aids such as diagrams, or models. • Among those implementing the change, create a clear vision of what the change looks like when fully operational. • If there is any shared vision in the organization, if possible, link the change to it.	
Physician compact	• Identify expectations ("give") that would support this change and that the organization would be able to deliver on (the "get"). • Among those who need to implement the change, discuss the current give-and-get promise and how it might be a barrier to change. • Involve others as much as possible to react to and modify a set of expectations related to what individuals can look to each other and to the organization for as they work to implement this change.	

TOOL 9-2. Build a Work Plan for Change

PURPOSE: To help those leading a change to visualize the work to be done and develop a timeline for steps in the change management process.

INSTRUCTIONS:

- On large self-stick notes, list the key steps that will be important in the change management process. A sample list of steps follows. Not all may be relevant to your change, and you may have already completed some.

  - Identify a change team.
  - Develop alignment among change team members.
  - Clarify the scope and purpose of getting others' input or feedback.
  - Design and implement a process for input.
  - Close the loop and get back to those involved.
  - Plan and implement a pilot.
  - Communicate about pilot results.
  - Develop ways to generate a felt need for the change.
  - Communicate proactively about the change to minimize resistance.
  - Be sure leaders have crossed the bridge and are committed to the change.
  - If there is any emotional transition that appears to be necessary, create opportunities for physicians to talk about and let go of the past.
  - Prepare leaders to address resistance.
  - Assess the consistency of supports for the change.
  - Ensure that the capability needed is provided.

- On a blank wall, arrange the steps relevant to your change in a column at the left-hand side. Put the steps in an order that makes sense to you, given the specific change and the organizational context in which it will be made.

- Across the top from left to right, again with large self-stick notes, identify blocks of time for the process to occur. You can use weeks, months, or quarters; sometimes, a combination works best that starts with weeks, goes to months, and then to quarters to make a 12-month timeline.

- Look at every step you posted on the wall in the left-hand column. Identify, at a high level, the various activities involved in that step. List each activity and who will be responsible for it on a self-stick note, and stick it in the appropriate time column. Do not be overly concerned about small details. Work to identify important activities that need to be accomplished for each step to ensure a successful process.

- The result of this "wall work" exercise is a road map that can be printed, and shared. The road map is a useful tool to help all those involved in leading and supporting a change to know what has to happen, in what order it will happen, and who is responsible for the various pieces.

CHAPTER 10 | Accelerating Change When You Are an Outsider

Assessing the Current State

If you are an "outsider" with respect to physicians in your own organization or in another organization you seek to influence, how effective are you typically in supporting them to implement needed change?

Not at all effective ←——————————————→ Highly effective

1	2	3	4	5

What do you think contributes to your general level of effectiveness? Consider:
- Factors in the physicians' control, including how they view you.

- Factors in your control, including how you view physicians.

The Influence of Outsiders

Increasingly those whom physicians perceive as "outsiders"[1] have responsibilities for the performance of physician organizations or seek to influence some aspect of the organization's performance. Often, their outsider status makes it difficult for them to be effective. For example, consider the following:

- *Dr. Hemmer, the health plan's medical director, is passionate about clinical improvement. Recent HEDIS data show that the largest practice associated with the plan is scoring below the median on all parameters. When Dr. Hemmer meets with the managing partner of this practice to talk about the need for improvement and resources the plan will provide for a pilot project, his offer is met with, "When you have some decent data, we'll talk."*

- *Another system's executive team reviews the quarterly performance of acquired physician practices. The losses associated with several are far greater than projected. They look at what it will cost the system to divest these practices and conclude it is almost time to cut losses. They agree that the doctors have had ample opportunity to improve; they schedule another meeting to prepare one final directive to the lagging practices, with dates and consequences for nonperformance clearly defined.*

- *Pat Burns is the department director of gastroenterology in an academic medical center. The CEO has communicated to her management team that patient service needs to be the number one priority in the coming year. Pat prepares a presentation for physicians that explicitly makes the case for increasing clinical hours and improving access. She takes the initiative, knowing the department head is under extreme pressure to finish a grant renewal. In the past, he has shied way from taking action that makes him appear to be too aligned with the CEO. At the meeting, few physicians show up on*

Building Shared Accountability
GARY A. VAN HOUSE

Gary Van House heads up practice management services for Partners First, the physician practice consulting division for Ascension Health, a Catholic health system serving communities through 35 ministries with more than one 150 facilities located in 15 states and the District of Columbia. His division serves 1,400 physicians employed by Ascension Health as well as independent practices associated with the System's hospitals.

For a number of reasons, physician organizations do not make the easiest partners. The way in which physicians organize and govern themselves and would-be partners' lack of understanding of the particulars of physician cultures cause most partnership difficulties.

Physician organizations exist in many different stages of evolution. When doctors first come together to practice, they tend not to set up their organization to deal with issues much beyond delivering care to patients. Many times, they are not particularly mindful of building durable governance and tend to under-invest in time and money to build systems. They organize themselves to deliver care but with inadequate understanding of strategic and business planning.

Many organizations were formed around a single strong, charismatic physician or simply the one willing to take the lead. When one physician takes charge of finances and decisions, the others do not get experience in how the business works. This model might work for the doctors, but when these physician organizations become partners or parts of systems, their infrastructure and communication processes work against their being able to deliver what they promise.

The sluggishness of the physician organization and/or its inability to follow through on commitments frustrates its partners. When a physician organization is part of a hospital system, for example, the physician board might buy in to a proposal the hospital makes, but the other doctors may not approve of it because of a lack of understanding of process within the group. The hospital falsely believes it and the doctors are building toward something together without realizing that one or more of the elementary building blocks are not in place.

For their part, hospitals and others have low tolerance for the way in which doctors make decisions. They don't understand how fundamentally different physician cultures are from their own. Many hospital executives

time. When the presentation gets under way, phones ring and doctors come and go. Looking at her audience, Pat senses few are engaged in her presentation.

Given the need to become more customer-focused and cost-competitive and the partnerships and alliances that physician organizations are now commonly a part of, outsiders are often in the position to "demand" or facilitate physicians to improve or adopt change. However, the baggage that "outsider" status carries makes it difficult for these individuals to sponsor change or be effective change agents. Those who are not physicians are almost always suspect, and physicians typically treat them with less respect than they would afford fellow physicians. Even a physician in an administrative role will be labeled "not one of us."

Baggage Gets in the Way of Partnership

Given physicians' lack of receptivity to being told what to do, relationships between physician organizations and their owners or partners are frequently contentious. Those who need to function as partners do not trust each other, choosing instead to protect their own self-interests. As in most relationships, when one party is frustrated by the other's behavior, both parties are experiencing similar feelings. Not all relationships between physician organizations and other entities are ineffective or dysfunctional. These relationships are as varied as the cultures and personalities involved. The growth of corporate medicine, however, and the economic imperatives forcing physicians to look for partners who can provide needed capital or resources have created alliances that, generally speaking, have been problematic.

Unfortunately, prejudice and mistrust are not uncommon. We have talked with doctors who feel discounted by administrators and system executives. For every hospital administrator or insurance manager who asks, "Why don't the physicians do what we've asked them to?" there are physicians who want to know, "Why don't they leave us alone to practice in the way that we know is best?"

Many physicians feel that what attracted them to medicine in the first place is now lost to them. The changed doctor-patient relationship, having too little time to spend with each patient, and the losses with regard to autonomy and the exercise of independent judgment have all taken a toll. Alan Sheldon, in *Managing Doctors*, writes of the impact of these losses, "Physicians are therefore realistically paranoid and, as such, sensitive and suspicious. Innocent actions, however well intentioned, may be misinterpreted. All managers need to be aware of this fact."[2]

Resentment, frustration, and wanting to dominate or control doctors are corrosive and the root of many ineffective relationships. Some, not all, professional managers and executives who work with physicians have built up negative stereotypes over the years. Managers' view of physicians as greedy or interested primarily in protecting their incomes is understandable, given how some physicians react when their incomes are threatened. Physicians can also be arrogant and patronizing to those they do not view as legitimate peers. They tend to hold their own profession in the highest esteem and to see managers' jobs as not adding much value and not all that difficult. Having heard stories of how unmanageable physicians are or having had direct experience, some outsiders conclude that it is better to try to control physicians than to risk being controlled by them.

It is our belief that outsiders' actions will not positively influence physicians' willingness or capacity to change if undertaken with resentment or hostility. The first step in being able to have any influence on physicians is investing in the relationship, and, to do that, you have to move beyond mindsets and prejudices that cast physicians as untrustworthy and purely self-interested. The second step toward effectiveness is acknowledging interdependence. If your organization has partnered with a physician organization, it has done so because of the potential for some gain. The right context for supporting physicians to change can be developed if you understand how a strong and effective partner benefits you. In the sidebar, page 160 and right, one senior administrator with a good deal of experience shares his observations on the perceptions that nonphysicians sometimes hold about physicians and how difficulties in partnering with physician organizations can be overcome.

Use Levers to Facilitate Change

Outsiders who want to be constructive can draw on the change management framework and get results.

---

have come to expect that doctor organizations may not be able to deliver; when the physicians do not, their perceptions are confirmed. To be able to influence physicians' practices and create effective partnerships, health care leaders need to begin by accepting that physician cultures are different and that their organizations do not operate as hospitals do.

People who are most effective in working with doctors, in my experience, share certain skills and characteristics. Typically they are:

- Able to simplify complex issues and present them in a logical way so that doctors can readily understand the issues in the context of their work. From their training, physicians are used to straightforward, reasoned arguments, and they want to see business issues laid out in a similar way.

- Skilled at listening, because many physicians today have a lot of pent-up anger and loss related to changes in the health care system

- Assertive and direct. Physicians have more respect for administrators who challenge them and are willing to be challenged.

- Hard-working, with high integrity and a work ethic that physicians can relate to.

- Comfortable sharing decision making with physicians and do not need to be center-stage.

At Partners First, we are fostering a model for shared accountabilities as a way to build partnerships between physician organizations and others. We think the key is building a team that fully understands and agrees on the strategic need for the partnership. We also try to put money in perspective as a motivator of change. If administrators think that, with the "right" compensation system, they will get long-term improved performance or greater cooperation from physicians, they are wrong. Accountability has to involve giving responsibility to physicians through vested governance and authority. If a hospital administrator tells a practice that it is not performing financially, most likely the administrator will get an earful about how poor the hospital billing system is. In an accountable model, responsibility for the business office would be given back to the doctors, with the expectation they will do what is in their control to improve. Making them responsible and not enabling their old internal dynamic helps physician organizations be better partners and leads to win-win outcomes.

Pat Burns, at the academic health center, could have been more effective. What might her efforts have produced if she had consulted the framework and done the following:

- Understood the importance of all three change roles. If she put herself in the change agent role, she could have enlisted the physician department head to be the sponsor of the change, and, working collaboratively, they could have identified physicians to call on to be champions. If they had been able to meet as a team, chances are good that they would have come up with a strategy for educating physicians about the need for change that would have achieved better results.

- Supported the formation of a task group, with the department head as sponsor, to look at the relationship between available clinical hours and patient satisfaction and to evaluate threats to the patient base from outside competition as a result of the department's poor service. She could have staffed this group to keep it focused on patient-service issues. The involvement of physicians would have helped spread the message about the need to consider change.

- Gotten the task group involved in identifying the level of complacency and how it and others could create tension to make physicians uncomfortable with the status quo.

- Met occasionally with two or three champions who buy the need for change and are willing to talk publicly about other physicians they know at the medical center who have seen their incomes decrease because they did not change.

- Prepared the department head with talking points for discussing needed changes in one-on-one meetings with other physicians. Coached him in effective listening when physicians express concern that time away from research is more likely than lack of patient access to compromise the department's reputation.

- Included a member of the information technology department at a task group meeting to educate physicians about the center-wide patient service analysis and to help them be able to explain the data methodology and results to their peers.

Likewise, the system executives facing losses from physician practices and the medical director who wants one practice to begin an improvement project could have benefited from applying the framework in their situations. Using it just as an assessment tool could have led to several key questions:

- Who are the leaders who could sponsor change? Who else would need to be on a change team or could add value to the team?

- To what extent have physicians been involved in any improvement efforts to date? How were they included, and what were the results?

- To what extent do physicians feel any need to change, or is the status quo completely comfortable? What are the costs of the status quo? What risks are associated with changing? Has the case for change been made in a compelling way?

- Why might physicians resist what they are being asked to do? What might they need to give up? They are intelligent people who basically want to do the right thing. Therefore, what are they saying when they resist change? What can be learned from their resistance about how they see the change?

- If the doctors did implement the change, is there any support in their environment? Are the potential supports, such as resources, staff, and rewards, consistent with what physicians are asked to do, or would physicians actually be penalized in some way for doing what is asked of them?

Build Overall Change Capability

Outsiders with responsibility for change in physician organizations can also work at a different level—at building change capability. In these efforts, the focus shifts from a single change project, such as getting a guideline implemented or putting a service guarantee program in place, to the organic capacity of the organization to be successful at implementing change. The greater the change capability in a physician organization, the more agile and adept it is at change. One way change capability grows is through ongoing engagement with change—implementing large- and small-scale changes that are sustained and that make delivering care easier or better for doctors and staff.

It is our experience that there is another, more fundamental way in which outsiders can help a physician organization become more adept at change—fix broken relationships and help it develop its internal capability to change. We believe the following actions can be extremely helpful for those on the outside to take to build change capability in a physician organization. Not all may apply to any one situation, but all can help move toward the ultimate goal of change being internally generated and sustained.

- If the relationship is broken, heal it.

- Support the physician organization to get strong.

- Stop reinforcing the old compact.

- Give physicians responsibility, authority, and resources and provide consequences.

- Align incentives.

- Build business literacy among doctors.

- Support the spread of learning and new ideas.

- Support information technology development.

- Help doctors feel valued.

- Use your authority or influence to spread constructive interaction.

If the Relationship Is Broken, Heal It

The relationship between most physician organizations and their partners or owners has room for improvement, but most are far from being totally broken. Most often, we find that, even though achieving improvements through joint efforts can be inefficient and difficult, there is sufficient goodwill to get work done together. Unfortunately, as economic pressures continue to bear down on physicians and other parts of the health care delivery system, some relationships break down and the behavior of physicians and others make it very unlikely that any positive outcome is possible. Parties have little trust or respect for one another, and accusations and finger pointing make problem solving impossible. One or both sides may feel the other is out to "get them," and communication is not constructive. Getting to this end state typically involves broken promises, poor communication, unresolved conflict, and battles for control.

If your relationship with a physician organization is in this state, there are two options: invest in trying to heal it or find some way to end it. Choosing neither limits your influence and further erodes the likelihood that the relationship can be salvaged. Fully healing a broken relationship takes time and a series of consistent experiences that build trust and respect. Nonetheless, when there is a commitment to improve the relationship, actions that heal old wounds can be taken.

Healing a relationship begins with acknowledging that a problem exists that must be addressed for any business or clinical outcomes to improve. It also takes owning your responsibility for why things are the way they are. Then it is appropriate to engage the other party if he or she is willing to put forth the effort to improve the relationship. Airing concerns and deciding on next steps might need to be done by two individuals, two leadership teams, or between one senior executive and all physicians in an organization. To have the difficult conversations that can heal feelings of injustice or of being wronged, it can be helpful to involve a third party as a facilitator. A neutral third party can play several functions, including:

- Develop a report on issues that can be used as the basis of conversation. In some cases, making an objective assessment of the situation is a helpful place to start. The facilitator can separately interview relevant parties to develop a picture of what needs to be resolved for the relationship to improve. These interviews might include:

  - Each person's view of the current situation.
  - What each feels needs to be changed or resolved.
  - What each feels he or she needs to change to make the situation better.
  - What each feels the other party could change to make the situation better.

Any report of findings should be written in a way that is clear and non-accusatory and that expresses sentiments without attributing specific comments to individuals. This report can be the departure point for one or more conversations that focus on what each party can do to heal the relationship and move it forward. It is helpful if there is one project, not too large in scope, that the parties can agree to work on together; this provides a way to learn to

FIGURE 10-1. Instructions for Perceptions Dialogue

The objective is to help two teams understand current perceptions, how they contribute to them, and what they can do to alter perceptions that are a block to a productive relationship. Allow a minimum of four hours to complete this structured discussion.

1. Set ground rules that support candor and safety

2. Allow 30 minutes for each team (separately) to identify the following on large newsprint sheets:
   - The perceptions we think you have about us
   - The perceptions we think you think we have about you

3. As one large group, each team shares its answers and the other team has an opportunity to ask questions about the behaviors or experiences that contributed to the perceptions that were shared. Team members are encouraged to ask questions for clarification (for example, "What does that mean? Can you give us a concrete example?"), but not to explain their behavior or to take issue with the perceptions.

4. Divide again into teams and give each team the newsprint sheet from the other team. The team should review what was said about it point by point with two questions in mind:
   - Do we think this perception is accurate?
   - If not, what questions do we need to ask to better understand where that perception is coming from?

5. Bring both teams together. Each team shares thoughts and explains the items on their two lists that they understand and asks questions about what they don't understand or connect with. The purpose of the discussion is to develop insights into why others hold the perceptions they have.

6. Then, engage in a discussion regarding what would need to change to diminish the perceptions that are not productive so the relationship can move forward.

---

trust one another and helps build confidence that everyone wants the situation to improve.

- Facilitate conversations that focus on the perceptions fueling the current dynamic. A facilitator can help leaders from both sides express their perceptions in a structured way. Talking about perceptions is a powerful way to delve into the basic drivers of a poor relationship. In a structured experience, all parties have the opportunity to digest and acknowledge one another's perceptions. One exercise that is particularly helpful in stimulating conversations that are healing is described in figure 10-1, above. This exercise is built around each side sharing with the other:

- How we think you see us.
- How we think you think we see you.

When all parties are willing to be both vulnerable and honest, questions such as those in the exercise stimulate authentic conversation. The discussion leads all parties to a better appreciation for what they are contributing to the current relationship and what they can stop doing, and start doing, to build greater trust and to be perceived more positively. Fisher and Brown, in *Getting Together,* capture a truth about human nature: "Each of us tends to see things in ways that take our own interests disproportionately into account. And the facts we know best are those closest to us."[3] The perception exercise is a way to surface other "facts" and to check out if the conclusions one party has drawn about another party's intentions and actions are accurate.

- Help parties develop ground rules to support a productive relationship going forward. Even when both parties acknowledge how their past behavior was unproductive and are willing to improve the relationship, old patterns are very hard to break. A facilitator can support the parties in developing new ground rules for how they will behave toward each other going forward. Some examples could include:

  - If someone acts in ways that seem counterproductive or not in the spirit of relationship-building, do not automatically assume ill intent. Bring the behavior to the individual's attention and ask questions to find out what you might have done to stimulate that behavior.

  - Do not engage in false agreements. If you disagree with a position or a decision, make your concerns known at the time. Do not say you commit to something you are not going to follow through on.

  - Do not "take shots" at the other party and do not tolerate that behavior among others in your organization.

It is impossible to devise ground rules to guide every interaction. A general approach to rebuilding a relationship is choosing behaviors that Fisher and Brown label "unconditionally constructive." This means doing only those things that are both good for you and good for the relationship, whether or not the other side reciprocates. Being unconditionally constructive does not require you to trust before you act. It simply means that you avoid engaging in behavior that erodes the relationship, regardless of how the other side behaves. Being unconditionally constructive reinforces the value of the relationship even if the other party seems to be engaging in unproductive behavior. Your actions demonstrate your commitment to make the relationship work.

Support Physician Organizations to Get Strong
Trying to control physicians generates unmanageable resistance. By the same token, trying to do business

with physicians is very frustrating when they are not able to deliver on their commitments. When physicians are unable to speak with one voice, have little capacity to implement improvements, or appear to act only out of self-interest, the most useful approach a partner or an owner can take is to support building the foundation in the physician organization. This involves providing needed support so that the organization can develop physician leadership and build a shared vision and a new compact. A weak or disabled physician organization does not, under any circumstance, make a good partner. It is in your best interest, their best interest, and ultimately in patients' and payers' best interest for the physician organization to be able to adapt to market demands and be a professionally satisfying place to practice. By helping the physician organization become stronger, you are also creating a better partner in care delivery. There are several ways an outsider can contribute:

- Provide expertise to help physicians develop a shared sense of mission and vision and a compact that is consistent with today's realities. This might mean finding an outside consultant who can facilitate this work or lending a trusted individual from your organization with the expertise and experience to support the leadership and the physicians through the kind of work described in the first part of this book as the foundation for change.

- Provide resources or lend your own expertise to help the physicians critique, and restructure as necessary, their organization so that they can be more effective in achieving the vision and implementing change.

- Support the development of physician leadership. This can include sending leaders to courses to develop skills, funding retreats that focus on leaders' responsibilities, and making available any other resources from your organization to support their leadership development.

The sidebar, pages 166-167, describes the steps one system CEO took to support a medical group's development.

Besides providing funds for these activities, outsiders can lend support by mentoring or by sharing contacts that have a good track record in these kinds of activities. In some cases, physicians might perceive they

Supporting Medical Group Development
TERRY BROSSEAU

Terry Brosseau is President and CEO of Medcenter One Health Systems in Bismarck, North Dakota. This integrated system includes the Q and R Clinic, a 135-physician multispecialty group, and other outlying physician practices and smaller clinics.

Being right accomplishes nothing other than being right. When you're frustrated, however, it's an easy trap to fall into. Our hospital system merged with the Q and R Clinic in 1994, and for a few years we struggled, with limited success and lots of disappointment and suspicion on all sides, to make it work.

The hospital and the medical group had been interdependent for years, but, with increasing pressure to improve quality and lower costs, total integration looked like it made sense. Three or four years after integrating, however, we weren't as far along as we should have been. I could not take the organization I had spent years to build into the future on my own. The doctors were the ones who had to get us where we needed to go.

To support the medical group's development, I brought in a consultant to work with the physicians. Part of that work involved developing a vision they felt ownership for and a physician compact that spelled out how they would relate to each other and to the system. Over the course of several months, the doctors developed greater cohesion and trust. That laid the groundwork for everything else we accomplished.

We restructured the clinical departments into service lines, including children's health, women's health, and adult primary care, each led by a service line chair and an executive partner. These two individuals are held accountable for their service line's performance. I purposely did not define the responsibilities for each partner. The pair is given responsibilities and accountabilities, and they work out the roles among themselves.

To help make the integration work, we needed a full-time medical director. A team of physicians interviewed candidates and made the selection. They needed to own the decision. I reserved veto power but never used it. They chose a physician from outside the clinic who has years of leadership experience. She's gifted in building relationships and is able to work effectively with all personalities.

have an acute need for help in an area that does not look to you like the ideal place to start. If you offer to help with resources and other support, it is important to start with the issue of most concern to them. There is no magic order when it comes to building the foundation. If physician leadership is convinced of the need to revise the compact, help them to do that. The foundational issues are all intertwined; chances are good that, as they engage in compact work, physicians will recognize their need for a shared business vision and more effective leadership.

Stop Reinforcing the Old Compact
A physician compact that includes expectations of autonomy, protection, and entitlement is antithetical to building change capability. Some administrators who work in physician organizations enable physicians to maintain the old compact even though it is detrimental to organizational success.

> *Erica Jones is the administrator of a 250-physician IPA. While she would like to see physicians work more effectively together to improve service and cut cost, there is a part of the physicians' compact she has not been willing to challenge. The physicians have come to expect her to take care of business so that, as much as possible, they will be left alone to see patients. The doctors look to her for protection from the vagaries of the local health care market. She takes this expectation of her for granted and does as much as possible to fulfill it. From all the signals the physicians send, she perceives her worth to them to be very linked to her ability to keep their practice lives as steady and predictable as possible.*

Erica would likely be ambivalent about pushing the doctors to revise the compact if it led to her having less power or having to step away from her role as the doctors' protector. Outsiders like Erica either support the old compact or help doctors come to terms with a new one. When no effort is made to educate physicians about what can be gained by formalizing a different compact, doctors assume that the old compact can and must be preserved. Every outsider, practice administrators in particular, needs to reflect on how the old compact makes change and improvement hard to implement and sustain, what they might personally get out of having the old compact in place, and how they might be reinforcing it. If administrative leaders are willing to give up the power they get from the old compact, they need to identify where they have leverage to support physicians to take up the issue.

Give Physicians Responsibility, Authority, and Resources and Provide Consequences

Physicians tend to be goal-directed. They are more likely to step up and make change happen when they have a clear picture of what needs to be accomplished; are given responsibility, authority, and resources; and are exposed to the consequences of their actions. Owners or administrators undermine physicians' active engagement in improvement when they try to control physicians by telling them what to do—"Do what we say because we know best"—or when they hold them accountable for a result the physicians cannot control—"You're accountable for collections being down even though the billing office doesn't report to physicians." Systems undermine physician effectiveness when they appoint a medical director and give him or her great responsibility but little authority. Outsiders also undermine physician ownership when they micromanage resources rather than allow physicians to take responsibility and live with the consequences.

Supporting physicians in building the foundation for change and improvement—leadership, a shared vision, and a compact that supports success—sets the stage for clarifying authority and giving physicians control. Several tactics can be employed to build physicians' readiness to accept authority and responsibility for change, all of which relate to treating them as respected business partners:

- Set targets and goals that are consistent with physicians' responsibilities and that are within the span of their control. Some health care system executives communicate to physician practices that they are responsible for a large deficit when, in fact, they are not in the position to address the entire loss. That does not mean that the physicians are not responsible for addressing some part of the loss. Physicians are more likely to own, and work to meet, targets that are realistic and specific.

Educating all doctors, not just service line chairs, has been a priority. We need all the doctors to understand the business, how Medicare works, and industry trends. In the old environment, this education wouldn't have been nearly as effective. Regular retreats for all service line leaders have also been educational. Meeting a few times a year has built teamwork within and across service lines. Insularity of service lines could have been a problem if not for the kind of interaction that these retreats have fostered. I've also focused on educating other hospital people as to why physicians have to lead us into the future. Historically, there were negative opinions about the doctors. We won't tolerate those now. In reality, as the doctors have developed as leaders, I've delegated more decision making and they've stepped up and taken responsibility.

We'll never be done with the work we have started, but, in two years, we've become a better, more efficient health system. On every parameter important to success, we've improved. Communication is better, everyone's satisfaction is higher, the doctors' understanding of the industry is deeper, and our associates and physicians are interacting in constructive ways. Physicians support major decisions. Our quality of care is better, because the doctors communicate with one another more effectively.

In retrospect, too much time went by between integration and the investment that resulted in our being a system that produces results. Strengthening our physician partners was the right thing to do. Those in a similar situation should understand that every day they don't do it only makes things worse. A successful system is built on physicians' understanding the complexities of health care, operating as a team, and fully participating with you in the business.

After 35 years as an administrator, I'm being rewarded and having fun watching our doctors develop as leaders and take responsibility for their future and ours.

- Give physicians responsibility and authority. To build change capability, physicians need to be given responsibility and authority. In our experience, some system leaders give authority to physicians to make a change and provide resources and support but withdraw them a few months into a change process if the practice does not measure up to some expectation. From the system perspective, the doctors had their chance, progress was slow, and the project could be better managed centrally. When outside leaders are concerned about physicians' ability to meet targets, there are other ways to deal with the situation. Let physicians know what they and their organization are expected to achieve and the level of authority they have to achieve results, and then be consistent in your support and communication. If it appears that physicians are not going to be successful, offer additional support and help without diminishing their responsibility or authority.

- Hold physicians accountable. Giving physicians control over resources produces results when they are also held accountable. Not holding physicians accountable sends the message that improvement or performance targets are optional and the lack of consequences can enable poor performance. It is useful to build in both positive consequences for physician organizations when they meet or exceed targets and "downside" consequences when targets are not met.

Align Incentives

Physicians behave in ways consistent with their own best interests, as do executives, administrators, and managers. It makes no sense to expect physicians to do otherwise. However, outsiders sometimes set themselves up for frustration when they expect physicians to behave in ways that are inconsistent with how they are being paid. While money plays a stronger role in motivating physician behavior in some organizations than in others, few physicians will act against their economic interests as long as their decisions do not harm patients. When physicians express concerns and frustrations that the incentives used to promote one change are misaligned with other expectations of them, outsiders need to listen. Even if realigning incentives is not your top priority, tackling the issue in response to physician concerns sends a message to physicians that you want to structure the business relationship in ways that make good sense to all parties.

Build Business Literacy among Physicians

Many physicians find it hard to accept that their profession is a business. When they have not integrated sound business principles into their practices and have not grappled with the implications of business realities, it is difficult to get them to engage in improving their business performance. The more physicians understand about the sources of the pressure to improve health care, the more likely they are to engage in efforts to improve business performance. Improving business literacy, that is, understanding of market forces and the economics driving health care, is an important role that many outsiders can play because of their perspectives and skill sets. They can provide physicians with a window into the health care market.

Physicians commonly assume that the pressure for lower costs or shorter hospital stays is generated by their partners, the owner, or the health plans with which they contract when, in reality, it comes largely from those paying the bills. To help physicians understand market pressures and underlying causes, it can be helpful to invite local purchasers to meet with physicians to explain their perspective.

Beyond understanding the marketplace in general, many physicians can benefit from education about the finances that affect them and the organizations with which they are affiliated. When the books are not open, physicians tend to suspect that they are being manipulated in some fashion. Share data about system and physician performance on a regular basis. In our experience, the more open you are with physicians about performance issues, the more engaged they will be in making improvements. The issue of data credibility is an important one to consider whenever you share performance data. (Chapter 8 has a fuller discussion of using various types of data and feedback as part of a change process.)

Support the Spread of Learning and New Ideas

Outsiders can play a valuable role by fostering collaboration and opportunities for physicians to learn from other parts of the system or organization about what works and does not work. The "not invented here" syndrome is a real barrier to the spread of ideas in many cases, but it should not deter outsiders from using the experience of others as a strategy to build change capability. Outsiders can ask leaders who have succeeded at implementing a change to share their experiences. It is most helpful to create an environment in which physicians are encouraged to ask questions not just about the specifics of the change but also about the challenges in the change process and how they were overcome. Important issues are the leaders' role, if there was a felt need to change, and how the change is being reinforced. The purpose of these conversations is not necessarily to focus on getting one group of physicians to replicate a change implemented elsewhere; it is to stimulate learning a perspective or skill that can be applied to any change in the physicians' own setting. Another way outsiders can bring value and stimulate interest in change is by sharing new ideas from related health care businesses or other industries. Physician organizations can become very insular. Introducing innovations that have been useful and productive in other settings can help generate interest in change if it is done without implied criticism of current practices.

This kind of sharing and learning can take place in person, over the Internet, or using phone or video conferences. General Electric's Jack Welch incorporated cross-fertilization of ideas and changes into regular, standing meetings of executives. His goal was to force learning and transfer of ideas from one part of the corporation to others.[4] Some modification of this approach could be used to encourage greater spread of changes.

If there is a lot of innovation and testing taking place in the organization or system, it can be helped to spread through opportunities for physicians to meet face-to-face with other physicians involved in implementation of a change. Outsiders can take the lead in fostering that kind of doctor-to-doctor communication.

When seasoned senior leaders from the outside develop trusting peer relationships with physicians, they can add value by sharing their experience and knowledge about change and implementation. When outsiders have advice and wisdom and offer it in the spirit of being helpful rather than controlling, physicians can develop their own change skills.

Support Information Technology Development

Develop and implement a strategy so that information technology supports the physicians in making improvements. When it comes to change, the better the data, the more powerful they will be in influencing physicians. Change efforts would be more successful if physicians had timely access to appropriate data and if useful reports and displays of data were provided.

Outsiders can help improve the data capability of a physician organization and thereby enhance the organization's change capacity. They must be careful to recognize differences in data requirements in the inpatient and the outpatient settings. Many physicians have expressed frustration that "hospital people" do not appreciate the data requirements of an ambulatory setting. When hospitals and systems invest money to build information technology capability in physician practices, too often the result misses the mark from physicians' perspectives. That kind of waste is tragic.

Help Doctors Feel Valued

In our observations, too little acknowledgment is shown toward physicians. The cycles of mistrust and disappointment in which many physicians and outsiders are trapped leave little room for acknowledgment of each others' positive contributions. In a relationship fraught with disappointment, it is understandably hard to acknowledge those you see as uncooperative or self-interested. When outsiders do not see the changes or improvements they expect, they often point out physicians' shortfalls and failings. The content and tone of the messages sent to physicians is that they "had better shape up." If physicians are made to feel like losers, other efforts to help them change are undercut.

If the doctors do not feel valued, two things happen: their energy and motivation to improve and change are sapped and the relationship that tethers the two organizations, or "two sides of the house," together is strained. You cannot be an effective change sponsor or agent if you are viewed with resentment or

Effective Partnerships
STEVE YOUSO

Steve Youso is Vice President, Health System Development, at Blue Cross/Blue Shield of Minnesota, where he manages the organization's partnerships with physician practices. Prior to joining Blue Cross Blue Shield, Steve worked as a practice administrator for physician-owned groups and an integrated system.

The quality of the relationship I establish with physicians is of paramount importance to my being able to influence them. Collegiality is a very important physician value, and I have always focused on developing relationships of mutual respect and trust. If you view physicians as superior or authority figures and always defer to them, your ability to have any influence is cut off. At the other extreme is advice I got early in my career from a hospital administrator. He said that I had better learn to manipulate the doctors, to work one side against the other. He believed that dominating doctors was the best way for him to get his work done. But that only breeds distrust in my opinion.

If you undervalue your own contribution or are intimidated, doctors won't respect you. While you have to know your boundaries, you also have to be confident of your contributions. Developing this helps you to be an effective partner. My most important message to a young MBA that I mentor is to know what you bring to a situation. I give him a lot of exposure to medical directors so that he can sit around the same table with physicians and learn when to jump in and when to listen to and respect their expertise.

Some health plan and insurance people have negative views of physicians. Because their only interactions with doctors are around money, they see them through a very narrow window. Some view physicians who bargain for higher reimbursement or claim to not be paid enough as greedy. This, in my opinion, leads them to take actions that undercut trust and therefore to lose any leverage they might have to help practices accept change.

At Blue Cross/Blue Shield of Minnesota, our partnerships focus on improving quality and efficiency of care using methods that align the economics between the organization and providers. Our ultimate goal is to yield benefits for patients. Actions we've taken to bring change to the practices with which we partner include:

hostility by physicians you hope to influence. Making conscious efforts to acknowledge physicians is effective in conjunction with other tactics, such as giving physicians responsibility and authority, investing in their building capable leadership, and holding them accountable for what they promise. Even in the absence of any other effort to shore up their change capacity, acknowledging their value can have an impact. It is essential to appreciate the intensity of the negative messages bombarding physicians. Any positive acknowledgment in this context can be meaningful.

One practical example is to acknowledge the contribution physicians make, even if their own balance sheet shows a loss. Explore ways they do add value to the organization—by having a positive reputation or adding other revenue not captured on the balance sheet—and demonstrate that those contributions are valued. The way to deal with losses from physician practices is to give physicians some control and hold them accountable for reaching specific targets—not to beat up on them.

Use Your Authority or Influence to Spread Constructive Interaction

Helping a physician organization develop greater change capability cannot be just one person's responsibility. The wider the circle of people willing to take the actions described, the greater your organization's ability to influence physicians. As an outsider, your impact on physicians can be magnified if others also understand how they can be positive influences. If you tolerate others' talking about the physicians as losers or allow incentives that are misaligned to continue, you undercut your own effort. If there is a negative history between administrative leaders and doctors or between a partner or owner and a physician organization, someone needs to step up and lead toward a different future.

First and foremost, leadership needs to act in constructive ways. Then, clear expectations need to be communicated to others about how physicians or the physician organization will be treated. Share the concept of being unconditionally constructive. Also, have others look at how they currently relate to physicians; if the relationship is less than effective, ask them to consider how their actions contribute to the dynamic. The message that needs to go throughout the organization is that investing to make physicians strong, capable partners is in everyone's interests. If this message is counter to what others currently believe or how they behave, it will have to be communicated repeatedly. Tool 10-1, pages 172-173, is designed to help outsiders examine their beliefs and attitudes toward physicians in order to become more effective at supporting them to make needed changes.

"It takes two to dance but one to change the dance." If you are not a physician or not a member of the physician organization you are trying to influence, take the first step. Do not wait for physician leaders to make the first move. Your efforts, multiplied by others in your ranks or in your organization, have the power to get results when physicians are treated as business partners. The sidebar, on page 170 and right, offers one health care executive's observations and experiences building partnerships with physicians.

- Provide actionable information. Physicians are competitive, hard-working people who will strive to do better if they have the information they need to do so. I focus on getting information into doctors' hands to show where they are different—data that compare their organization to others and individual doctors to other doctors whenever possible.

- Provide incentives and reward positive changes. Doctors play to win once they know the rules for success. When it comes to care improvement, we tell them the rules. That means aligning expectations and economics and identifying measures of success that make sense to physicians.

- Structure equal partnerships. We're structuring relationships with the clinics with which we have financial arrangements so that they and we are equal partners. For major decisions, both parties need to reach agreement. This eliminates one-upping each other and supports us in getting down to the real issues.

- Invest in building physician leadership in the clinics. You need to have someone with whom to partner. It's to our advantage to have effective physician leaders in the clinics with which we have relationships. Taking physician leaders to conferences and financially supporting their development is a win-win arrangement.

- Create the expectation that change is a constant. A reasonable expectation for a physician to have of a hospital or insurance partner three years ago very likely isn't appropriate today, given how much is changing. I keep pointing out to physicians that change is part of the landscape. When physicians have realistic and flexible expectations, disappointments and a sense of betrayal are minimized.

Tools for Taking Action

TOOL 10-1. Support Physicians to Change When You Are an Outsider

PURPOSE: To identify ways in which individual leaders who are not physicians from "inside" the organization can effectively support change among physicians.

INSTRUCTIONS:

- Part A is an exercise for personal reflection. Answer the questions thoughtfully.

- If you are willing to see physicians in a positive or new way, go to Part B. Review the list of actions that can support change. Check off a few areas (up to three) in which you think you personally could be more effective at supporting change capability among physicians.

- On a separate page, list the areas on which you want to work and identify specific actions you can take that would significantly help build change capability.

PART A. Personal Reflection

My general feelings toward the physicians I need to influence to change:

What are these feelings based on?

In what ways do my perceptions about or attitudes toward doctors affect my ability to facilitate change among them?

How effective have I been at facilitating change among physicians?

Are there any ways in which I could be more effective by seeing physicians in a different way? How open am I to changing how I see them?

PART B. Actions that Build Change Capability

_____ If the relationship is broken, heal it.

_____ Support the physician organization to get strong.

_____ Stop reinforcing the old compact.

_____ Give the physicians responsibility, authority, and resources and provide consequences.

_____ Align incentives.

_____ Build business literacy among the doctors.

_____ Support the spread of learning and new ideas.

_____ Support information technology development.

_____ Help doctors feel valued.

_____ Use your authority or influence to spread constructive interactions.

CHAPTER 11

Moving Forward: Mindset and Action

A Broader Perspective

The view from above is always different. It only takes an airplane window seat to remind us. As you fly out of Boston's airport, you can see the massive hook of Cape Cod stretching eastward into the Atlantic and then curving back onto itself. What you cannot see as the plane taxis down the runway, but you know is there, gets revealed when you lift off and gain altitude. Reflecting on our work in physician organizations brings to mind how much getting a higher view allows for a changed perspective and new insights.

In the nearly 20 years we have worked with physician organizations, we have found each organization to be unique and challenged by its own set of circumstances. Some have struggled in their attempts to accelerate change and progressed only in fits and starts. Others, with minimal intervention, moved to higher levels of change competence in relatively short order. In looking across the successes and the failures, one observation that stands out is the importance of leaders' being very clear about their role in the change process and their willingness to take action to make change happen. We know from first-hand experience that a leader who tries to influence physicians but does not have the right mindset will not be effective. If the leader is not coming from a constructive place, those they encourage to change through involvement, data, or education will feel manipulated. Being enlightened and determined to be helpful, without initiating action, also will not result in change.

Wanting to produce a practical guide, we provide a lot of detail and specific advice in earlier chapters. We hope readers find the specificity helpful. As useful as new knowledge and new insight may be, however, we think leaders would gain most as they undertake change efforts by understanding from a broad perspective the mindset and actions that support success.

Leader Mindsets

Whether a leader is from inside or outside the organization, his or her mindset about the role of the leader is a key determinant of successful change. We have observed success when leaders see their job as:

- Clearing away the miasma that blocks physicians and others in the organization from engaging in change.

- Kindling internal motivation for change.

- Building and strengthening relationships.

- Making heroes of those on the front line.

- Demonstrating the courage to see reality as it is and to be the first to change.

Leaders Clear the Miasma

Leaders who are successful in helping physicians through change believe that physicians basically want to do the right thing. That includes changing, experimenting, and innovating when the case for change is clear and when supports are in place to facilitate trying out the new way. Unfortunately, we know of many health care leaders who doubt that physicians are motivated toward improvement if it means they personally have to change. Through their lens, they see physicians as change-adverse, self-interested, and disillusioned. In Pygmalion fashion, when physicians are treated as if these are their only characteristics, they respond as such and the self-fulfilling prophecy confirms a negative stereotype.

Leaders who shared their experiences in the sidebars in earlier chapters would attest to the natural inclination of physicians to positively engage in change when supported to do so. This is not to say that every physician will be willing to give up the status quo or to experiment with untested ways. By and large, however, when physicians resist change, invest in preserving the status quo, or are frustrated with or hostile toward those who expect more of them, there is a deeper problem. The energy for improvement is stifled by a kind of miasma that could be a compact that is out of step with reality, individual and conflicting visions for where the organization is headed, ineffective leadership, unwillingness to have honest dialogue, hostility from business partners, and so on. Lifting the fog that dampens creativity, innovation, and even professional satisfaction is leaders' job.

Leaders Build Internal Motivation for Change

Another mindset that facilitates success is a belief that models, such as the change management framework described in this book, are a means to an end that is larger than ongoing implementation of discrete changes. That end is proficiency among those leading and implementing change and internalization of the model as a set of guiding principles. The model is not, and must not be seen as, a mechanism to manipulate doctors and staff.

By helping physicians and staff have successful and positive experiences of change, leaders contribute to greater curiosity about improvement. When changes that make care better for patients and that are more professionally satisfying are successfully implemented, it primes the pump for greater involvement.

Leaders Value Relationships

From what we see, many health care leaders think they can reshape their organizations and build alliances by wielding power and applying economic pressure to physicians. The trend toward building integrated systems and growing them has started to unwind. Many of the systems slapped together for market dominance or to have clout with payers have failed miserably in their primary objectives—to reduce redundancies, lower costs, and improve quality and service. Mismatched cultures are one often-cited reason for the inability to achieve any real value-added integration.

Behind mis-matched cultures, we often find a mindset that is counterproductive. When leaders hold, and reinforce in others, a win-lose mindset, the relationship between entities that should be collaborating becomes dysfunctional. When leaders tolerate this way of thinking among parts of a system, or within an institution, they sub-optimize performance and contribute to cultural conflicts. If leaders do not pay conscious attention to ingraining a win-win mindset throughout the enterprise, mistrust and infighting often prevail.

An effective change leader understands that judging physicians or seeing them as wrong, difficult, or greedy cuts off influence. A colleague who spent years as a clinic administrator once said, "You can be right or you can have a relationship." If you believe that you are right—and that doctors are wrong—you are certain to stifle change.

Leaders Make Heroes of Those on the Front Line

Leaders who develop more change-resilient organizations know who the real heroes are in their organizations. Some physician organizations value their dealmakers to an extent that undermines the status of those who take care of patients day in and day out. When front-line physicians and staff go to large-group meetings, all too often what they hear about are the new lines of business, the acquisitions, the work that excites the people at the top. Their day-to-day work seems to be old hat and not really valued. Most doctors care deeply about their patients. Do you as a leader care that they care? More important, do those on the front line know that you care? The mindset that it is leaders' role to ennoble and acknowledge the work of doctors and staff is one hallmark of effective leaders.

Leaders Demonstrate Courage

Above all else, leaders who are building change capability in their organizations understand the importance of courage. Taking a critical look at current reality and what is on the horizon in the marketplace takes a good deal of courage for most leaders. This is particularly true for those who have been guided by the traditional mental models of physician leadership discussed in chapter 1 and who believe that communicating the need for fundamental changes will be unpopular. In addition to seeing reality, taking responsibility for how one has contributed to the current state is an act of courage.

The individuals with whom we have worked who have succeeded in taking others to a place they might not have wanted to go to on their own all had the courage to make their personal transition first. No leader can lead anyone to a place where he or she is not personally willing to go. Being willing to cross the bridge first may not seem like such a courageous action, but it takes a mindset that not all leaders have cultivated. Consider the physician and administrative leaders in Beth Briere's case on compact change (chapter 9). The transition work they called "crossing the bridge" was all about taking on a new mindset that included willingness to lead this change. Leaders in the organization credit this work with substantially aiding their change effort.

Actions

It takes more than the mindsets identified above to move change forward. High-level actions that leaders can take to bring greater change capability to their organization and to renew their own commitment to change include:

- Focus on a few fundamental changes that help achieve the vision.

- Integrate work on your change foundation with implementation of operational changes.

- Get beyond hostility to build true partnerships.

- Seek like-minded colleagues for support.

- Do something—don't feel overwhelmed to the point of not taking any action.

Focus on a Few Fundamental Changes That Move the Vision Forward

Most leaders would agree that implementing change in physician organizations is like trying to change the tires on a car speeding down the freeway. The leader's role in change implementation can seem overwhelming when there is so much ongoing change and pressure for more. Likewise, physicians who are asked to incorporate more change into their practices when their days are already packed wonder where they will find the time to do so.

We know of very few executives and operational leaders who do not feel overwhelmed by competing demands for their attention and energy. One of the most common complaints we hear is how full everyone's plate is. Given the amount of planning and active sponsorship that it takes to successfully implement significant changes, choosing a few changes to focus on is essential.

In addition, most physicians feel pushed to their limits by patient care, paperwork, call-backs, hospital rounds, and keeping up with the changes immediately affecting their practices. Asking physicians to take on too many changes at once only increases resistance and resentment. Physicians and others do best when they have the experience of actually making things better. Again, this requires focus and support.

Identifying which changes to focus on and which to not pursue is a leader's responsibility. Deciding what not to do can be the more difficult call. If leaders fail to make those calls, they end up pushing agendas that are far too ambitious—agendas that, like a tidal wave, engulf everyone in the organization. Often what is behind the failure to focus is leaders' fear of abandoning any strategy. They worry that any initiative not pursued might later prove to be the one that could have secured the organization's future. Leaders would do well to consider focusing on a small number of large-scale changes that have three characteristics in common: they powerfully advance the business vision, they confer a competitive advantage in the marketplace, and they inspire a strong sense of commitment in all leaders and managers. Scoring potential changes against these three criteria would be a helpful way to narrow the list.

Integrate Work on Your Change Foundation with Implementation of Operational Changes

As earlier chapters explain, it is ideal if the foundation for change is in place—aligned leadership, shared vision, new compact—when an organization launches other fundamental, organizationwide changes. In reality, many physician organizations do not have the luxury of time to work in that order. A health plan announces it will reduce reimbursement to its affiliated physicians with the next contract. An IPA is told it needs to dramatically improve its patient satisfaction scores or jeopardize losing its largest contract. Significant change may need to happen quickly in response.

In addition, regardless of the importance of foundational issues to the success of the whole organization, physicians may view them as idealistic, impractical, or irrelevant. Under these circumstances, taking the opportunity to address foundational issues in the course of implementing a significant change is often a sound strategy.

Beth Briere's experience with compact and other changes, described in chapter 9, is an excellent example of advancing leadership, compact, and shared vision, while implementing operational changes related to access and capacity. This approach helps build the organization's change foundation and advance key business strategies at the same time. Conversations about vision and compact cease to be theoretical when discussed in connection with operational changes such as re-engineering for improved access or greater patient satisfaction. Physicians' expectations about how much flexibility they have in their schedules or that their day will end at a specific time may need to be revised for an open-access system to work. Talking in general terms about how physicians need to revise their expectations about work hours could well be unproductive. However, by connecting the need for greater physician flexibility to getting a more patient-oriented access system up and running, the conversation becomes more relevant.

Break Through the Hostility and Build Partnerships for Change

Throughout this book, we have encouraged leaders to reach out across the boundaries of clinical specialties, organizational hierarchies, and institutions in order to build support for change implementation. We know that, in many organizations, the current state of relationships does not support collaboration. It is not uncommon to find palpable hostility between the affiliates in an integrated system, between physicians and a health system, or between an IPA and an insurance company. In some organizations, primary care doctors and specialists are engaged in struggles around control and money. In some parts of the country, shrinking resources have intensified intraorganization competitiveness. As the saying goes, "When food gets scarce, table manners go to hell." When hostility goes unmanaged, it escalates and makes any opportunity to collaborate less likely.

When tension, distrust, or anger blocks partnership, it is up to leaders to put an end to negative and inciting behaviors. This does not require becoming idealistic, liking the other party, or giving in. First, care less about being right. Hold yourself accountable to act in ways that build the relationship for you and for them. Put your focus on results, not personalities or style. Let go of unproductive assumptions and judgments when someone fails to live up to what he or she committed to do.

To start a new dynamic and move away from a history of hostility requires courage and patience. Even a dysfunctional dynamic is predictable, so changing it represents a risk. But what if the olive branch in your hand goes unnoticed? It is difficult to continue efforts to build collaboration when the other party fails to notice

or dismisses our efforts. Breakthroughs in relationships that have been stormy, or from which the reservoir of goodwill has been drained, typically require a willingness to act constructively for some period of time, regardless of what you get back. The alternative, keeping up the tension, carries a higher price.

Seek Like-Minded Colleagues for Support

The company you keep has an effect on your success as a leader of change. It can be extremely helpful to spend time with colleagues who share your vision and commitment to fundamental change and improvement. Leaders who find themselves surrounded by constant negativity can only "hold out" and work for change for so long. Misery doesn't love company; it demands it! If the environment in which you find yourself is negative, it takes a good deal of energy not to be sucked downward, too.

We would encourage leaders to seek others who are also committed to learning about and developing greater proficiency in advancing change. When leaders support one another, they can learn from one another's failures and successes, challenge one another's observations and theories, encourage one another to dream, provide acknowledgment, help one another not to fall back into old behaviors, and share the joy of self-discovery. Building a network of leaders who can be vulnerable and authentic with one another can provide the self-renewal every change leader needs.

Do Something

It takes a lot of work to get change right. From the acknowledgment that an improvement or change is needed to the point at which the new way is implemented and humming involves numerous steps and interactions. We do not want to downplay the energy, time, and challenges that successful change requires. By the same token, we do not want any leader to be put off or feel overwhelmed by having to do it all to make any difference. Building a change foundation and applying all the levers have been shown to get results. At the same time, applying any one of the levers can make a specific change process more positive for those involved. For example, if all you do is clarify your own thinking about why and how you will involve others, the participation process can be more effective. If you respond to resistance in a way that acknowledges and honors the other person's perspective, that action will reduce tension and improve the relationship. From the ideas, examples, and tools for taking action provided in this book, pick one or two that you have largely in your control. Choose to work in ways that help to lift the fog in your organization that prevents engagement with change. Refuse to let feeling overwhelmed by change become another barrier to experimenting and improving your personal capability to facilitate change. Do something.

For physician organizations, much depends on whether they will be able to adjust to new competitive demands and make the necessary improvements in quality and service while they simultaneously reduce costs. In addition to facing today's market imperatives, these organizations will also be increasingly challenged to incorporate new technology (e.g., electronic communication with patients) and re-invent themselves as new therapeutics reshape physicians' work (e.g., as gene therapies or bio-tech breakthroughs cure some chronic diseases). Leaders and others who are in a position to support change play critical roles. They have the potential, by leading successful change, to secure a positive future. "Only connect...," wrote E. M. Forster in *Howards End*.[1] This simple exhortation has special significance for today's health care leaders. Paradoxical as it sounds, we learn best and develop personal competence when in relationship to others. Connecting is therefore an essential part of learning. Seek connection. Ask for coaching. Share your successes. Too much is at stake to not learn how to change.

Tools for Taking Action

TOOL 11-1. Write Your Own Success Story

PURPOSE: To help individual leaders envision the future and their role in supporting successful change in their organization.

INSTRUCTIONS:

- Imagine a time in the not-too-distant future when successful change is being made and you are contributing in a positive way.

- Identify one change that you will implement or be responsible for helping others implement and imagine that it is being implemented successfully. The change could be a foundational change that affects the organization in some very substantial way, or it could be an important operational change.

- Envision that you are being interviewed for an article about this change. What answers would you give the interviewer to the following questions?

  - What is an appropriate title for this article?

  - What is the triumph?

  - What did the individuals do, and how do they feel about the accomplishment?

  - What is your role in the process? How did you contribute?

  - What did you learn from this success that you would want others to know?

- How will you use this reflection exercise and any insights you got out of it in your work to support change among physicians today?

References and Footnotes

Chapter One

1. Mental models, as used by Peter Senge, refer to "deeply ingrained assumptions, generalizations or even pictures or images" that influence our understanding of our world and our actions." Senge, P. *The Fifth Discipline: The Art and Practice of the Learning Organization.* New York, N.Y.: Doubleday Currency, 1990.

2. Kotter, J. *Leading Change.* Boston, Mass.: Harvard Business School Press, 1996.

3. Senge, P., *op.cit., p.78.*

4. Savage, T. *Seven Steps to a More Effective Board.* Kansas City, Mo.: National Press Publications, 1994.

5. Pointer, D., and Orlikoff, J. *Board Work: Governing Health Care Organizations.* San Francisco, Calif.: Jossey-Bass Publishers, 1999.

6. Silversin, J., and Kornacki, M. "A New Dynamic for Medical Group Governance: Enhancing 'Followership' and Organizational Performance." *Group Practice Journal* 49(2): 27-34, Feb. 2000.

7. Wills, G. *Certain Trumpets: The Nature of Leadership.* New York, N.Y.: Simon and Schuster, 1994, p. 17.

8. Bradley, B. *Values of the Game.* New York, N.Y.: Broadway Books, 1998, p. 15.

Chapter Two

1. Collins, J., and Porras, J. "Building Your Company's Vision." *Harvard Business Review* 75(5):65-77, Sept.-Oct. 1996.

2. Sanders, B. *Fabled Service: Ordinary Acts, Extraordinary Outcomes.* San Diego, Calif.: Pfeiffer & Company, 1995.

3. Senge, P. *The Fifth Discipline: The Art and Practice of the Learning Organization.* New York, N.Y.: Doubleday, 1990.

4. Herzlinger, R. *Market-Driven Health Care: Who Wins, Who Loses in the Transformation of America's Largest Service Industry.* Reading, Mass.: Addison-Wesley Publishing Company, 1997.

5. Nanus, B. *Visionary Leadership.* San Francisco, Calif.: Jossey-Bass Publishers, 1992.

6. Senge, P., and others. *The Fifth Discipline Fieldbook: Strategies and Tools for Building a Learning Organization.* New York, N.Y.: Doubleday Currency, 1994.

7. Collins, J., and Porras, J. *Built To Last: Successful Habits of Visionary Companies.* New York, N.Y.: HarperBusiness, 1997.

Chapter Three

1. Argyris, C. *Personality and Organization,* New York, N.Y.: Harper Row, 1957.

2. Schein, E. *Career Dynamics: Matching Individual and Organizational Needs.* Reading, Mass.: Addison-Wesley, 1978.

3. Bartlett, C., and Ghoshal, S. "Changing the Role of Top Management: Beyond Systems to People." *Harvard Business Review* 73(3):132-142, May-June 1995.

4. Strebel, P. "Why Do Employees Resist Change?" *Harvard Business Review,* 74(3):86-92, May-June, 1996.

5. Silversin, J. "Want to Enhance Physician Satisfaction? Change the Compact!" *Group Practice Journal* 47(5):32-6, May 1998

6. Silversin, J., and Kornacki, M. "Creating a Physician Compact that Drives Group Success." *MGMA Journal* 47(3):54-62, May/June 2000.

7. Robbins, T. *Even Cowgirls Get The Blues.* New York, N.Y.: Bantam Books, 1990.

Chapter Five

1. Rogers, E. "Lessons for Guidelines from the Diffusion of Innovations." *Joint Commission Journal of Quality Improvement* 21(7):324-8, July 1995.

2. Harvey, J. *The Abilene Paradox and Other Meditations on Management.* San Diego, Calif.: University Associates, 1988.

3. Rogers, E. *Diffusion of Innovations,* 4th Edition. New York, N.Y.: Free Press, 1995.

Chapter Six

1. Tichy, N., and Charan, R. "The CEO as Coach: An Interview with Allied Signal's Lawrence A. Bossidy." *Harvard Business Review* 73(2):69-78, March-April 1995.

Chapter Seven

1. Eisenberg, D., and others. "Trends in Alternative Medicine Use in the United States, 1990-1997." *JAMA* 280(18):1569-75, Nov. 11, 1998.

2. Senge, P. Radio interview. "The Connection" on WBUR (Boston), May 10, 2000.

3. Kübler-Ross, E. *On Death and Dying: What the Dying Have to Teach Doctors, Nurses, Clergy, and Their Own Families.* New York, N.Y.: Touchstone, 1997.

4. Bridges, W. *Managing Transitions: Making the Most of Change.* Reading, Mass.: Addison-Wesley Publishing Company, 1996.

5. Gardner, H. *Leading Minds: An Anatomy of Leadership.* New York, N.Y.: BasicBooks, 1995.

6. Armstrong, D. *Managing by Storying Around: A New Method of Leadership.* New York, N.Y.: Doubleday Currency, 1992.

7. Tichy, N. *The Leadership Engine: How Winning Companies Build Leaders at Every Level.* New York, N.Y.: HarperBusiness, 1997.

8. Lipman, D. *Improving Your Storytelling: Beyond the Basics for All Who Tell Stories in Work or Play.* Little Rock, Ark.: August House Publishers, Inc., 1999.

9. Gordon, T. *Parent Effectiveness Training.* New York, N.Y.: Wyden Books, 1970.

10. Gordon, T. *Leader Effectiveness Training.* New York, N.Y.: Wyden Books, 1977.

11. Rogers, C., and Roethlisberger, F. "Barriers and Gateways to Communication." *Harvard Business Review* 69(6):105-11, Nov.-Dec. 1991.

Chapter Eight

1. McGregor, D. *The Human Side of Enterprise.* New York, N.Y.: McGraw-Hill, 1960.

2. Herzberg, F. "One More Time: How Do You Motivate Employees?" *Harvard Business Review* 65(5):5-16, Sept.-Oct. 1987.

3. Scholtes, P. *The Team Handbook.* Madison, Wis.: Joiner Associates, 1990.

4. Deming, W.E. *Out of the Crisis.* Cambridge, Mass.: MIT Center for Advanced Engineering Study, 1986.

5. Kohn, A. *Punished by Rewards: The Trouble with Gold Stars, Incentive Plans, A's, Praise, and Other Bribes.* New York, N.Y.: Houghton Mifflin Company, 1993, p. 139.

6. Levine, F., and Fasnacht, G. "Token Rewards May Lead to Token Learning." *American Psychologist* 29(11):816-20, Nov. 1974.

7. Deci. E. L. "Effects of Externally Mediated Rewards on Intrinsic Motivation." *Journal of Personality and Social Psychology* 18(1):105-15, Jan. 1971.

8. Deci, E., and Flaste, R. *Why We Do What We Do: Understanding Self-Motivation.* New York, N.Y.: Penguin USA, 1996.

9. Berwick, D. M. "Controlling Variation in Health Care: A Consultation From Walter Shewhart." *Medical Care* 29(12):1212-25, Dec. 1991.

10. Berwick, D. M. "Developing and Testing Change in Delivery of Care." *Annals of Internal Medicine* 128(8):651-6, April 15, 1998.

Chapter Ten

1. "Outsiders" can be nonphysician executives and managers working inside or outside a physician practice, or they can be physicians who work for an entity other than the physician practice, such as an insurance company, a hospital, or a corporate owner.

2. Sheldon, A. *Managing Doctors.* Homewood, Ill.: Dow Jones-Irwin, 1986, p. 41.

3. Fisher, R., and Brown, S. *Getting Together: Building a Relationship That Gets to Yes.* Boston, Mass.: Houghton Mifflin Company, 1988.

4. Tichy, N., and Charan, R. "Speed, Simplicity, Self-Confidence: An Interview with Jack Welch." *Harvard Business Review* 67(5):2-9, Sept.-Oct. 1989.

Chapter Eleven

1. Forster, E. *Howards End.* New York, N.Y.: Signet Classic, 1998.

Index